TINA ARENA

Now I Can Dance

Tina Arena
with Jude McGee

HarperCollins*Publishers*

HarperCollins*Publishers*

First published in Australia in 2013
by HarperCollins*Publishers* Australia Pty Limited
ABN 36 009 913 517
harpercollins.com.au

Copyright © Positive Dreaming Pty Ltd 2013

The right of Positive Dreaming Pty Ltd to be identified as the author of this work has
been asserted by them under the *Copyright Amendment (Moral Rights) Act 2000*.

HarperCollins*Publishers*
Level 13, 201 Elizabeth Street, Sydney NSW 2000, Australia
Unit D1, 63 Apollo Drive, Albany, Auckland 0632, New Zealand
A 53, Sector 57, Noida, UP, India
77–85 Fulham Palace Road, London W6 8JB, United Kingdom
2 Bloor Street East, 20th floor, Toronto, Ontario M4W 1A8, Canada
10 East 53rd Street, New York NY 10022, USA

National Library of Australia Cataloguing-in-Publication entry:

Arena, Tina, 1967– author.
  Now I Can Dance/Tina Arena ; with Jude McGee.
  978 0 7322 9756 5 (pbk)
  Includes index.
  Arena, Tina, 1967–
  Singers–Australia–Biography
  Women singers–Australia–Biography.
  Other Authors/Contributors:
  McGee, Jude, author.
782.42164092

Cover design by Hazel Lam, HarperCollins Design Studio
Cover photography by Pierre Baroni
Typeset in Plantin by Kirby Jones
Printed and bound in Australia by Griffin Press
The papers used by HarperCollins in the manufacture of this book are a natural,
recyclable product made from wood grown in sustainable plantation forests. The fibre
source and manufacturing processes meet recognised international environmental
standards, and carry certification.

8 7 6 5   14 15 16

To Gabriel, Louis, Matéo, Sofia and Valentin

In 2012 my family and I moved from our home in Paris to Australia for six months. While I was down under, I appeared as a mentor on a family entertainment TV show called *Young Talent Time*. The show featured a team of kids performing popular songs, as well as children from all over Australia who appeared as contestants each week. My job, alongside dancer and choreographer Charles 'Chucky' Klapow, was to help and advise both the YTT team and the guest performers.

It was a wonderful time. My little boy, Gabriel, attended the local primary school and had the chance to experience Australian life. He loved every minute of it, and so did I. It was great to be back in Oz, and it was great to *give* back. It was also a trip down memory lane in a lovely way. Because, of course, my career as a singer began on a show called *Young Talent Time*.

I was only eight years old when, in 1976, I joined the team on the enormously popular show hosted by Johnny Young. Dubbed 'Tiny Tina' (I've always been vertically challenged!), I appeared on that show every Saturday evening right up until two weeks before my sixteenth birthday.

For many years after, I felt like I couldn't escape from 'Tiny Tina', that I was dragging her around like a ball and chain as people struggled to accept me as an adult performer. But eventually, I not only broke free from Tiny Tina but came to appreciate *Young Talent Time* for what it was – innocent, joyful family entertainment from another, simpler era.

As it turned out, YTT was just the beginning of my career in music. Or should I say careers – sometimes I feel like I've lived seven lives and had at least seven careers! I've sung onstage and in the studio in English, French, Italian and Spanish; I've written songs with all kinds of artists; won awards; performed in musical theatre in the West End of London, and around Australia; and I've performed onstage all over the world. I've been pretty busy since I first appeared on *Young Talent Time* singing ABBA's 'Ring Ring' all those years ago.

In fact, in my early thirties, while at the top of my game, I left Australia for success in Europe. There, I fell in love. So to find myself back in Oz, working on YTT *mach* II, made me realise that things had come full circle. And as I reflected on the past three and a half decades, I had to admit it had been an amazing ride. There've been incredible moments, funny moments, and some tough moments. I've met and worked with some extraordinary people, including brilliant musicians, writers and visionaries. I've experienced the gifts of love, family and children. And, of course, I've been blessed to have a wonderful career that allows me to do what I love to do, which is to sing and make music.

It was time to tell the story, to try to make sense of my colourful life so far. It's the tale of a young girl who lived to sing, and a woman who, whatever the cost, tried to stay true to herself and her vision of music. It's taken faith, hard work, courage and a thick skin! But finally, here I am, in a happy place, humbled by – and grateful for – my past and excited about what lies ahead.

So here it is. Sure, you can find out on the internet just about anything you want to know about me, but it's not the same as hearing it from the horse's mouth. If you really want to know *who* I am, and what made me who I am, you need to read this book.

But be warned. I've still got a lot to do: more albums, more concerts, more dancing, more joy – and more stories, of course. So there may be further instalments down the track. I just hope you enjoy this one.

Melbourne, September 2013

1999

What had I done to deserve this? What had I done wrong?

It was 1999 and according to Prince in his famous song, I should have been partying like there was no tomorrow. After all, my career as a singer and now songwriter was going gangbusters.

Since childhood I'd been able to follow my passion – music – and had great success doing it. From the age of eight until I was sixteen, I'd enjoyed a career as a child performer on the Australian TV show *Young Talent Time*, so much so that 'Tina Arena' was now a household name in my homeland. Then, during my twenties, I'd had three hit albums, two of them recorded in the US with some of that nation's top musicians and producers. I'd gone on to sell millions of records around the world. I'd won a World Music Award and six Australian Recording Industry Association (ARIA) awards, including Song of the Year for my bestselling single 'Chains', and Album of the Year, an award never previously won by a woman, for my second record, *Don't Ask*. I'd sold out national concert tours. I'd performed major roles in several musical theatre productions. The previous year I'd finally performed at the Royal Albert Hall and Wembley Stadium in London and had begun to break into the French market in a big way.

And now the boss of Sony in the US, Tommy Mottola, the man who had guided the career of Mariah Carey (then married her), had taken a personal interest in my career. He'd chosen the song that his company hoped would help me crack the tough US market – 'If I Was a River' – and Sony had footed the bill for an expensive video to promote it as well as a two-month promotional tour of America. To have a major record company backing me in the US was a dream come true. And to top it all off, I'd found love, marrying in a beautiful white wedding a man who, very conveniently, was also my manager.

And yet, as I boarded a plane bound for the US and the start of that promo tour, all I could think was: 'I'm dying.'

You would be forgiven for thinking I was simply spoiled and ungrateful – a right diva (which, in all honesty, is usually just another word for 'difficult brat').

But I'd only ever been *deeply* grateful. Grateful for the opportunity as a child performer to learn my trade. Grateful to be able to continue pursuing my passion as an adult. Grateful to learn the craft of songwriting from true artisans. And, more than anything, eternally grateful for a love of music that had buoyed me up every day of my life.

The truth was, though, by 1999 things had gone pear-shaped. Not my career, obviously. That was powering along, thanks to more than twenty years of relentless hard work. I guess I'd inherited my capacity for work from my Sicilian parents – they'd arrived in Australia in the 1950s and had been toiling away ever since. But that capacity for hard work, for never giving up, for keeping on keeping on, had become a double-edged sword. *Because* I fronted up every day, no complaining, and just got on with it, no one – not me, not my then manager–husband, not my record company – had ever thought to stop, not even for a minute. I'd been twisted and pulled in every direction, to the point where I'd been wrung dry. And now I felt I had nothing left to give.

How had it happened? How could I find myself at the age of thirty-one so completely burnt out? Stressed and full of fear, I was waking every night in a cold sweat. It had become so bad I'd taken to showering in the middle of the night. By the morning I'd look like a ghost, haggard, pale, with hollow eyes. The curvy, fresh-faced girl I once was had become a tiny slip of a thing. I hadn't lost my appetite – quite the opposite – but I was burning so much energy I couldn't put on any weight.

For the most part, I realise now, it was my own bloody fault. My capacity for hard work went hand in hand with a desire, a need, to fit in, to keep everyone happy, to always give my best. I always said yes, to everything. I'd never learnt how to say no.

For ten years I'd been struggling to find my own voice and my freedom. I wrote my hit song 'Chains' about that struggle, about trying to break free of my past as 'Tiny Tina'. I wrote the song 'Now I Can Dance' about experiencing that freedom in a foreign land, where no one knew who I was or had been. But now, if I was honest with myself, I had to admit I'd failed to break free from all that. I was still 'in chains'. Underneath, I was still that little girl on TV, the smiling poppet with the big voice doing her very best to please everyone, regardless of the price paid.

Unfortunately, that price was turning out to be high. I had no personal life at all – when I married my manager I'd unwittingly forfeited it completely. What had seemed in the beginning to be a match made in heaven had turned out to be a mistake. And as that realisation slowly dawned on me, my marriage and my work became increasingly untenable. How or where would it end? I couldn't even begin to imagine.

Sitting in the plane, counting down the hours until I landed in LA, I asked myself again: *What did I do wrong? And what am I supposed to be learning here?* But I had no answers.

All I knew was that the flame that burned in my heart for music, for life, was slowly, painfully fading. Soon it would fizzle out. Inside my head, a voice repeated over and over again: 'I'm dying.' And for the first time in my life I didn't care.

CHAPTER 1

You're My World

Perhaps it was Aunty Gisella who brought out the singer in me. Gisella was Egyptian – she wasn't really my aunty – but like me, she was of Italian descent. There were lots of Italian families in our neighbourhood and she lived just behind us. When Mum went off to work – back then she was a machinist in Flinders Lane in Melbourne – sometimes Gisella would look after me. She and Mum were good friends.

I was only three or four, but Aunty Gisella impressed me enormously. For one thing, she was tall and striking, and she dressed like an Italian movie star. She also happened to speak seven languages, sometimes, it seemed to me, in the same sentence. When we spent the day together we'd play records all day long: Italian singers such as Massimo Ranieri singing 'Rose Rosse' or Orietta Berti singing 'Fin Che La Barca Va'.

'What will we listen to today, Filippina?' she'd say. Filippina – or Pina for short – is the name my parents gave me. I'd choose a record, she'd put it on and then I'd dance, flouncing around in her floaty dresses, chic hats and gloves and Italian shoes to die for. Gisella would sing in her rich and sultry voice – she sounded like Anne Bancroft. Soon I was joining in. I was better at singing than dancing, I discovered. It was Aunty Gisella who introduced me, when I was four, to Edith Piaf. Now there was a voice that commanded the attention of a little Italian–Australian girl growing up in the suburbs!

Or maybe it was my older sister Nancy's fault. She was already six when I was born on 1 November 1967, and she had a pile of records, top forty singles and LPs too, that she'd bought at 100 Puckle Street, a rambling variety store just down the road in Melbourne's Moonee Ponds, where we lived. We played that vinyl over and over on the stereo in the huge sunroom at the back of our house. Nancy always had a way with fashion, and in the days when too much satin was barely enough – it was the early 1970s – she'd dress me up in her version of cool. Then she'd stand me on a chair in my borrowed high heels and have me sing along to her favourite songs, things like Alvin Stardust's 'My Coo Ca Choo', Sweet's 'Ballroom Blitz' or ABBA's 'Waterloo'. I'd have memorised every lyric and would belt out the number into an unplugged power cord while Nancy choreographed.

You could say I was Nancy's muppet, but I wasn't complaining. Soon I was buying my own records to sing and dress up to, captivated by what I'd heard on the radio or seen on TV: ABBA's Agnetha and Frida sending out an 'SOS' in pageboy haircuts and knee-length white boots, or Daryl Braithwaite, Sherbet's lead singer, bare-chested but for a cream satin waistcoat, singing 'Summer Love'. Then there was rock, which I fell hard for straight away: Suzi Quatro goin' down to 'Devil Gate Drive' in top-to-toe leather, or Bon Scott grinning wickedly as he sang 'It's a Long Way to the Top' while Angus rocked out in his little school uniform.

Mum and Dad adored music, too, especially big voices and crooners. Tom Jones and Mario Lanza or Italian singers like Little Tony and Ada Mori serenaded us on Saturday mornings while my mum, Franca, scrubbed our old bungalow from top to bottom or cooked and cooked for us, and for our cousins, aunties, uncles, friends. When my dad, Joe, wasn't at his job (for years he worked for VicRail, maintaining the *Southern Aurora*), he'd be toiling in the garden, his pride and joy. So much of what we ate he grew: olives, tomatoes, eggplants, fava beans, figs, basil, zucchini, prickly pears – you name it.

That was my parents: working all week, then never stopping all weekend. They loved to entertain and as they both came from large families – six of Mum's eight brothers and sisters had migrated to Australia, and Dad had several siblings out here, too – the house always seemed to be full of people. And full of music. That was my world.

So, however it happened, I was singing as soon as I could mouth the words. Even before, in fact. Mum remembers that at a wedding when I was nineteen months old, I wriggled out of her arms and ran to the singer and insisted he hold me while he sang. I couldn't talk but I wanted to sing along. I just loved singing – it was as natural and easy as breathing.

In every other respect I was your average little girl. Which is why, when I was asked to be a flower girl at my cousin Gaetano's wedding, I was mad with excitement. And when I tried on the long white dress, I thought the biggest moment of my life had arrived. The funny thing was, in a way it had. Because if it hadn't been for Gaetano's wedding in early 1976, I might still just be singing to myself in the shower.

It was a big, loud, sumptuous Italian affair. More than 300 guests were invited to the Springvale Town Hall in south Melbourne for the reception. To my eight-year-old eyes, the building looked like an ancient palace, with imposing stone columns and a grand staircase. In reality, it was built of brick and concrete, probably in the 1960s, and is all clean lines and modern functionality. But when I tripped up those stairs and entered that grand vestibule, I felt like I was part of some fairytale pageant. Nancy was just in front, one of the bridesmaids dressed in pale green, and all the men were wearing brown velvet suits with cream trim. Even back then, I loved a good show!

Through the glass doors we went, into the cavernous hall, which would be shared by two big weddings that evening. Table upon table was swathed in white and decorated with what looked to my childish eyes like the most beautiful arrangements of flowers I had ever seen.

We kids – Nancy, my little sister, Silvana, my cousins and I – all sat together, which added to the excitement. And when the food and speeches were over, the music started and the real fun began.

Our large extended family took celebrations seriously, so the music that night wasn't a few tapes or a DJ spinning records. At Gaetano and Theresa's wedding there was a real live band, with drums and guitars, even a brass section, and a crooning singer. They performed on a real stage, and in the honey glow of the stage lights they played music to please all ages: old Italian standards such as 'Mare, Mare, Mare, Mare' and 'Volare' for the grandparents, Tom Jones and Frank Sinatra for my mum and dad's generation, and a few top forty hits for the kids.

Everyone danced, even the oldies. Nancy and I ran around, free as birds, while our parents socialised. What a night! Then, at some point during the evening, I had an idea. Or was it a feeling? Perhaps Nancy put me up to it – I can't remember. But I do recall running off in search of my dad. I was on a mission, and I was in a hurry.

Dad was easy to find, his loud voice audible above the music and the chatter. He was sitting down the front, talking with my uncle, probably about the new house we were building. That didn't stop me. I knew I could bail my dad up anywhere, anytime, and he'd give me a big hug and stop to listen.

I tugged on his jacket. 'Dad, I want to sing.'

Dad turned and looked at me. As always, he was smiling. 'Go and dance, Pina. Find Nancy and have a dance.' He kissed me on the forehead.

'But Dad, I want to sing. Please?'

Dad's a big softie, but he was always firm with us girls. 'Not tonight, *Pinuccia*. Look, there's already a singer up there. He's doing the singing tonight.' He kissed me again and sent me on my way.

But Dad should have known: we Arenas don't give up without a fight. In fact, my little idea had become a need.

Five minutes later I was back.

'Please, Daddy, pleeeeeease? Just one song.'

No doubt I was wearing my sweetest, most innocent expression, but again he sent me away.

Finally, after constant nagging, he agreed, and when the band stopped for a break he got to his feet with a sigh. Taking my hand, he led me to the front of the hall where the master of ceremonies was chatting to the band singer.

My dad may be loud, warm and affectionate with his family, but he's very polite and quietly spoken with strangers. Still, he put my case: *Pina loves music and she would love to sing a number. Would it be possible at some point in the evening?*

I stood by Dad's side, my fingers crossed behind my back. The singer listened intently, then turned his gaze to me and winked. 'But she's tiny, Mr Arena,' he said in Italian. 'Just a little child.'

He was right – I was small for an eight-year-old. But

being an Arena, Dad gave it another go. 'She is, but she can sing. Why don't you let her sing for you? Listen to her. She's good!'

The singer smiled but shook his head. 'I'm very sorry, sir. But we have a repertoire. We don't usually do requests.'

Butterflies of anticipation settled into dull disappointment. I stuck out my bottom lip.

Dad gave me a squeeze and led me away. I suspect he was quietly relieved. Now he could go back to his conversation and I back to dancing. But half an hour later, the singer approached my dad. He wanted to hear me sing.

I have no idea what changed his mind. Perhaps someone had put in a good word for me. Or maybe he just felt sorry for a little girl. Whatever the case, minutes later I was backstage with my dad and the band, ready to sing my heart out.

I'd already picked out the song, a number-1 hit I thought was perfect for the occasion. I'd practised it endlessly in the sunroom with Nancy, singing along to the seven-inch single. I knew every word, every nuance of phrasing, every pause, every whisper – and the big note at the end.

I sang for the band, and they clapped and cheered. Then we worked out what key to play in, although I had no idea what they were talking about. Finally the singer nodded at my dad. 'Okay, Mr Arena, we're going to put her on.'

As I climbed onto the stage, a bunch of kids followed and gathered around. The singer introduced me and then handed me the microphone. It would be the first time I'd ever sung into a mike, but as far as I was concerned I knew what to do, thanks to all that practice with a power cord.

The band started up: drums, bass, organ. It was loud! I looked around for Mum and Dad. There they were with my cousin Frank Belbruno, smiling and waving from a table near the front. I was nervous under the spotlight, but the funny thing was, it felt perfectly natural. Then the band leader caught my eye and nodded. Off I went.

Like so many hit songs, the hook line was right up front: 'You're my world'. My version of the classic was based on Daryl Braithwaite's, his first solo single. He'd sung it (or mimed it) on the first episode of *Countdown* in November 1974, and it had become a hit overnight. I have no doubt Nancy and I watched that first show, just as we watched every episode afterwards. Like most Australian kids in the 1970s, we were glued to the TV at 6 pm every Sunday night for our weekly dose of essential vitamins: bands, singers and, in the early days, the *Countdown* dancers, performing our favourite songs.

I know I had a ball singing that song up there. But my sister Nancy remembers it better than I do. She was down the front, her eyes fixed on me. Then, halfway through the song, she glanced behind her. All around, she says, people had stopped and were listening intently. Maybe it was simply because my eight-year-old voice sounded so different from the previous singer's. But when Nancy looked around again, she saw a crowd of people standing at the glass doors at the back, peering in as if they were lining up for a concert. And as the song built to a crescendo they pushed through the doors and crowded towards the front. By the time I hit that high note at the end, looking up at me was a sea of faces.

Nancy says she knew then it was a special moment. Maybe I did too, because when I'd finished, it seemed that all of Springvale Town Hall was on its feet cheering, whistling. I glanced left, I glanced right, I stared straight ahead. Then I burst into tears.

Through my tears I looked across at Mum and Dad. My cousin Frank jumped to his feet, ran to the foot of the stage and opened his arms out wide. I fell into them and he carried me away. Which was just as well, because my feet no longer touched the ground. It was an incredible feeling, of freefalling, almost – euphoric. Nancy says I fainted.

I still think about that moment when I cried. Sure, I was little girl doing something new and exciting for the first time – it was overwhelming. But part of me wonders whether there was more to it than that. Because, even as a kid, for me singing was feeling, a connection. It was how I could truly express myself. It wasn't only about the words or the melody, either. It was also a physical thing. It made me feel happy, it made me feel good.

For me, singing was that simple. Well, it was back then, when I was eight years old and still Pina Arena.

CHAPTER 2

Ring Ring

Dad left Springvale Town Hall that night with a business card in his top pocket. On it was the phone number of a singing teacher called Voila Ritchie.

Mum was still wiping away my tears after my performance when the band singer pressed the card into Dad's hand.

'Your daughter's got something. Take her to Voila. See what she says.'

No doubt Mum and Dad thanked him graciously. I was only half-aware of the conversation, and by the following week I may have even forgotten about it. But my parents must have given it some thought, because they did ring Voila.

When Mum told me she'd made an appointment for me to audition with the singing teacher, I bounced around our tiny kitchen, shouting for joy.

Mum stopped me and looked me in the eye. She had never

pushed me into anything, and she wasn't going to start now. 'Are you sure you want to do this, Pina? You don't have to, you know.'

I knew I didn't have to, but I was already beyond the point of no return. Learning how to become a singer was the thing I *did* want to do more than anything else in the whole wide world.

Voila Ritchie's studio was through a plain door and up a narrow flight of stairs on Sydney Road in Brunswick. I sat next to Mum in the little anteroom, the sheet music for 'You're My World' open on my lap. While we waited, I stared at the posters that covered the walls, huge photos of Johnny Farnham, Rick Springfield and other Australian singers. I found out later these were some of Voila's former students.

A woman with dark hair, bright blue eyes and a warm smile appeared in the doorway. This was Voila. She ushered us into her studio and led us over to the piano. I handed her the sheet music.

Voila sat at the piano and began to play. I sang, giving it my all as I did at the wedding, and ending on that high note.

All the while Voila watched me, smiling encouragingly as her hands moved across the keys.

'Wow!' she said when I'd finished. 'That was lovely, Pina!' She glanced over at Mum and nodded.

Then we chatted, and it felt like we'd known each other forever. Finally she said: 'If you want to come back, I'd be happy to teach you. I think you've got something wonderful there.' Then she turned to Mum. 'I'm impressed. Why don't we make an appointment this time next week?'

For the next few months I attended a singing lesson once a week. Voila gave me lots of exercises to practise and taught me how to use my diaphragm. She also taught me how to hold myself and how to use facial expressions to communicate emotion.

It turned out that Voila knew Johnny Young. A former singer, songwriter, DJ and record producer who had penned a bunch of Australian hits in the 1960s, including 'The Real Thing' for Russell Morris, John was the executive producer and host of a TV show called *Young Talent Time*. YTT, as it was often called, was on every Saturday evening at 6.30 pm.

The show featured a bunch of kids, the Young Talent Team, who performed the hits of the day and other favourites. They got to dress up in the latest fashions – lots of white flares, matching boleros and polyester satin shirts – and always looked like they were having discoballs of fun. Then there were the kids who competed each week. Ordinary kids like me, who loved to sing or dance or play the piano.

Nancy and I had been fans of *Young Talent Time* since it started in 1971. And as my little sister, Silvana, got older, she became a fan, too. The clothes, the songs, the sets: it was like another world to the Arena girls growing up in Moonee Ponds. I never believed I could be one of those kids, even though I thought I could sing as well as they could. Somehow, those children on the telly didn't quite seem real, despite all the fun they appeared to be having.

To Voila, however, *Young Talent Time* was not only real, it was an opportunity for her newest recruit. In a matter of weeks, she'd put a call through to Johnny Young and got me a spot on the show as a contestant.

I couldn't wait and counted down the days. Every afternoon after school I practised, singing into the power cord. Nancy was on hand to give advice and direction. She was even more excited than I was. Where it all might lead I had no idea. All I knew was that I wanted to sing on that show.

When the day finally arrived the whole family piled into the car and we drove across Melbourne to the TV station at Nunawading. The trip seemed to take forever but finally we pulled into the carpark.

Inside the studio people were rushing around. There were painted sets and lights and big cameras on wheels that looked like Daleks out of *Doctor Who*. I'd never seen anything like it but it appealed to me immediately. It looked like so much fun! During a quick rehearsal I was told where to stand and which camera to look at. Then I went with Mum backstage to get ready.

For my first appearance on national television in early 1976, I fittingly wore my flower-girl dress, but this time I sang ABBA's 'Ring Ring', which I'd chosen myself. Mum, Dad, Nancy and Silvana were in the audience, and I could see them as I sang.

At the end of the show, before Johnny and the team cooed 'All My Loving' for the thousandth time, the winner was announced. Little Pina Arena.

Of course, we were all thrilled – my parents, my sisters, Voila and I. But my main thought then was that I wanted to do it again. And again. Soon.

Just weeks later I was back on the show, this time in red and white silk pants with a matching bomber jacket that Mum made especially for the occasion. I sang 'Save Your Kisses for Me', the song that won the Eurovision Song Contest in early 1976 for the British act Brotherhood of Man. It had been a hit in Australia and Nancy had bought the record.

I appeared as a contestant twice more on *Young Talent Time* and was lucky enough to take the prize on three out of those four occasions. My sisters and I were still huge ABBA fans, and for my third and fourth appearances on YTT I convinced Voila to let me sing two of the Swedish band's most recent hits: 'Rock Me' and 'Money, Money, Money'.

By my fourth TV appearance I thought I was quite the little professional: Mum had made me a twenties flapper costume that Nancy probably dreamt up. Voila had taught me how to handle a microphone, when to look straight into the camera, when to smile and when to look pensive. But the wiggling shoulders and hair-flicking I came up with myself, and they stood me in good stead for the next few years.

That year we moved to a brand-new home in Keilor East, a few suburbs north-west of Moonee Ponds. Mum and Dad kept the old house, renting it out to a bloke who turned it into a nursing home. Typically, Dad continued to maintain the garden there as well as establishing one at the new house.

To my parents, the move to Keilor East represented everything they'd worked so hard for since they'd arrived in Australia from Sicily in the mid-1950s. They'd bought the land and built their dream home, a large modern red-brick four bedder with a grand curving staircase, fancy white balustrades, a gleaming new kitchen and terrazzo floors. For Nancy and me it meant moving school – me to Keilor Heights Primary and Nancy to Keilor Heights High.

Many of the neighbours in our little cul-de-sac had stories like ours: parents who'd migrated to Australia from Italy after the war and had worked hard to give their children a better life. Our neighbourhood was built on work and family. That was what bound us together and gave meaning to our lives.

Nancy, Silvana and I soon hooked up with kids in the street and became great friends with the Solars, in particular, who lived two doors down.

I was out riding my bike with Linda Solar one day, not long after my most recent appearance on YTT, when Mum called me in.

I thought I was in trouble. You didn't mess with Mum – she took no prisoners – so with a pounding heart I rode back down the road and up our drive.

I was sitting on my Dragster looking up at her there at the top of the front stairs when she told me the news. John Young wanted to meet us to talk about me joining the Young Talent Team.

I'll never forget that moment. Hooting and shouting, I threw my bike down and jumped up and down, both hands flapping. 'Yes, Mummy! Yes, yes, yes!' Then I was back on my bike and steaming down the driveway and out into the street, shouting all the way: 'Linda, Linda! Guess what? I'm going to be on *Young Talent Time!*'

In fact, when Neville Kent, the show's executive producer, had rung Mum a few days earlier to invite me to join, Mum told him thanks but no thanks. 'I have two other daughters, we both work, and we only have one car,' she said. 'We can't do it. It would be too hard.'

But Neville wouldn't take no for an answer. They 'had to do something', he told Mum. The show had had so many letters and phone calls from viewers, they had no choice but to add me to the team.

Mum had held her ground, but she agreed to think about it.

Now she called me back to explain. 'Pina,' she said once I'd wheeled my bike back up the drive. 'I don't think we can do it. You'd have to go to rehearsals after school as well as do the show all Saturday. It's too much.'

Mum says my response was: 'Mummy, if you don't let me do it, you'll break my heart!' Not a bad effort for an eight-year-old!

Mum didn't give in right away, but she didn't say no, either. And when Neville Kent rang again, she agreed to meet him to discuss it.

*

Mum, Dad and I met John Young and Neville at their production office in a grand Victorian building called Television House in Lennox Street in Richmond.

I'd met John a few times before and already I'd warmed to him. It may be that he understood where I was coming from: his parents were Dutch immigrants who'd settled in Perth, so in some ways our backgrounds were similar.

With John there, we Arenas didn't feel too intimidated. John kicked off by saying how much they'd enjoyed my performances on the show. He said he could hear a big sound growing out of my little-girl voice. He reiterated that they'd had countless phone calls and letters from viewers begging them to make me a team member.

While the adults talked I admired the decor: oversized leather sofas, gold records decorating one wall, and huge posters of current and former *Young Talent Time* stars. I recognised Karen Knowles, Debbie Byrne, Philip Gould, Jane Scali, Sally Boyden and Jamie Redfern – all household names at the time. Most of them I'd never met, but I'd watched that show religiously and I felt as if I knew them all like old friends.

The discussion was wide-ranging: what my schedule would be, how much I'd be paid, how they saw me fitting into the team. My parents listened politely, asking questions only every now and then. English may be their second language, but they're both sharp as tacks and no doubt they understood in a way I couldn't that our daily lives would change irrevocably if we agreed. But in the end that didn't discourage them. They knew it was what I wanted to do.

There was one condition my mother would not budge on, though. When we went on tour (which happened during many school holidays), she or Dad would go with me. 'No Franca, no Pina,' Mum said to John.

When my parents were happy with the deal, they agreed. But there was one issue they hadn't been prepared for. The production team had talked it through and felt strongly that I should alter my name, for the show at least. Filippina was too much of a mouthful for television, and Pina was a little too foreign for Aussie ears, they argued. On *Young Talent Time*, they'd like me to be Tina, not Pina.

I listened in on that part of the discussions and it seemed like a good idea to me. Just a one-letter change, and I liked the sound of 'Tina'.

For Mum, though, it wasn't that simple. I'd been named after her mum, my *nonna*, Filippa Catalfamo, who was still living back in Sicily with my *nonno*, Francesco. I'd met them just once, when I was four, on a family trip to Sicily to meet the rellies. So my name was important to Mum – perhaps it was a little piece of her mother and the life she'd left behind.

But my parents are practical people, and they understood and appreciated the thinking behind the name change. So when we left that office an hour or so later, I had a brand-new stage name.

Tina Arena. Or Tiny Tina Arena, as I became known.

The two names summed up my life from then on. For half the time I was Pina, the girl in year three at Keilor Heights Primary who liked to ride her bike, hang out with her sisters and watch *Countdown*. But for the rest of the time I was Tina, a professional performer who worked several hours a day, five days a week, rehearsing, recording and performing. And it was Tina who appeared on national television every Saturday night, watched by three million Australians – almost a quarter of the entire population of the country back then.

And I was still just eight years old.

CHAPTER 3

The Way We Were

How to summarise seven years of your life in a few pages? Especially when those years made you who you are. It's probably lucky, then, that I don't remember specific days or performances or shows. What I recall are moments and feelings, flickering memories of how it was.

Mum once told me that, years before I was born, she'd seen a child perform at the theatre and had turned to Dad's mother, my *nonna* Nunzia Arena, and said: 'I'd love to have a child like that one day.' As they say, careful what you wish for. Because, from my first *Young Talent Time* rehearsal in mid-1976, our lives changed, just as my parents knew they would.

Being a YTT cast member was almost a full-time job. We worked at least twenty hours a week, Tuesday to Saturday, all squeezed in around school and whatever else we had on. The show ran virtually year-round, so we did that for eleven months of the year.

It was a tough, rigorous schedule, not only for me but for the whole family. After school on Tuesdays we rehearsed and recorded the backing vocals for the coming Saturday's show. For the first few months I was on YTT, we spent those nights at Channel 0's studios in Nunawading, east of the city, a forty-kilometre drive across Melbourne from Keilor East where we lived. The sessions would start around 4.30 in the afternoon and finish around eight o'clock at night. My parents played tag team – Mum would drop me off, and when Dad finished work at night he'd pick me up. I remember those long drives home with Dad. I'd be flaked out in the back seat; he'd be listening to the radio. When we finally got home I'd fall into bed, exhausted.

Not long after I joined we began recording backing vocals at studios in St Kilda then Richmond, while weeknight rehearsals were moved to John's production offices at Television House. The change took a little of the pressure off.

Television House became our second home. It was where it all happened. Wednesday night was reserved for publicity: public appearances, photo calls, promos, interviews. Or we might use the night for costume fittings, answering fan mail or to put the finishing touches on the songs. Sometimes, we got Wednesday nights off.

We learnt the dance routines and practised all our moves on Thursday and Friday nights. And then, starting midmorning on

Saturdays, we'd be in the TV studio doing camera rehearsals, lighting rehearsals, costume rehearsals, then hair and makeup.

Late on Saturday afternoon the show was recorded with a live studio audience, and either went to air live or was broadcast around the country soon after recording. In the early days Mum and I travelled to Nunawading by train on Saturdays, leaving home at around 6 am. After a while my parents bought a second car so we could drive there instead.

Sunday was usually our day off. Then we'd wake up on Monday and the whole cycle started again.

It may have been a punishing schedule, but for me, working on YTT was like going to Disneyland five days a week. I loved every second of it: the painted sets, the satin and sequins, the makeup, the hairdos, the songs – it was the best game of make-believe I'd ever played, and I got to do it most days.

When I joined, the team consisted of Karen Knowles, Nicole Cooper, Debbie Hancock, John Bowles, Robert McCullough and Steven Zammit. Very quickly I was teamed with little Johnny Bowles, as he was known, a boy who had started on YTT not long before I did. John was a couple of years older and a bit taller. We made a cute duo singing 'You're the One that I Want' dressed in white flares and bright yellow satin tops; or 'Everybody Needs a Rainbow', strolling hand in hand down a garden path at the Melbourne Show; or 'Jeans On', with John sitting at a table in a VicRail cafe (I popped up into frame to do the 'chh chh' between choruses, which must have inspired the train theme).

John and I spent so much time with each other he became the brother I never had. We laughed our heads off together, perfected that 'smile into each other's eyes' look as we harmonised on choruses, and forgot our dance steps together – well, okay, I forgot *my* dance steps.

Not long after I joined *Young Talent Time*, someone, probably John Young, had the idea to make a record of 'Tiny Tina and Little John' singing a bunch of show favourites, including 'Ring Ring', which I performed again on the show as a team member. We also sang 'Somewhere Over the Rainbow' and John sang 'Ben', a song about a pet rat that gave a fourteen-year-old Michael Jackson a number-1 hit in 1972.

That album, which apparently went gold, has gone down in history as my first release. The cover was surely a powerful selling point: John and me dressed all in white (I was clutching an oversized teddy bear), hand in hand on a little brown wooden bridge with brown painted trees and a brown rainbow in the background.

I remember recording my vocals for that album standing on a hill of sandbags so I could reach the mike. It's something I've done ever since.

By the end of that first year I was already a seasoned professional performer, with all the skills that went with that: memorising, recording and performing new songs every week, working with TV cameras, understanding how the recording process worked, singing live. It was seat-of-the-pants stuff when the show was done live to air (which depended on whether

Studio A at Nunawading was available). We often had just the thirty-second commercial break to change costumes and redo hair, and performing the next song with an open fly or your shoelaces undone was a common occurrence. Doing the show on Saturdays was exciting – fun, but gruelling. It was nonstop and required absolute concentration.

So it was hard going, but we had a great working environment, starting with the lovely John Young, who was as gentle and sweet as he came across on TV. *Young Talent Time* was his baby. He was involved in every aspect of the show, but he'd surrounded himself with an interesting, solid bunch of people. They taught us an enormous amount, and were great with us kids – supportive and nurturing. Which was just as well, because sometimes it felt like we saw more of the *Young Talent Time* team and crew than our own families. Or to put it another way, the team and the crew on *Young Talent Time* became my second family.

Clips from those early years are time capsules. The hilarious 1970s fashions, the pop songs of the day, the innocence – all are forever captured there, as are we kids, growing up in front of the nation's eyes. In 1980, still a little girl and decked out in a powder-puff fairy godmother dress, I sang 'When You Believe in Magic'. That same year, I was dressed as a fluttering angel with a tinsel halo while John Bowles sang Gene Pitney's 1974 hit 'Blue Angel'. And as part of a round-the-world special I sang 'Mare Mare Mare Mare' in English and Italian, dressed in a sequinned ocean-green shirt with the biggest collar you'll ever see. I'd heard that song at home, probably the original version by Ada Mori (the Australian singer Judy Stone later covered it). It's about a lover leaving, crossing the sea, never to return, and it must have struck a chord with Italian migrants like my parents.

In fact, I became quite a hit with Australia's Italian community, who *loved* their music. When, in 1978, Italian superstar Gianni Morandi toured (and I mean *superstar* – he's estimated to have sold fifty million records worldwide), I appeared live with him, aged just ten, singing his 1976 hit 'Sei Forte, Papà' (You're Strong, Dad). It was the first time I ever sang at the Sydney Opera House. I would also perform at Italian variety shows featuring Italian and Australian–Italian performers.

It had taken only a couple of weeks on the show for people to recognise me in the street and at school. Wherever I went, kids and often their mums and dads would stare or sidle up to me with anything they could find to get an autograph. As months and then years passed, people truly believed they'd come to know us personally. In a strange way they had, because they spent quality time with us – we were in their lounge rooms every single Saturday night.

Part of our education on the show was learning how to cope with that kind of notoriety. It was simple, and something I had no trouble understanding because Mum and Dad had drummed it into me since I could talk. 'Treat others the way you'd like to be treated' was the basic rule. Always show respect and always be polite. Always introduce yourself – never assume people know your name.

But the instant notoriety, the fame, still came as a shock. Because not everyone was a fan. Having strangers call you names, sometimes racist names, when you're ten years old is confusing, even frightening, and it was something that stayed with me. I also learnt that sometimes people were only interested in the girl on the telly rather than Pina the person. It was a crash course in the complexities of human nature.

Some of the kids on the show found all the attention difficult to deal with. And there's no denying that many child performers suffer or struggle later with self-esteem issues, drug or alcohol addictions, eating disorders, depression. *Young Talent Time* members weren't immune: Debra Byrne had an awful experience, which she wrote a book about later, and there were others who struggled after they left the show.

I don't know why my experience was relatively positive when some others' clearly weren't, but I do know that my very traditional, very strong parents had a lot to do with it, Mum in particular. Both my parents had strict upbringings in Sicily – I remember when I met my *nonno*, Mum's dad, on that trip back to their homeland, I thought he was the grumpiest man I'd ever met. We celebrated my fifth birthday in my grandparents' dark little house in Valguarnera, the town where my mother grew up. Nonno was there as I blew out the candles, and he looked as gruff and cross as if I'd just tipped the cake all over the floor. I never really came to know him, even though I felt a connection with him, but I got the sense he'd been a hard disciplinarian.

In our house, respect for tradition, for the people around you, was demanded. We were expected to follow the rules, and to do things honestly and to the best of our ability. There was a lot of love, but it came hand in hand with discipline, and an assumption that you worked hard and didn't let your family down. It kept it all pretty straightforward for me growing up.

One way my parents showed their love was by always being there. When YTT went on tour, which we did during many school holidays, Mum or Dad always came, just as they promised. By then Mum was working from home, sewing on an industrial machine in the laundry. She'd pound away on it every day in between cooking, feeding us, dropping us off and picking us up – she more or less worked around the clock.

My parents never once made me feel guilty about the effect my ridiculous schedule had on the family. As Mum has said since: 'Do it with love or don't do it at all.'

I'm sure Nancy and Silvana wondered more than once why I seemed to get so much attention or why their schedule had to fit in around mine. But we'd all been taught that family came first, above everything, and when you love and respect your family you stick together through thick and thin.

This became a necessity when Mum had a car accident and was bedridden for almost a year when I was twelve. It threw the household into chaos, but somehow we held it together. Because there was no one to drive me to the studios on Saturdays, the network sent a car. The other YTT kids razzed me mercilessly for that. They thought I was a total upstart!

The kids at Keilor Heights Primary had never made a fuss about me being on the show. Occasionally I got a bit of stick, but it never felt like anything I couldn't handle. However, when I attended a week-long orientation at the local high school, the kids just ripped into me.

I was mortified. On the fourth day I came home and burst into tears. 'I can't go to that school, Mum, I just can't,' I said.

Mum got it, and went to work. Through a family friend a meeting was arranged with the principal of St Columba's in Essendon. Sister Helga Neidhart was gorgeous, cultivated, an arts lover, and she and her team welcomed me with open arms.

No one gave me a particularly hard time at St Columba's and I made some true friends there, girls who knew me as Pina, not Tina. It was at St Columba's that I met Julie Field, who remains a dear mate more than thirty years later. Julie was a year older than me but we just hit it off – she had such a warped and comical outlook and we spent most of our time together laughing. Julie is almost six feet tall and I always looked like a stunted mushroom beside her, but her generosity and friendship got me through tough times on more than one occasion. Then there was Morena Miceli, another mad Sicilian like myself. Morena and I still laugh like schoolgirls whenever we see each other. Danielle Bernardo was, and still is, a great mate. And there was Clare Heasly, a good friend and arts lover. Clare and I ended up working together on and off.

It was also at St Columba's that my enduring love of musical theatre was born. The school staged a production every year and I always got involved if I could. In 1980 I played Polly Browne in *The Boy Friend*; in 1981 we did *Bye Bye Birdie*; and in 1983 I was Charity in *Sweet Charity*.

Saint Columba's was another rock under my feet, as were the lifetime friends I made there.

In 1981 John Bowles turned sixteen and left the show. I missed him terribly – we'd been such good mates. Bobby Driessen took John's place as my counterpart, and that year, on the 500th episode special, Bobby and I sang 'I Believe in Music'. Things had changed, though, and I had, too. Tiny Tina had suddenly grown up and my little-girl voice had matured into something stronger and richer.

By the following year I had come into my own, whether I was singing 'Day by Day' in a glittery red belted mini or 'I Love the Nightlife' in a silver metallic frou-frou skirt. That year – 1982 – was the year Dannii Minogue started on the show. I adored Dannii – I still do. She was such a beautiful child, sweet-natured, kind and funny, who, like me, had a wonderful family around her.

But for the first time since I started as an eight-year-old in 1976, it all began to feel a little laborious. Homework had increased, there was more social pressure at school, and I began to feel twinges of dissatisfaction.

Sometimes, performing with the littler kids, I felt a bit too big or a bit too old for it all, not that I ever made a fuss. I think I was starting to look ahead and think about the next chapter.

My musical tastes had developed as well, starting with Barbra Streisand and Liza Minnelli. I remember seeing Liza live at the Palais in St Kilda when I was thirteen or fourteen and being mesmerised by her performance. Then there was Dusty Springfield, especially her versions of Burt Bacharach's classics, as well as contemporary female artists like Kate Bush and Debbie Harry. I'd also fallen in love with R & B, and was listening to Diana Ross, the Pointer Sisters, Sister Sledge and, most inspirational of all, Donna Summer. It was Donna's 1978 version of Jimmy Webb's classic, 'MacArthur Park', that inspired my first performance of that song on the show in 1982. Perhaps the sentiment of the song reflected how I was feeling: the magic of *Young Talent Time* was passing, as was my childhood. And as the song says, I'd never have that recipe again.

I remember the day I decided it was time to call it quits. I was going to perform 'Happiness' by the Pointer Sisters. I wanted to sing live with a live band, which John and the crew thought was a good idea. Then I picked an outfit I wanted to wear: a lavender silk number with bat wings and a big belt that had been one of Jana Wendt's outfits for reading the news. It was very eighties and quite sophisticated for a fifteen-year-old. I was excited at the thought of wearing something more grown-up instead of the usual frilled skirts and ankle socks. But John made me change it – I guess he thought it was too old for me.

It was then I decided I had to leave soon. I couldn't be that kid on YTT forever. It was time to grow up.

By mid-1983 I was ready to go, even though John wanted me to stay on. I gave a lot of thought to what I'd sing for my final appearance on *Young Talent Time* and two songs stood out. I'd sing 'MacArthur Park' again. I would also sing a song that, when I look back now, captures the nostalgia for those simpler times when a kids' song-and-dance show like *Young Talent Time* entranced an entire nation. It's a song that was written for Streisand. On my last show, I decided, I'd sing 'The Way We Were'.

CHAPTER 4

Turn Up the Beat

Grief. I suspect lots of teenagers go through it, whether they realise or not, as they leave their childhood behind. Grief for innocence, for how things were. Knowing life can never be like that again.

Young Talent Time had been a huge part of my childhood. Leaving the show meant growing up and saying goodbye to my own little Disneyland forever. Coming to terms with that was going to be a huge adjustment.

But by the time I'd made my decision to leave I was already through the first stages of grief. I was starting to feel trapped, something we Scorpios hate. I knew it was time.

My final show was to be 22 October. The year was 1983. When I arrived at the studio that Saturday morning it was like a dream. The mood was sombre and everyone was sad. I guess it was the end of an era, in a way – for many of the crew, the team, and the musicians, I'd always been there.

We had a great day but by the time 6.30 came around, sadness descended. Still, I knew that, like every Saturday for the last seven years, I'd just get up and do my job. I'd keep smiling.

When it was my turn to sing, I walked out onto the stage, and the floor manager, Greg Petherick, positioned me for the cameras. I peered out into the audience and spotted Mum, Dad, Nancy and Silvana. Nancy gave me a little wave. When John introduced me, the crowd cheered. At that point I blocked out everything around me and went into my own little bubble. As soon as I sang the first words of 'The Way We Were', boom, I immediately felt the beauty of the song and everything was all right. Just like the night at Gaetano's wedding, my feet were barely touching the ground. It's a poignant song and it was an incredibly poignant moment in my life.

As the last notes of the song faded the audience applauded and I started to cry.

John appeared with all the team. Gorgeous little Dannii Minogue, who only came up to my elbow at the time, presented me with a huge bouquet of flowers. Someone else handed me a gift – a stunning gold and garnet necklace from Channel Ten that I still own. John – ever the practical Dutchman – gave me a box of tissues. It was nearly over. Just 'MacArthur Park' to sing.

In keeping with Donna Summer's version, the song started slow before launching into a full-on disco anthem. It was a great way to go out – singing and dancing like there was no tomorrow.

But there would be a tomorrow, and it would be without YTT. From here on there'd be no more recording sessions, no more dance rehearsals, no live performing, no sparkly costumes. It was a brutal ending to what had been a hardcore but exciting routine.

Turning sixteen a week and a half later seemed to seal the deal: I was no longer that little kid on TV. I was back to just going to school, back to being Pina (or Peen, as my sisters and old friends still call me).

But I'd walked away from YTT with two incredibly valuable gifts. The first was a trade: working on the show had been a wonderful apprenticeship and I came out of there a seasoned professional. The other thing the show gave me was a regular salary, even if I'd never seen much of it – Mum and Dad, always looking to the future, had put most of it away.

They'd certainly never used the money I earned to buy me loads of material things: my sisters and I were far from spoiled, and Mum still made lots of our clothes. But at sixteen I was beginning to discover all those things money can buy – movies, clothes, records, *stuff*. It occurred to me that I could be using the money I'd earned from YTT to get myself some of those things sixteen-year-old girls think they need. I remember one day having a fight with my mum about that: I wanted the latest Fabergé stretch jeans and she wasn't going to waste money on them.

'Well, I'll use *my* money!' I said. 'I earned it. I can spend it how I like!'

Mum wasn't having any of it. We were in our blue Ford Falcon (god, I wish they'd kept that car!), so without another word she drove all the way to Brunswick. She stopped in Albion Street in front of a fish and chip shop with a little Victorian house attached. 'See that on the left?' she said, pointing.

I nodded, having absolutely no idea what we were doing there. Was she mad? All I cared about was getting a pair of expensive jeans.

'Well, that's what your money's bought. So stop whingeing!'

Mum doesn't mince words.

I was speechless. And I realised, maybe not at that moment but soon after, just how lucky I was. I knew there were not many sixteen-year-olds who owned a house.

So YTT had given me much, and I'd be forever grateful. But what now? I had no plan except to finish school. Dad and Mum were very firm about that – they weren't going to let me quit, that's for sure. In fact, Dad had always quietly hoped that I'd go to university. That was a big thing for people of his generation – they wanted their kids to have all the opportunities they'd never had. Mum and Dad would have been happy if I'd pursued another career.

But I knew what I wanted to do – I wanted to keep singing. In fact I think I *needed* to sing, especially back then. Singing was just about the only way I could express how I felt. Working as a professional performer for so much of my childhood had given me immense discipline – I'd learnt to work hard, fit in, follow direction and behave appropriately. The downside of that was

I didn't know how to let loose, be myself, or express my own feelings. I didn't even know what they might be. Singing was my outlet.

My parents were prepared to support me as I followed that dream, but their primary concern was that I concentrate on school, especially since neither had any illusions about the music industry. 'It's a dirty business, Pina,' my mum told me more than once. 'There are pitfalls.'

I didn't have illusions either. And when it came to pitfalls, well, they were looking more and more like craters. I'd begun to work it out while I was still on YTT: in many people's minds I'd always be Tiny Tina Arena, the smiling poppet on TV with the big voice. It was the main reason I left when I did.

So I knew it was going to be tough. What I didn't realise was just how tough. I'd made a lot of friends and contacts in the music business through YTT. But now, when I started to ask around, I constantly came up against the same thing: no one could see how I'd be able to break from the past and launch a career as an adult performer. I began to feel like I was cooped up in a pigeonhole with no escape hatch.

But it was early days, and I wasn't going to give up so easily. While I was still at school I started playing music with Greg Petherick, the YTT floor manager. He was interested in songwriting and producing and he'd come over to my place and we'd play around with song ideas. Greg was a funny, sweet guy and he and I were great mates. Mum and Dad liked him a lot but they weren't that keen on my spending so much time on music at that stage – they were worried it would distract me from school.

But for me it was the first time I'd given any thought to writing songs rather than just singing them. Singing was how I communicated, and now I was discovering that it was possible to write your *own* songs. A little candle was lit in my head. Maybe one day I could too.

Greg was the first person to believe I had a future beyond *Young Talent Time*. Finally, we had demos of some original songs that might be the start of an album. Greg shopped the demos around, but still no one was interested. Greg changed tactics, keeping my identity a secret until his record company contacts had at least heard the songs. But as soon as he told people who I was, that was the end of it. 'Tina who? You mean Tiny Tina Arena?' they'd say, shaking their heads. 'Maybe she should change her name,' someone suggested.

Greg knew a lot of people in the music business (he ended up helping to launch Kylie Minogue's music career, demoing 'The Loco-Motion' then passing it on to Mushroom Records), and finally he put me in touch with Brian Cadd. Brian's an Australian music legend. As well as having several hits in the 1960s and 1970s, he ran his own record companies and penned hits for countless Australian and international artists, including Cilla Black, Glen Campbell, Gene Pitney, Wayne Newton, Bonnie Tyler, and the Pointer Sisters. Oh, and the Little River Band, Joe Cocker and Ringo Starr. Not a bad track record. Brian had moved to America in the late 1970s but he'd come back to Melbourne for short stints to set up a new record label, which he called Graffiti Records.

I knew all about Brian. He knew a bit about me. But he'd been living in LA since the mid-1970s so while he knew what I'd done and what I could do, he hadn't been in Australia during those years I was on YTT so perhaps didn't have such a fixed idea of who I was. He liked my voice and he liked what I could do. He also liked the idea that he could launch his new label with an artist like me, someone with a profile.

I was the first artist Brian signed to Graffiti. The label was so new he didn't have a logo. Nancy, my older sister, who by this time was working as a graphic designer, designed the label for him, and we all thought it looked cool – white graffiti-style type on a red background.

Brian had hooked up with some great songwriters and musos during his time in LA, so rather than choose one of the originals Greg and I had been working on, we trawled through cassette tapes of demos Brian had, looking for a good song. Soon I thought I'd found it – a brilliant song called 'How Will I Know' by Shannon Rubicam. I just knew it was a winner and was excited about it, but when we enquired it turned out that Arista boss Clive Davis had the song on hold. In early 1985 it was released by Whitney Houston and became a world smash hit. *C'est la vie!*

Instead, we settled on a song Brian had bought the rights to, by American songwriting team Pam Reswick and Steve Werfel. I'd never heard of them or met them. But I liked the song.

It was called 'Turn Up the Beat', a piece of rocky pop in a similar vein to Kim Wilde's 'Kids in America' (though more upbeat), which had been a big hit in Australia a few years earlier. I liked it because it was up-tempo and fun, a song about how sometimes music is more important than just about anything else. It appealed to my inner rock chick and would be a chance to say, 'Hey! I'm here, I'm all grown up and I'm ready to take on the world!'

We recorded the song at Armstrong Studios and went for a live rock sound. The B side was a song Greg had written called 'Dreamer'.

Brian had big plans for the single as it would not only launch my solo career but also launch his label. We decided to shorten my name to just 'Tina', à la 'Madonna'. It seemed like a good idea, as they always do: I guess we thought it would help me shake off the Tiny Tina Arena label, and get people thinking about me a bit differently.

Brian had what I thought was a great idea for the clip. It was made to look like a live performance with a bunch of hard-rockin musos (well, except for the marimba player!) and a huge crowd getting down to the beat. I strutted and bopped around the stage, my name in huge neon letters behind.

It wasn't a bad first effort, but it didn't chart and plans to make an album were shelved. I think I was the first and last artist to be signed to Graffiti, apart from Brian himself – he put out a couple of his own records on the label after mine.

*

Around the same time I hooked up with a guy called Fab. Suddenly, I was not only juggling school and music, but a new boyfriend. Mum and Dad mustn't have got a wink of sleep during those last two years of school. Fab (short for Fabio) was a handsome, strapping Venetian, loud, funny and fun. I'd hear Fab coming long before I spotted his hotted-up car rumbling down our little street, his subwoofers booming U2's 'Sunday Bloody Sunday' or Simple Minds' 'Love Song'. Fab introduced me to English and Irish rock and pop. He loved his food but I could still eat him under the table – we'd go out to Enzo and Mario's in Keilor Road and eat a pizza each for entree followed by a big bowl of pasta each. Tortellini with cream and mushrooms was my favourite. I'm sure we made our mothers proud, at least in the food department.

That said, Fab's mum Narcisa, like all true Venetians, wasn't easily impressed. 'Don't expect me to speak English or Sicilian. In this house we speak Venetian so if you want to understand anything you better learn it,' she said to me by way of greeting when I finally plucked up the courage to meet her. She was speaking in Venetian, which is so different to Sicilian I had no idea what she was saying. Afterwards, Fab translated and eventually I did what I was told and learnt Venetian. Anything to keep Narcisa onside!

Months after 'Turn Up the Beat' came out I graduated from high school. I'd just turned eighteen, was at last an 'adult', but in many ways I was very naive. I'd had a traditional upbringing, and I'd been too busy working through my teen years to ever really rebel against my parents or teachers. I'd just tried to do what was right. But what was right now? I felt lost. I knew I could sing, I knew I had a voice, but I had no idea what to do with it.

No one else did either, it seemed. Still no record company was willing to take me on. I guess after the failure of 'Turn Up the Beat', they figured I wasn't much of a commercial proposition.

That summer I went with Fab and some friends down to the Mornington Peninsula. Years earlier, Mum and Dad had bought a beach shack for not much at all down at Rosebud, not far from Sorrento, and while I was growing up our family spent part of every summer there. As we girls grew older we began to go down there with our cousins and friends, sometimes just for the day. We'd take our music and books and hang out on Sorrento Back Beach. In the days before we had boyfriends, we'd perve at all the blond, tanned surfer boys – who didn't? – dreaming that one of them would walk up and ask us out. It never happened, and we envied the blonde, tanned girls in their string bikinis who carried the towels, bought the Chiko Rolls and waited patiently on the beach for those boys to come in from the surf.

For me, Sorrento represented the innocence of being a kid, when anything seemed possible, but that year it felt like my childhood dreams were slipping away forever.

When the summer break was over I had to decide what I was going to do. I'd had a shot at launching a solo music career and I'd landed on my arse. I felt like I was still dragging Tiny Tina around like an old stuffed toy. Perhaps it was time to let those dreams go, and move on. I knew that it would make things easier for Fab and me – he was set to study architecture at RMIT and so would be tied to Melbourne for at least the next few years. If I quit music I wouldn't have to travel. We could spend as much time as we liked together.

Then my good friend Julie Field called, all excited. 'I've got a job! With an insurance company. I start next week! Peen, why don't you try? We could work there together.'

I wasn't sure. It wasn't that I was work-shy. I'd been working since I was eight. But it was so far removed from what I'd been doing and what I'd dreamt of. Still, over the years people had told me I wouldn't know what it was like to work in a 'proper job'. Maybe they were right, I thought then. Maybe I should give nine to five a try. I had nothing on the horizon and no idea what else to do.

I applied for the job and they hired me.

CHAPTER 5

Don't Stop 'Til You Get Enough

I lasted three months at the insurance company. Having a nine-to-five job to go to every day was fun in the beginning, but I quickly found out it wasn't the place for me. Maybe it was having to start from scratch – it didn't take me long to find out I was a much better singer than I was an office worker.

So I was back where I began and desperate to get work, but this time in the only profession I knew – music. In my family no one sits around doing nothing. I was still living at home but now I was out of school I was determined to be financially independent.

I decided I'd get whatever singing work I could. Someone suggested I try to get some work in jingles. It paid okay and it was a job. The best-known jingle writer in Melbourne at that time was Mike Brady. He'd written 'Up There Cazaly' to promote Channel Seven's Australian Rules football coverage. He'd then released it as a single and it went to number 1 on the charts. (In later years he wrote 'Lucky You're with AAMI', among many other well-known jingles.) After the success of 'Up There Cazaly' Mike had recorded Joe Dolce's 'Shaddap You Face', and when no one else would release it Mike did. It also went to number 1, both in Australia and the UK, and charted all around the world. Jingles were Mike's bread and butter, and he agreed to give me some work.

Loud, hilarious and smart, Mike was fun to work with, even if singing jingles didn't exactly knock my socks off. There was Ollie's Trolley chicken, Movieland, Haymes Paints. But I needed the money – every bit I earned I planned to reinvest in my career.

Mike's musical arranger was a guy called Ross Inglis, a highly talented musician and songwriter with a great feel for pop music. Ross also happened to play lead guitar for a band called Network, who had a regular gig at the Grainstore Tavern in King Street in Melbourne. Ross was supportive and sweet, and we got on well.

The Grainstore was a happening place back then, and Network were a brilliant nine-piece with a hot brass section and a percussionist. They could play just about anything you threw at them.

Mike suggested to Ross that they give me a go as a guest vocalist. I love performing live and I love rock 'n' roll so I jumped at the chance. I went down to a rehearsal and we tried a bunch of songs and it worked well. We had a bloody great time together.

The first night was brilliant: the place was thumping and the band was rocket-tight. I remember singing 'Rich Girl' by Hall & Oates, Aretha's 'Freeway of Love', the Jackson 5's 'I'll Be There'. Van Halen's 'Dreams' literally rocked the building's foundations, which was disconcerting, to say the least. And when we played 'Don't Stop 'Til You Get Enough' the place went off.

When I first started singing with the band, the guy who booked the entertainment, Peter Hoyland, was so worried I'd turn people off, he tended not to mention that I was appearing, even though he knew I was up to the task. And it was true. When people came through the door they'd ask who was guest singer. When they heard it was me, they'd laugh. 'What, Tiny Tina from YTT? We've got to see this!'

But those punters came back, week after week, and from the stage I could see them start to come round. I remember one Friday night we were about to start a song when some drunk screamed out: 'Show us your tits, Tina!'

I'd always been pretty timid on stage and off, and once I would have just ignored him. But that was the first time I grasped the advantage of being the one behind the microphone. 'Not until you show me your little weenie first!' I replied, smiling sweetly.

The guy turned around to his mates and they all yelled 'Ohhhhh!' But it changed the tone of proceedings and I think that was when the audience began to realise I wasn't Tiny Tina anymore. I began to realise it too.

Those nights at the Grainstore were the start of a change of attitude, I'm sure. Week after week the place grew fuller and fuller until it was jam-packed. It was a lot of fun and I learnt so much – how to handle and work a raucous audience, and how to stand on my own two feet.

Fab and Nancy and our mates would come along and we'd hang out together before and after the show.

That's what I did for most of 1986 – jingles and live work. As they do, one thing led to another. I got a call from Harley Medcalf, an Australian music promoter who'd toured countless great artists, including Elton John, Rod Stewart, Queen, Bob Dylan, Dame Edna and many more. He was touring Lionel Richie, who had just had a worldwide smash hit with his album *Dancing on the Ceiling*. In the States, the support act had been Sheila E. Harley was looking for a support act for the Australian shows and he offered me the gig.

I was grateful to Harley for showing confidence in me and giving me such an opportunity. I'd always loved performing live, and the last few months working with Network at the Grainstore had reignited that passion. And this was going to be huge: I'd be performing in stadiums and the largest concert halls all over the country.

The only downside was I'd be away from Fab. He'd be in Melbourne working and studying. He was cool about it – he knew how much the job meant to me – but it was the first of many separations and we felt it.

The Outrageous Tour, as it was called, kicked off in Melbourne in January 1987 with shows at the Sports and Entertainment Centre. When we turned up for that first gig we were bowled over by the scale of the production. The crew was the size of an army; the gear filled a fleet of semitrailers, the members of the band were too numerous to count and the entourage even larger. It was the height of the 1980s, and Lionel was an international megastar, so the whole production was lavish, with no expense spared – quite an eye-opener for a girl from Moonee Ponds. That tour was the first time I'd ever seen, let alone tasted, Evian water – bottled water hadn't made it to Australia by then. Lionel had brought in crates of the stuff and he and his band and friends drank it constantly. (It must have made an impression on me, because I still love Evian water.)

It was an incredible tour. We stayed in the same hotels as Lionel and his band and entourage – in fact, together we probably just about booked them out. Lionel was a gorgeous man – still is – and he treated me like a daughter. One afternoon I was in the laundry when his then wife, Brenda, came in. She was washing Lionel's Calvin Klein underwear and I was washing my Target lingerie. We got talking and she told me that they were in the process of adopting a little girl. I was genuinely excited for them. That little girl turned out to be Nicole Richie.

When the tour was over I returned home to Keilor East. Mum and Dad were spending a lot of time over at the old house in Moonee Ponds. They'd taken over managing the nursing home, but the place was very run-down and Mum was spending every day there, scrubbing on her hands and knees. As well, she'd taken on caring for the elderly clients with almost no help. She bathed and dressed them, cooked their every meal using the fresh produce from Dad's garden, and put them to bed at night. Dad would shuttle back and forth between the two houses, helping out when he wasn't at work. Finally Mum decided she'd have to move back to Moonee Ponds – running the nursing home was an around-the-clock job.

It was an extraordinarily courageous choice for my parents to make, but not surprising. Hard work and sacrifice were nothing new to them or to us, and while they were already in their fifties, slowing down or taking time to smell the roses was an alien concept.

The timing was tricky, though. Nancy had recently married her boyfriend, Walter Bilic, and moved out of home. But my younger sister, Silvana, was still at high school and living at Keilor East, and she had trouble coping with Mum being away from home so much. Silvana was rebelling, not happy. I tried to keep an eye on her but I was only five years older and couldn't be the mother she needed. It was a tough time for everyone, and Silvana and I, in particular, resented the time Mum devoted to the old folk in the home. It clearly wasn't just a job for Mum – it was a calling. Not until years later did we come to understand why she had to do what she did.

Soon after, I was asked to audition for a role in the Australian production of *Nine*, a musical by Maury Yeston based on Federico Fellini's autobiographical film *8½*, which had run for almost two years on Broadway. *Nine* was about a famous Italian film director, Guido, who is turning forty and faces a crisis in his work and love-life. Apart from Guido, the cast were all women. I won the role of Renata, an Italian girl; I was also understudy for Peta Toppano, who was to play Claudia Nardi, a main character based on actress Claudia Cardinale.

The show ran for several months at the Comedy Theatre in Melbourne and starred John Diedrich, who also directed and produced, as Guido, and some remarkable women – Peta Toppano, Maria Mercedes, Nancye Hayes as Liliane La Fleur, Caroline Gillmer, Alison Jiear – so many great Australian performers. It was the first time I'd appeared in a full musical production at a professional level and what an extraordinary experience it was!

It was a beautiful production. The sets were magical, stunning, and for a girl who always appreciated a good frock, the costumes were divine. What I learnt from doing that show is that musical theatre is unbelievably physically and mentally demanding. We did eight shows a week. I wasn't part of the main cast, but I was on stage for almost the entire show.

When Peta Toppano was sick for a few days, I suddenly found myself in the deep end. There I was, a nineteen-year-old suburban girl trying to play a thirty-something Italian screen goddess. (Having met Ms Cardinale since, I now realise they were quite some shoes to fill!) How on earth I pulled it off, or how convincing I was, I have no idea.

After the Melbourne season, *Nine* travelled to Sydney, but I stayed behind. Ross Inglis and I had begun working on some demos with Mike Brady's brother, Doug, who was a sound engineer. Ross had written the songs and we had the idea to release them as an album – my album. Ross and Doug approached Mike to see whether he'd use his contacts to score me a recording deal. Mike agreed.

I was over the moon. With Mike's help maybe this time I would crack it.

So I stayed in Melbourne to continue work on the demos. Now all we needed to do was find a record company to take me on. How hard could it be?

CHAPTER 6

Strong as Steel

Scoring a recording deal turned out to be too hard. Mike tried all the majors and was knocked back each time. Finally he decided to fund the project himself with a view to finding a label to release it later. It was an incredible vote of confidence on his part. In the end, Mike did a deal with a label called Avenue Records, which had had success with Mondo Rock, Jimmy and the Boys and a few other Australian acts. My album would be released through EMI. But Mike would be footing the bill.

We began work on the album in 1988. We had the songs Ross Inglis had penned, but we needed a couple more, so we trawled through a pile of songwriters' demos. In addition to Ross's songs we chose 'Strong as Steel' by Diane Warren, who'd written hits for people such as Cher, Tina Turner and Gloria Estefan. The song had been a hit for UK band Five Star and I knew it was a great song. I'd always loved Stevie Wonder, so we added to the list his 1972 classic 'I Believe (When I Fall in Love It Will Be Forever)'.

The album was recorded at Metropolis Studios in Melbourne. Mike was executive producer, Ross produced and Doug engineered. One afternoon we were sitting around the mixing desk listening to what we had so far and arguing about which song should be the first single. Mike was clear on his preference: 'I Need Your Body'. It was one of Ross's songs, a piece of electro-dance pop with a driving synth riff, classic eighties drums and a (slightly) raunchy hook line. It had a catchy, in-your-face chorus and was perfect for radio and clubs. Ross and Mike both felt it would grab people's attention and would send a strong message that Tiny Tina had finally grown up. Mike strongly believed that getting that message across was the key to the album's success, and I think he was right.

I knew 'I Need Your Body' was a good, memorable song with all the ingredients, and that it would help me lose the YTT baggage that we knew was still holding me back. But the song itself wasn't one of my personal favourites. Its message was hardly subtle and I had different musical tastes that were perhaps a little more sophisticated – I still loved and listened to the greats like Dusty Springfield, Barbra Streisand and Aretha Franklin, and R & B divas like Donna Summer and Chaka Khan.

The truth was, however, I was twenty years old. I didn't feel confident enough to believe in my own opinions, let alone express them clearly. All I knew was that I needed to explode once and for all the image of that cute little girl that seemed to be everyone's idea of who I was. So I agreed.

It was around that time that Mike started talking about getting me a manager. He could see I needed someone to help coordinate media appearances and performances, especially in the lead-up to the release of 'I Need Your Body'.

One morning he rang me at home. 'I think I've found someone who might be interested in managing you,' he said. 'I want you to meet him this afternoon. He's only in Melbourne for one day.'

I'd heard a bit about Geoffrey Schuhkraft. He'd been working in the business for years, and had been an offsider of Glenn Wheatley, John Farnham's manager.

We met at Mike's office in Batman Street, West Melbourne. When I walked in a tall, slim man in a black suit stood to greet me. Probably in his mid-thirties, he had curly, sandy hair, rosy cheeks and a wide smile. His manner was very polished and professional but he radiated warmth and charisma. I liked him straight away.

I sat down and we got talking. Geoffrey was living in Los Angeles looking after Little River Band, among other projects. He told me he had a business partner, an American manager called Paul Palmer. They were clearly well connected in the US music industry. Mike filled Geoffrey in on what we were working on. As Mike saw it, we needed someone to take on the management of day-to-day stuff.

Geoffrey and I talked some more. He came across as honest, straight-talking, caring, but with a wicked sense of humour that had me laughing every second minute. We just seemed to click.

After we'd chatted for a while, he said: 'Now, Mike's told me a lot about what he thinks you need, and what the plans are. But what do *you* think, Tina? I know you want to sing, but what's the bigger picture for you?'

I think I stared at him like he was a four-eyed alien out of *Lost In Space*. While I'd never been pushed, or told what to do, I'd never really questioned what I was doing or why. He was right, I wanted to sing, but beyond that, I wasn't sure.

I stammered something about a music career, recording, performing.

He peered at me through narrowed eyes and pursed his lips. It seemed to me that he knew more about what was in my head than I did. 'Perhaps we can talk more about that later, Miss Tina,' he said. And he laughed.

When we finished up, Geoffrey left to think about it. He hadn't said no, but he hadn't said yes. I went home that night with my fingers crossed. I'd liked him so much and thought we'd hit it off. I just hoped he felt the same way.

I also couldn't get his question out of my mind. It's one thing to know you want to be a singer; it's another thing to know what kind of singer and why. Sure, I had a voice, but how would I use it?

Geoffrey had hit on where I was at. While I was loving making the album, sometimes I felt like I was little more than a voice on tape. Put me in front of a microphone and I could sing for hours – I was a workhorse. But that's all I was doing. Every song on the album had been written by other people. They weren't my own words or my own thoughts or feelings. I was just the interpreter.

The next morning Geoffrey rang me from the airport. 'I couldn't possibly say no,' he said. 'We get on too well.'

He was right. We did.

The first thing Geoffrey did was look at my agreement with Mike. He came back to me with a few thoughts. 'I'd like to renegotiate it,' he said. 'As an artist you need more control. The contract needs to allow for that.'

I thanked him from the bottom of my heart and left him to it. Mike probably wouldn't be thrilled, especially as he'd introduced me to Geoffrey. But Geoffrey was putting my interests first, and that was his job. I'd been bumbling along doing my own deals as best I could, but I was still young and had no head for business. I didn't have the balls to push hard for what I wanted. For one thing, I wouldn't have known what to push *for*. I'd simply been grateful to get any work. Now at last I had someone in my corner, someone who would look at the bigger picture and plan accordingly. Geoffrey was a godsend who came at the right time in my life.

For the rest of that year I gigged live for money while putting the finishing touches to the album.

We also filmed the video clip for 'I Need Your Body'. Mike lined up Melbourne film and ad director Salik Silverstein to direct. Salik was looking to create something lush and mysterious. He decided to film the clip in Melbourne's Regent Theatre, which was out of commission, having been earmarked for demolition. It was a stunning space – classic 1920s Italianate architecture – but freezing.

Mike was a mate of Melbourne fashion designer Jenny Bannister, and he suggested to Salik that Jenny dress me. Salik agreed and he and Jenny designed an outfit. It was beautiful and I still have it: black velvet, handmade, lined. But when I tried it on I was embarrassed – all I could see were curves and cleavage. Everyone else loved it, so being an old pro and a trouper, I just got on with it.

When I look at that video clip now, I see a curvy young woman who I guess is not *too* hard on the eye. And as someone recently commented, the dress covers so much that, these days, I could be mistaken for a nun. But when I saw the rough cut of the clip back then, I was mortified. To my eyes I looked like a chunky Italian girl who loved her food (which was exactly what I was!). Today, people pay good money for boobs like that, but in 1990 I would have given them away for nothing. I *cringed* every time I saw that clip. It certainly shouted the fact that Tiny Tina had grown up, but it just wasn't me. Still, I swallowed my pride and went along with it. After all, it was too late to change it now.

But when it came to naming the album I was more assertive. 'It's called Strong as Steel,' I said at a meeting.

'Why?' Mike very much saw this album as his baby – after all, he'd funded it – so I knew he'd have firm views regarding the title.

I had good, clear reasons for my choice. 'Strong as Steel' was a great song by a well-known songwriter and I was proud of my version. As well, the phrase struck a chord with me: I was finding out that in the music business you had to be strong just to turn up every day to work. More often than not the odds were stacked against you, and every time you put yourself in front of a microphone you risked hanging yourself out to dry.

The truth was, I still didn't know if I had it in me. Especially since, to be strong, you've got to know what you're being strong *for*. Even back then I was coming to the realisation that to have a career in music would mean making compromises, especially in my personal life. I'd been raised to value family above everything else, and I knew that one day I'd want a family of my own. Already Fab and I had had to compromise. Fab had always been understanding when it came to my work, but I knew it wasn't easy for him. To balance work and family in this business you needed backbone. 'Strong as Steel' summed up how I *wished* I felt.

Mike, Ross and Geoffrey all liked the title so that was that: *Strong as Steel* it would be.

Those recording sessions and making the video clip for 'Body' were a lot of fun, but I needed paying work. In the music business paying work is usually live work. I'd been living off my savings from *Nine*, plus a few gigs here and there, but funds were running out.

Geoffrey put out feelers and I was offered and accepted a part in a new live show. Called *Dynamite*, it had been conceived by David Atkins, one of Australia's great song-and-dance men, and written by Tony Sheldon, another brilliant Australian singer, writer and performer. The show was a collection of set pieces built around popular songs – 'Man in the Mirror', 'Diamonds Are a Girl's Best Friend' and 'Age of Aquarius' were just some of the numbers I sang. There would be three months of rehearsals in Sydney, where the first leg of the show's national tour was scheduled, at the Footbridge Theatre. The show would run for ten months in all, touring to Surfers Paradise, Adelaide, Melbourne and elsewhere.

So in late 1989 I headed for the Emerald City. It was the first time I'd moved away from home for any length of time. It was exciting but daunting, complicated by the fact that it wasn't great timing for my family: Mum was still living over at Moonee Ponds caring for her clients night and day, and Silvana was only sixteen.

I also had to leave Fab behind in Melbourne, which was hard, but, as always, he was patient and supportive.

I moved into a place in Coogee Bay Road with Alyssa Lloyd, one of the dancers on the show. It was my first introduction to cockroaches. As a fastidious Sicilian who'd been born with a sponge in her hand, I spent every minute when I wasn't working scrubbing and vacuuming.

Collaborating with David Atkins on *Dynamite* was exciting. I've never met anyone who worked so hard. He was tough on me – he's such a perfectionist and my dancing skills were not exactly on par with his own – and yet what a gentleman!

David's then wife, Sheree da Costa, a former principal with the Australian Ballet and Sydney Dance Company, was one of the lead dancers. Bless her heart, Sheree was very generous when it came to my own dancing. I guess she and David figured my talents lay elsewhere.

The show premiered on 6 April 1990. By turns dramatic and tongue-in-cheek but always entertaining, *Dynamite* was physically demanding for the performers. Every night I'd drive home almost asleep at the wheel.

One of the numbers was set to Sting's song 'They Dance Alone'. The song was originally written about Chilean women protesting the 'disappearing' of their loved ones, but David had reinterpreted it, and the piece included images of Australians going to war. It became an especially poignant moment in the show once the Gulf crisis developed in August that year.

A month after the *Dynamite* premiere, 'I Need Your Body' was released. The song was picked up by radio stations around the country as well as the dance clubs. It very quickly charted, reaching number 3.

I was bowled over. I'd given it my best shot, but the success of that song still came as a shock.

Geoffrey swung into action and began organising interviews and appearances, which I'd squeeze in between my *Dynamite* performances. It was crazily busy but fantastically exciting. However, soon it became apparent that no one wanted to talk much about the song. Everyone seemed to be obsessed with one thing: the video clip. Or, to be more precise, my *cleavage* in the video clip.

CHAPTER 7

Woman's Work

Australian comedian Gina Riley added to the clamour around the video for 'I Need Your Body' when she performed a parody of the song on the Australian TV skit show *Fast Forward*. Gina's version was called 'I've Got This Body'. The clip looked something like the original. Gina had been poured into a tight black velvet dress that barely covered her spectacularly augmented boobs, which, in the song's chorus, she implied were 'running free'. I had to laugh. I may have been the one in the firing line, but Gina was hilarious, and at least this time it wasn't me in that dress!

Always two steps ahead, Geoffrey pointed out that it could only help raise my profile and sales of the single. And he was right. The fact Gina thought I was worth parodying was a compliment in itself.

We followed up 'I Need Your Body' with another single written by Ross – 'The Machine Is Breaking Down' – which also charted. Finally the album came out in October 1990 and went gold, reaching number 17 on the album charts, which wasn't a bad effort. I was stunned but grateful – to Mike, Ross, Geoffrey and everyone out there who bought the record and believed in me when I wasn't sure I even believed in myself. In November of that year we released 'Strong as Steel' as the next single.

I was still working on *Dynamite* but as soon as the season finished we headed off on a promotional tour. Geoffrey had lined up a troupe of dancers called the Ramjets, which included Todd McKenney, who choreographed, Jason Coleman, Kelley Abbey and my old Sydney flatmate, Alyssa. We performed to backing tapes at clubs and venues around the country. My old schoolfriend Clare Heasly was tour manager and did an excellent job. Clare was always by my side, and we had buckets of fun.

Ten months of *Dynamite* had improved my dancing skills, but I still felt like I had two left feet compared to the pros behind me. They didn't mind – they were incredibly kind and always patient. On the road we were like one big happy family. We laughed our heads off.

Up in Queensland we caught up with Geoffrey's mum, Betty, who was soon treating me like her long-lost daughter. Geoffrey was starting to seem like a brother. We had so many good times together.

That tour culminated in an appearance at the Sydney Gay Mardi Gras (as it was then known) in early 1991, and it turned out to be the best wrap-up ever.

The venue was the Hordern Pavilion in what was then the Sydney Showground. The stage was an elevated 'boxing ring' right in the middle of the space. As soon as the crowd heard the first few bars of 'I Need Your Body', they cheered and began to dance crazily. I appeared, slowly rising from the stage on a hydraulic lift. I was wearing a mesh bodysuit with a black leather corset, a black leather cap on a black bobbed wig, a suspender belt and fishnet stockings. I had a whip in my hand – it was as close as I've ever come to being a dominatrix.

When the audience saw me they went absolutely mad. There was so much love in that room. It felt like they were all saying, 'Yeah! She's finally grown up and isn't she gorgeous!'

In a funny way, that night was like *my* coming out. It was another nail in the coffin for Tiny Tina and it felt *great*.

Todd, Jason, Kelley and Alyssa – a whole bunch of dancers – performed with me, and the girls were dancing with the girls and the boys with the boys. The music was so loud it blew my ears off. It was an awesome night that I'll never forget. Ever.

It had been a big year not just for me but for Geoffrey as well. He was also co-managing the US act Nelson, made up of the twin blond rock-god sons of rock 'n' roll legend Rick Nelson. With their song '(Can't Live Without Your) Love and Affection' then at the top of the US charts, Gunnar and Matthew Nelson were the third generation of Nelsons to have a number-1 US hit. Geoffrey was jetting back and forth between Australia and the States but he seemed to love every minute of it.

'Woman's Work', the fourth single from my album, was released in early 1991. Around the same time I was asked to sing 'Strong as Steel' live at Melbourne's International Comedy Festival. There was one catch. They wanted me to appear with Gina Riley, she of the 'I've Got This Body' piss-take.

I wasn't sure, but Geoffrey gave me the little push I needed. After all, it would be Gina and Tina, together. What could possibly go wrong?

Comedy legend Shane Bourne introduced me. I appeared, dressed in a black velvet outfit reminiscent of the 'I Need Your Body' dress.

I began to sing – but it wasn't me, it was Gina. Then I did appear – the real Tina. Geoffrey *literally* pushed me onto the stage, hissing in my ear as he did so: 'Get out there and have a good time.' After a bit of banter I threw Gina offstage and started the song again, this time in tune! (Gina, who is a fantastic singer in her own right, generously underperformed that night.) It was fun and I was delighted just to be a part of the festival, which is such a Melbourne institution.

That appearance was close to my last in Australia for some time. All the work we'd done on *Strong as Steel* had paid off and the album had been pretty successful. Now I was looking ahead, thinking about the next album and my next step. I might have been plugging away since I was eight years old, but this woman's work had only just begun.

From the day we met, Geoffrey had been in my ear, imploring me to think through what it was I *really* wanted to do.

Geoffrey was that kind of manager. He believed his role was to look after an artist's best interests, whatever that might entail. If it meant I gave it all away, then he'd support me in that, even if it meant he was out of a job. He knew I needed to find myself after more than a decade of fitting in with other people's agendas. 'You don't have to do all this, Tina,' he'd say. 'You've got to be true to yourself, and if that means going off to live on the top of a mountain, then so be it.' It was a conversation we continued to have for a long time.

One dream I'd had since I was a young girl was to one day make music in America. So many of my heroes – musicians, singers, songwriters – lived and worked there. When it came to popular music, the States was the place to be.

My other dream was to write. I realised that if I wrote my own songs I could put into words and music all the feelings and ideas I seemed unable to express in any other way. I didn't want to be forever just an interpreter of other people's songs.

When I admitted this to Geoffrey he jumped into action. 'Okay. Let's go to LA and get you writing songs over there,' he said. 'Now's the time.' With his US connections, Geoffrey could actually make it happen.

Geoffrey and his business partner, Paul Palmer, would be able to set me up with some songwriters and producers. It would be a six-month songwriting apprenticeship.

I loved the idea, and with the money I'd saved from working on *Dynamite*, I could actually do it. Mum and Dad gave me their blessing: they knew it was what I wanted and that, now I was twenty-three, it was time to go.

But as with all great opportunities, there would be sacrifices. I'd have to leave behind my family and Fab, who after five years had become an honorary member of the Arena family. Over the previous year, due to my work and his study commitments, Fab and I had spent very little time together. When I did see him, we had as much fun as ever and always picked up where we left off, but I think he began to tire of the media and public attention. He continued to support me, but he didn't much like the circus that surrounded it all.

He'd always been respectful of my choices and my commitment to the craft but deep down I think he knew it was going to be tough. With my heart set on going to the States we realised we were growing in different directions. We decided it was time to split. Young as we were it was very painful for both of us, but we still managed to laugh through the tears and we parted good friends.

When I arrived in LA, a black stretch limo from Music Express was there to meet me. Music Express is a legendary limousine company that has probably ferried around every famous person ever born. Geoffrey had organised it, of course. The limo took me straight to an apartment in West Hollywood. There I met up with Geoffrey and his friends, including Tim Keehn, who later became one of my good mates. After hugs all round we retired to the rooftop terrace to sip champagne and take in the view of the Hollywood sign and the city. It was a brilliant afternoon – I felt like I was free. It was Geoffrey's way of saying welcome and it set the tone for my time in that city.

Geoffrey had organised for me to stay in a 1930s Spanish revival-style Californian bungalow in West Hollywood that belonged to Paul, his business partner. It was as cute as a doll's house and as soon as I clapped eyes on it I knew I'd be happy there.

The next day we met Tim and his friends Victor and Scott, and we all went for a stroll around the neighbourhood. I was looking sparkly that day, in a pair of cherry-red and blue jeans, a tight black top, red lipstick and with a little hat and handbag. A young gay guy walking past clocked me and called out: 'My god, girl! Are those tits and lips real?' It wasn't the first or last time someone commented on my lips, let alone my boobs ('I Need Your Body' was not the end of it, by a long shot).

'You bet!' I shouted back, and we all squealed with laughter.

That incident summed up that trip. In LA I could just be myself, because no one there knew me from a bar of soap, let alone who I *had* been. Perhaps for the first time in my life, since I began working on TV as a kid, I felt free to be me and, more importantly, free to make mistakes. It was a weight lifted from my shoulders that I hadn't even realised was there.

Geoffrey wasted no time showing me a good time – with him, anything could be cause for celebration. Whatever we were doing, whether it was work or play, he made sure we had fun. But through his partner, Paul, he also introduced me to some interesting songwriters with whom I very quickly got to work, writing songs.

After initial introductions, when Geoffrey and Paul would send some of my recordings to give people an idea of where I was coming from, we'd get started. I'd hired a little car and most days I'd head off across town to spend the day with various songwriters, many of whom had studios in their houses. I drove all over LA, all by myself. It was liberating.

I'd begun jotting down words, feelings, thoughts, and slowly began to shape them into lyrics. It was a learning process, but it was also a process of discovering how to express myself, something I somehow needed to do after more than a decade of singing other people's songs.

The first song I wrote on that trip was called 'Message'. I wrote it with songwriters Annie Roboff and April Lang about, of all things, homesickness. Because occasionally I did get homesick while I was in LA. When it happened, I'd call Mum, who would talk me down from wherever I was. 'Stick it out, Pina,' she'd say. 'You're there to learn and you know it's what you want.' By the time I'd hung up the phone I was usually back on track.

Two songwriters that Geoffrey and Paul hooked me up with were Pam Reswick and Steve Werfel, who'd written 'Turn Up the Beat', the first single I'd released with Brian Cadd. Back then they'd been just names on a tape, and here I was in their home studio. One song that came out of those sessions was 'Be a Man', which eventually turned up on my next album. It was the start of a collaboration that continued for some years.

Work was balanced with play, which Geoffrey and Paul took almost as seriously. They introduced me to so many of their friends and clients, including the Little River Band boys and their families. Paul's wife Lyn and Glenn Shorrock's wife, Jo, took me under their wings. Then there were the Nelson twins, whom Geoffrey and Paul were managing. With a number-1 single and album, they were touring the States, playing huge auditoriums.

According to Geoffrey, when Gunnar Nelson saw a photo of me he said he wanted to meet me. He liked my lips, apparently. Geoffrey teed it up, of course, and there I was in New York for the first time in my life, to see Nelson play. But we arrived to discover that Gunnar had lost his voice completely and the show was cancelled.

I felt for Gunnar – I know how scary it is as a singer when your voice gives out – so we went to visit him in his hotel room. To look at, Gunnar was a Viking, out of this world – waist-length blond hair, perfect bone structure, tanned, tall – I won't go on – and he was just as gorgeous on the inside, as was his brother Matthew. Gunnar and I took a liking to each other immediately, but he wasn't allowed to speak so we spent the next two days writing notes to each other. It was sweet and romantic – somehow it was easier to write things than to say them.

In September I was packing my bags. Geoffrey had arranged for me to appear in the Pan-Pacific Festival's 'Women with Great Voices' showcase. I would be touring Japan with three other female artists who represented Japan, Indonesia and the US. The woman chosen to represent the US just happened to be one of my favourite singers – Chaka Khan. She's somebody I still consider to be one of the greatest voices ever, and I would have the privilege of performing on stage with her.

We all performed individually and then came together to sing the finale, 'Wind Beneath My Wings'. None of us liked that song. During rehearsals we would all moan and groan when we got to that bit. We couldn't wait for it to be over.

But it was a great experience. The Ramjets came with me, and together we had a ball. I remember singing with Chaka in the dressing-room and pinching myself afterwards. How lucky was I? One evening, we ended up in a nightclub in Hiroshima after a gig. An American band was playing, led by a black American woman. We'd all had few drinks and Chaka decided she needed to show this woman a thing or two. She climbed onto the stage, hair flying. 'What are you doing? Give me the mike!' she yelled at the lead singer. After we'd coaxed her offstage, she jumped on me and planted a big kiss on my lips. I looked across at Geoffrey. He was aghast – for once in his life he had no idea what to do.

At the end of the night we fell into the taxi. The cab driver, who was wearing long white gloves, sat motionless, staring straight ahead. I'm guessing he'd seen worse, even in Japan.

That tour of Japan was an education in itself for this good Italian girl. And for the whole time we were there, Geoffrey and I continued our discussions about what I wanted to do, and how.

'Stop trying to please everyone else,' he'd scold me. 'Be true to yourself.'

During my time in LA, I'd been able to do just that. I'd learnt and grown so much. I'd had some great times, met some colourful people and made some good friends. I'd also embarked on the journey of learning the craft of songwriting. Now I just needed to figure out my next step.

Mike Brady had put Geoffrey in touch with the then vice-president of Artists & Repertoire at Sony US, a guy called Randy Jackson. (Also a great bassist, Randy more recently became well-known as a judge on *American Idol*.) Randy liked *Strong as Steel* and was keen to hear the new material.

That Randy wanted to hear my new stuff, songs *I'd* had a hand in, was really exciting. I knew I didn't want to do another record like *Strong as Steel*. It had been great, and I would be forever indebted to Mike for setting me on this path, but next time around I intended to have songwriting credits and more control over my image.

Ultimately, though, Sony US decided against releasing *Strong as Steel* in America. In regard to new material, they suggested we talk to Sony Australia.

It was disappointing. Randy had shown quite a bit of interest, initially. It wouldn't be the last time I experienced just how difficult it was to crack the US.

There had been more sad news, too. Not long after we returned to LA after the tour of Japan with Chaka Khan, Mum rang to tell me that her dad, Nonno, had died aged ninety-three. She said he'd collapsed in the cellar. He'd been busy fixing something and died with a hammer in his hand.

I may have thought he was a grumpy old man when I was kid, but he'd made an impression on me, nevertheless. Now I was just thankful I'd had the chance to meet him.

Mum couldn't leave the nursing home to attend the funeral, so Dad went instead. It was a reminder of how hard it can be when your family is spread around the world.

Finally, to top it all off, darling Geoffrey, who had been such a supporter as well as a wonderful friend, had decided it was time to move on. He was looking to new horizons. An avid sports fan, he'd begun to move into sports management and was loving it. Music was doing his head in, he said, and he wanted to move back to Australia permanently.

I'd miss Geoffrey – he felt like family – but we knew we'd always stay friends. I'd be forever grateful for his hard work, tenacity, diplomacy and mentoring at a time in my life when I needed it. Geoffrey had brought me out of myself and helped set me on my journey. With his help, I'd begun to find myself and express myself through song. Plus he happened to be the best person to party with. LA would never feel the same without him.

CHAPTER 8

Any Dream Will Do

Geoffrey returned to Australia, but I stuck it out in LA. The Australian singer-songwriter Rick Price was recording his debut album there and he'd asked me to sing backing vocals. I'd met Rick at my twenty-fourth birthday party, which Geoffrey threw for me at my place in LA.

Singing with Rick gave me the chance to indulge my rock fantasies – somewhere inside me there was still a wannabe Suzi Quatro just waiting to come out. It also gave me the opportunity to see the brilliant engineer and producer Chris Lord-Alge at work. Chris was already a legend in the business, having worked on so many great records – James Brown's album *Gravity*, including the song 'Living in America', the *Rocky IV* soundtrack, Prince's *Batman* soundtrack, Chaka Khan's *Destiny*, the Rolling Stones' 'Too Much Blood' and Springsteen's 'Dancing in the Dark' and 'Born in the USA'.

And that was just in the eighties! Wow. How lucky was I to be in the same room. I just hoped something might rub off.

Spending time with Rick meant spending time with his Australian manager, Ralph Carr, a little guy with energy to burn.

It turned out I'd actually met Ralph a few years earlier at a restaurant he ran in Richmond called Churchers Wine Bar. It was a cool place. Ralph loved music and he'd get interesting people to come down to his bar and jam. I was seventeen when I went there with Nancy to celebrate her birthday and he had come over to say hello.

When we met again in LA, Ralph and I got on well. He was a bit older than me – thirty-two to my twenty-four – but he seemed warm, friendly and hard-working. Ralph, like me, was a Melburnian of Italian descent who'd changed his name (he had originally been Raphael Carnovale) and it felt like we had a lot in common. Like me, music was his passion. One thing led to another, as they do when you're two expats in a foreign land, and we started dating.

Meanwhile, Rick was due to appear in a six-night showcase of Australian talent called 'Wizards of Oz'. Scheduled for the second week of May 1992, the showcase also featured artists such as Kate Ceberano, Deborah Conway and the Angels. A few weeks later Rick's album would hit the shelves in Australia, where it quickly charted.

Rick asked me whether I'd sing backing vocals with him on the night. Of course I said yes. The trouble was, it was just a week after the LA riots, which had blown up after police were acquitted of bashing Rodney King. Having spread like wildfire, the riots raged for six days. The entire city was in lockdown and there was an 11.30 pm curfew. It put a dampener on the event and the turnout was not as great as expected. *C'est la vie* – there were bigger issues than Oz music on the agenda that week. But the industry response was positive, and apparently quite a few people enquired about me following Rick's show.

Before long, Ralph and I started working together. I think it had been Rick's idea that Ralph should take me on. Ralph listened to some of my demos and I think his ears pricked up, which was encouraging. I may have had a top five hit in Australia, but after Geoffrey and I parted ways, managers hadn't exactly been knocking my door down. Perhaps they saw the success of *Strong as Steel* as a fluke or a one-off. Obviously they didn't know me – I wouldn't be putting away my microphone just yet.

To his credit, Ralph saw I had more where *Strong as Steel* had come from. And being an ambitious man who wanted to be a manager, a record producer, publisher – you name it – he must have decided I had something.

There was no written agreement between us. Ralph just jumped in and got to work.

One of the first things Ralph did was to contact Sony Australia. My little pile of demos was growing and taking shape, and Ralph sent the latest batch to Peter Karpin there. It included a couple of songs I'd written with another expat,

Mark Holden, who'd had a hit with 'Never Gonna Fall in Love Again'. Mark had since written songs for a range of artists, including Belinda Carlisle, Donny Osmond and Fleetwood Mac. He had a great brain and was nifty with words and melody and we had a lot of fun writing together.

This time, Sony sounded interested, and after some toing and froing the bones of an agreement were in place. Sony offered me a four-album deal. My records would come out on the Columbia label in Australia. If the US decided to release them, they'd be on the Epic label there.

I couldn't believe it when we heard. I'd been fantasising about this moment – a recording contract for an album of songs I'd co-written. And with a major label. The news gave me the inspiration to keep writing.

When I told Mum and Dad they were as excited as I was. But, as ever, Mum warned me to keep my head and be careful. 'You know what I say, Pina,' she said over the phone from Moonee Ponds. 'Keep your eyes on the road and watch out for foxes.' It was good advice that I would do my best to remember.

At the same time, Ralph and I began to talk about what this new record would be and where I wanted to go. The discussions I'd had with Geoffrey were still fresh in my mind and I knew I wanted to do things differently this time around. For one thing, I didn't want to be 'packaged' the way I felt I had been for 'I Need Your Body'. That song and video clip had made a statement and put Tiny Tina to bed for the last time, but the girl in that video already seemed like a stranger, and the clip's New Romantic feel was now well and truly past. I'd never seen myself as an Aussie Madonna – I would never be comfortable with that kind of image. I needed to find my own look, one I could live with. The reality was, I needed to just be *me*. It sounds obvious, but in the entertainment business nothing is so simple.

Luckily, it was finally sinking in that being myself would have to be enough, not only for me, but for all those industry types and for the public as well. Writing songs was helping me get there. Songwriting had given me a way to formulate and express thoughts and feelings, which somehow helped me figure out who the bloody hell I was. At last I was finding my voice.

Shortly after the Wizards of Oz show, Ralph and I returned to Australia together. Not long after we arrived, Ralph came out to Keilor East to meet my parents. Mum cooked a big spread, much of it picked straight from Dad's garden. They were both as gracious and polite as ever, but I could see Mum wasn't entirely sure about Ralph. I guess mothers are often critical of their daughters' choices, whether it's hair colour, clothes or men.

Before we left, Mum spoke up. 'If you're genuinely here for my daughter and you both genuinely care for each other,' she said to Ralph, 'we will unconditionally support both of you. But if you're here for some other reason, please be careful.'

I realise now that Mum was concerned not so much about my taste in men as about the fact that mixing business and pleasure can get very complicated. Being a canny woman, she was all too aware that it could be a recipe for disaster.

Ralph and I just laughed it off – Italian parents can be so protective, especially of their daughters. And the truth was, I trusted Ralph. He was my knight in shining armour, someone who I believed would look after me and shield me from the worst of the music business. He was someone who believed in me. Our relationship neatly combined work and family. This could be *perfect*, I thought.

I was keen to keep up my songwriting while I was back in Australia, so Rick Price hooked me up with a writer he'd worked with and become very close to. Heather Field should go down in history as one of Australia's best songwriters, but somehow we never really 'got' her and she's since moved to Nashville. Blind and very spiritual, she has a gift when it comes to lyrics and melody.

I spent some time with Heather in her flat in Crows Nest, Sydney, and together with Robert Parde, another great Australian songwriter and musician, we wrote a song that will be forever dear to my heart. It was my farewell gesture to Fab, that gorgeous Venetian who had been such a big part of my life. 'Wasn't It Good' is a parting-of-ways song with a difference, a song about remembering and honouring the good things about a relationship rather than focusing on the heartache. Of the many songs I've written, 'Wasn't It Good' remains one of my favourites.

Back in Melbourne, I was running out of funds. The Sony deal was nearly nailed, but I knew there'd be no big fat advance to tide me over for a couple of years while I made the album. My options were fairly limited: live work or jingles. The pressure was on to rustle up something. Ralph had no regular income either, so I couldn't lean on him.

We hadn't been home long when someone from Andrew Lloyd Webber's company, the Really Useful Group, called Ralph. Apparently Mr Lloyd Webber had requested I have a private audition for the role of the Narrator for the Australian production of *Joseph and the Amazing Technicolor Dreamcoat*. They wanted me to fly to New York – straight away.

The musical, which had first been staged in the early 1970s, had been revived in 1991 in London, with Jason Donovan in the lead. A single from the recording, 'Any Dream Will Do', had reached number 1 on the UK charts that year, and the show had since been restaged in Canada. An Australian production was planned to premier in early 1993; a Broadway production was also on the cards.

I had three hours to get on a plane if I was to make the audition – at least they'd offered to fly us first class! I'd only ever done a handful of auditions, so it was scary territory for me, but I knew I couldn't say no to Andrew Lloyd Webber.

A limo was at the other end to pick us up, and we were driven to the Four Seasons Hotel, where we were to stay. The audition, the following day, was at a theatre on Broadway. When we arrived we were shown into the auditorium. There was Mr Lloyd Webber himself, full of thanks that we'd come so far at such short notice. He was also very complimentary about my voice, which, coming from the world-renowned master of musical theatre, was nice, to say the least.

The first song he wanted me to sing was 'Jacob and Sons', an up-tempo tongue twister.

'I haven't had time to learn all the words,' I admitted nervously. 'I'll have to read them from the script.'

Andrew's brow furrowed for a moment – I don't think he was hugely impressed. But he just nodded and let me get on with it.

I gave it my best shot. When the song was over, Mr Lloyd Webber seemed reasonably happy and asked me to sing two more.

Audition over, he thanked me and walked us out. I was still so naive – feeling excited and intimidated at the same time – but I was under the impression he liked what he'd heard. By the time we'd reached the door I was pretty sure I had the part. Andrew hadn't actually offered it to me, but he'd made it fairly clear that, if I was available and we could come to some agreement, the role was mine.

Sure enough, the offer came through. I accepted.

It was a fantastic opportunity and had come at the perfect time for me. Just when I needed a salary, *Joseph* came along to pay the bills. It would also remind people I was still around – it had been two years since *Strong as Steel* had been released, and listeners no doubt had already moved on. Best of all, *Joseph* is a fun, exciting piece of musical theatre. The Narrator is a huge role, second only to Joseph himself. I'd be onstage for the entire show. It would be a huge challenge.

Sealing the deal was the fact I'd be home in Australia for a bit. I'd been missing my family and friends and a couple of months hanging out in Melbourne would be just what I needed. I'd be able to spend some quality time with my sisters. By this time Nancy and her hubby, Walter, were living in Preston. Silvana was working as an assistant in Ralph's office, so I knew I'd be seeing a bit of her.

We were still finalising things with Sony when I started rehearsals for *Joseph*. Ralph and I had become more involved than ever, personally and professionally. I guess we were both so focused on work, it just seemed to make sense. Ralph was renting a little bit of office space from John Young, who, having sold Television House in Lennox Street, Richmond, was now based around the corner in Swan Street.

Finally, the Sony contract was ready to sign, and Ralph and I made a trip up to Sydney to do the honours. I was exhilarated and hyped up, but also a little overwhelmed. When we arrived at the Sony offices in Hargrave Street, East Sydney, Mr Sony Australia, Denis Handlin, appeared, bowling towards me, his arms outstretched. Peter Karpin was not far behind. Bottles of expensive champagne were popped and everyone seemed genuinely excited, which was enormously heartening. Not since John Young offered me a spot on YTT had I felt such a sense of anticipation and optimism.

I couldn't celebrate for long, though. Rehearsals for *Joseph* were still going, in preparation for the show's premiere. I'd already made lots of friends in the cast and crew. David Dixon, who was playing Joseph, was great fun to work with, as was dear Michael Cormick.

We did get Christmas Day off, which Ralph and I celebrated with my family at Keilor East. As usual, it was a full-on family affair with a spread so copious that even the army of cousins, uncles and aunties who dropped by couldn't put much of a dent in it. After a huge lunch, Ralph took my dad aside and asked for my hand in marriage. It was a very old-fashioned way of doing things, I know, but I wanted to do it properly. Dad is my favourite man in the world, and I wanted his blessing.

Whatever my family thought, they shared in the celebrations. Ralph and I would be tying the knot – if we could ever find the time!

Joseph premiered on New Year's Eve, 1992. After the Narrator sings the prologue, Joseph the dreamer who can interpret dreams sings 'Any Dream Will Do'. It's the song everyone remembers from the show, and I think the message is 'follow your dreams'.

Hearing the song just as the new year was upon us seemed somehow appropriate. Because, when it came to *my* dreams, 1993 was looking promising. With a record contract in my back pocket, a new manager and an engagement ring on my finger, I *almost* felt ready to take on the world.

CHAPTER 9

Chains

Joseph ran for almost nine months, touring to Brisbane, Sydney and Adelaide. The show was a full-time commitment, so the album remained on hold. But, as usual, I saved up my pennies, this time to fund the next songwriting adventure and cover expenses while I was recording the album.

A week after the show closed in September 1993, Ralph and I were on a plane bound for LA. I was so nervous I was in tears. This was it: for this trip I would not only be writing, but ultimately recording an album. It was exciting but gut-wrenchingly daunting – I felt like I'd been let loose in some strange and wonderful new land then told I had to find my way home alone. I just kept telling myself that I had a good bunch of songs that deserved to be heard. Hopefully they'd provide a strong foundation for the album.

The first songwriters I hooked up with were Pam Reswick and Steve Werfel. When I turned up on the doorstep of their home in Burbank, Pam gave me a hug. 'Look who it is! Tina, honey! So good to see you!'

Steve was in the hallway behind her, grinning. It was good to see them too. By now they felt like old friends. They were such cool, blissed-out people and always so easy to work with.

Pam and Steve led me through the house to their studio, and after a cup of herbal tea we got started.

An idea for a song had been kicking around in my head for months, maybe years. I wanted to write something about how it felt to be boxed in, to be oppressed by people's preconceptions of who I was and what I could do, and the frustration of being shackled to my past.

We started talking around that idea, then began to work on a melody. But it wasn't until the next day that the song came together. The night in between, Pam had dreamt the chorus, more or less, and once we had that, it all fell into place. What I didn't know was she and Steve were going through a lot of changes in their lives. So the song became a point of connection between us all, while meaning different things to each of us.

As is often the case, it came out as a song about love, about a girl who needs to break free from a relationship that's holding her back and sending her crazy. It was dark, bluesy and soulful, with a melodic change that took it somewhere else entirely, and the lyrics worked on a few levels.

Mum with me at a wedding when I was around one year old. Months later, at another wedding, Mum says I broke free from her arms and ran to the singer to try to sing with him. A few years on, at yet another wedding, I finally got my chance. Thank god for all those family weddings!

Where it all began. Here I am aged eight, singing 'You're My World' at my cousin Gaetano's wedding in early 1976. Just weeks later I appeared as a contestant on the TV show *Young Talent Time*, wearing this flowergirl dress. I won that night and soon joined the show as a cast member.

Nancy, me and Mum with Mum's parents Filippa and Francesco Catalfamo in Valguarnera, Sicily, where my Mum grew up. I thought my granddad was gruff and brooding. Almost forty years later I found out why.

With my granddad (far left), Uncle Felice and Aunty Rozaria, a neighbour (in stripes), Nancy (far right) and Mum (behind me – I'm in yellow). I celebrated my fifth birthday at my grandparents' place in Sicily. Nonno was gruff as ever – years later I found out he adored opera. I always knew we had a connection.

My dad, Giuseppe (Joe), and Mum, Franca, celebrating their engagement. I've always thought my parents looked like movie stars in this picture, which was taken in Sicily before Dad left for Australia in 1955.

Mum at her wedding reception with my four grandparents on either side. Dad didn't attend their marriage in Sicily in February 1957 – he is present in a photograph only, on the table in front of Mum. Dad was in Australia at the time, so my parents were married 'by proxy'. Not long after, Mum left for Australia too.

The cast of *Young Talent Time* circa 1978, a year or two after I started on the show. Clockwise from left: John Bowles, Steven Zammit, Debbie Hancock, John Young, Robert McCullough, Karen Knowles, Nicole Cooper and me. I became a seasoned professional working on YTT and John Young was a great mentor. Love the skivvies! *News Ltd/Newspix*

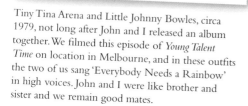

Tiny Tina Arena and Little Johnny Bowles, circa 1979, not long after John and I released an album together. We filmed this episode of *Young Talent Time* on location in Melbourne, and in these outfits the two of us sang 'Everybody Needs a Rainbow' in high voices. John and I were like brother and sister and we remain good mates.

Singing a duet with Italian superstar Gianni Morandi during his 1978 tour of Australia. It was the first time I ever appeared at the Sydney Opera House.

Nancy, me and Silvana out the front of our brand new home in suburban Melbourne. Apparently, Mum never got over the scene of Scarlett O'Hara dashing down the grand staircase in *Gone with the Wind*.

A few years later, here we are again, gone from sensible sunhats to 1980s big hair. How we've grown!

It's 1883 and Bobby Driessen and I are ready to sing a tune in the saloon. Actually, make that 1983, on the YTT set. For me, working on the show was like going to Disneyland every day. I loved every minute.

The Young Talent Team circa 1983, my last year on the show. I'm to the right of John Young. In front of me is Dannii Minogue, aged eleven, who went on to forge a career in entertainment. As a little girl, Dannii was gorgeous – she still is. *News Ltd/Newspix*

I made lifelong friends at my high school, St Columba's in Essendon, and there my love for musical theatre was born. Here I am playing Polly Browne in our school production of *The Boyfriend*. I was always a better singer than dancer, but I'd still have a go.

Hanging out with my sisters, Walter and a friend at Rosebud, near Sorrento on the Mornington Peninsula. Mum and Dad had a shack there, and we girls would take our mates down for weekends. My song 'Sorrento Moon' was about those carefree days.

All grown up and with a gold record for my first hit single, 'I Need Your Body'. The song charted at number 3 in 1990, but what really got people talking was the video or, to be more specific, my cleavage in the video. *Photo courtesy Geoffrey Schuhkraft*

With Molly Meldrum at the launch of my first solo album, *Strong as Steel*. The album went gold, which was great, but I was determined, next time around, to help write as well as sing the songs.

After the success of *Strong as Steel*, I took time out to learn the craft of songwriting. My then manager, Geoffrey Schuhkraft, hooked me up with some brilliant songwriters in LA. Here we are on the day of my arrival. I had a wonderful time. For one thing, no one knew who I was! *Photo courtesy Geoffrey Schuhkraft*

Geoffrey Schuhkraft also co-managed Nelson, twin brothers and rock royalty who had just had a smash hit in the States. We visited them in New York, but the show had to be cancelled because Gunnar Nelson lost his voice. For a day or two, Gunnar and I, who'd become friends, could only communicate by writing notes to each other. *Photo courtesy Geoffrey Schuhkraft*

In 1991 I toured Japan as part of the Pan Pacific Festival's 'Women with Great Voices' showcase. Also on the tour was the great Chaka Khan. Here I am rehearsing with the backing singers, getting ready backstage and grabbing some shut-eye on the road. It was an amazing experience and quite an eye-opener for a girl from Moonee Ponds. *Photos courtesy Geoffrey Schuhkraft*

As the Narrator with David Dixon as Joseph in Andrew Lloyd Webber's *Joseph and the Amazing Technicolour Dreamcoat*. I've always loved musical theatre and have appeared in many before and since. It can be a tough gig, though, involving usually eight performances a week. *Getty Images*

With a few Sony heavyweights around the time of *Don't Ask*. From left: legendary Brit Peter Asher; Peter Karpin, Sony Australia's then A&R boss; and Sony Australia boss Denis Handlin. Those were heady days, for everyone. *Photo courtesy Sony Music Entertainment Australia*

Performing live at the ninth ARIA Awards in October 1995. My single 'Chains' had reached number 4 on the charts in Australia and the album, *Don't Ask*, hit number 1, ultimately going ten times platinum in my homeland. *Nathan Edwards/Newspix*

With Janet Jackson, after winning four ARIAs, including awards for Album of the Year and Song of the Year. It was fantastic to be recognised by my peers and the industry. *Jacqueline Vicario/Newspix*

Marie Antoinette and her sisters, aka Nancy, me and Silvana at my surprise thirtieth birthday in November 1997. Also attending were Elvis, a monk and even a Sydney Swans player. The biggest surprise was seeing Silvana, who, without my knowledge, had returned from overseas for the occasion.

In 1997 my second album, *In Deep*, was released. Here I am in the video for 'Burn', the first single off that record, which we filmed in Richmond public pool. Photographer Pierre Baroni directed, and you can hardly tell that my skin is completely shrivelled after hours in the water! *Photo courtesy Pierre Baroni*

On set with the cast for the video of 'Now I Can Dance'. Directed by Pierre Baroni (behind, in the glasses) and filmed in Melbourne, the clip has always been one of my favourites. It featured the amazing Charo (bottom right), a legendary Flamenco guitarist and actress. *Photo courtesy Nicole Groch*

Recording 'If I Was a River' in 1998. Clockwise from left: Engineering magician Chris Lord–Alge, Peter Karpin, Sony US's gun producer Walter Afanasieff, Ralph Carr and yours truly. *Photo courtesy Peter Karpin*

On location in Egypt shooting the video for 'If I Was a River' in 1998. It was 50 degrees Celsius during the day. Pierre Baroni (in the hat) directed the video and did an amazing job. *Photos courtesy Nicole Groch*

With Marc Anthony and his then partner, Jennifer Lopez, at the 1999 American Latino Media Arts Awards (the ALMAs). We won a gong for 'I Want to Spend My Lifetime Loving You', which was the theme song for the movie *The Mask of Zorro*. That song opened many doors for me in Europe, and helped kickstart my French recording career. *Phil Roach/Ipol Globe Photos Inc*

Celebrating in Paris around the time of my first concert performance in France in 1999. From left: Sony international promotions manager Mitch Vanoni; head of Columbia France the late Virginie Auclair; my right-hand woman, Ann-Marie Meadows; live engineer Steve Scanlon; me; and Columbia marketing manager Valerie Michelin and her offsider, Sabine Feutrel. *Photo courtesy Ann-Marie Meadows*

When we sent the demo for 'Chains', as the song was named, to the guys at Sony the response was fantastic. They absolutely loved it. Sony's reaction gave my confidence a boost. Perhaps I did have it in me to pull this off and make a record I could be proud of.

After we wrote 'Chains', it was suddenly full steam ahead. All we needed was a studio, a producer and some musicians. Ralph, the Sony guys and I had talked about who should produce. A recent favourite song of mine was Alannah Myles' 'Black Velvet', which had been co-written and produced by Canadian Dave Tyson. The more I listened to Alannah's first album, the more I liked the sound and the feel. Okay, it was my inner rock chick coming out again, but hey, what a song!

Dave was based in LA, so we approached him. After he'd heard my demos, he said yes. I still felt like the girl lost in wonderland, but at least I now had Dave by my side.

Dave was fun, talented and sensitive. He was incredibly meticulous when he was working, but always generous and considerate, professionally. His partner in crime was another Canadian, Christopher Ward, a broadcaster and songwriter who had been Dave's co-writer on 'Black Velvet'. They made a good team.

Often we ended up recording in Dave's home studio. He had a beautiful house perched high in the hills in Laurel Canyon and his studio had big windows with views across the valley.

One morning we were mucking about at his place, trying to write something. Dave and Chris pulled out a tape and stuck it in the machine. 'Listen to this. We want to see what you think.'

The music started – guitar, a bit of bass and drums, a Latin feel. I sat back, took in the view and listened. It was one of those crisp but sunny Californian days. The music just seemed to carry me away.

'It needs a melody and some lyrics,' Dave said. 'Got anything?'

'Maybe,' I said. 'Play it again and I'll see if I can come up with something.' I went to the mike, put on the headphones and started to sing. The melody just came to me. It almost seemed to write itself. The three of us wrote the words together the next day. 'Sorrento Moon (I Remember)' came together just like that. It was a song about our summer family holidays in Sorrento, on the Mornington Peninsula, and the joys of childhood freedom. It had such a good feel, and a hint of bittersweet nostalgia.

Later, when Peter and Denis at Sony heard 'Sorrento Moon', I think they scratched their heads. Latin wasn't part of the Australian musical landscape back then. But they reported that, after a couple of listens, their feet were tapping and they were singing along, and that was that.

We wrote 'Heaven Help My Heart' on Dave's terrace overlooking the valley. Dave's friend Dean McTaggart was there with his guitar, smoking Cuban cigars. The bottle of red we were drinking probably should have also got a writing credit.

'Message' had started out in a major key, but when Dave got his hands on it he switched it to a minor, making it a little darker. All the songs evolved in some way as we worked on them.

We recorded 'Chains' there in Dave's studio. We started by putting down the vocals with just a guide track or two. The song remained quite bare, which gave the vocals plenty of space to shine. I added some backing vocals and later Marilyn Martin added her stunning voice. The finger snaps and handclaps were other minimalist touches that set the mood. Then we built it from there.

It took us five or six months to record and mix the album. Various session musos and backing vocalists came in to sprinkle their magic dust. Rick Price returned the favour and sang backing vocals, as did Robert Parde. Then there was bassist John Pierce, who has played with Donna Summer, Fleetwood Mac, Rod Stewart, Celine Dion and many more; guitarist Bob Mann, who has played with James Taylor, Barbra Streisand, Linda Ronstadt, Cher and Neil Diamond; Tim Pierce, also on guitar (he's played with the likes of Madonna, Michael Jackson, Elton John and Joe Cocker). On drums there was Carlos Vega (Herb Alpert and George Benson, among others) and Pat Mastelotto (Patti LaBelle, the Pointer Sisters, Hall & Oates, King Crimson and Mr. Mister – the list goes on).

A guiding hand was provided by Peter Asher, a legendary Brit whose illustrious musical career began with a stint as a musician in the 1960s before he became head of A&R at Apple Records. From there he signed and then managed and produced

James Taylor and Linda Ronstadt. Peter, who some say is the person Mike Myers modelled Austin Powers on, helped with production on my record and even played a bit of percussion. He had a particular interest in female vocalists, I think (as well as being Linda Ronstadt's producer he'd worked with Bonnie Raitt and Cher), and he took a bit of a liking to me.

And finally, there was the wondrous Chris Lord-Alge, who engineered during the mix.

Working with such an incredible bunch of musicians and artists was a huge eye-opener for me, and I learnt so much. I'd come a long way already from singing jingles for cash, and that felt good.

Making that record felt like falling in love for the first time. I just adored the process of writing and felt so liberated by it – I could write from the heart. And then to have musos of such a high calibre bring those songs to life meant so much to me – it was, dare I say it, awesome.

Technically, that record may have been my second album, but in many ways it felt like my first. The songs, while co-written, all gave expression to *my* experiences and feelings. It was *my* heart and soul in that record, which was truly satisfying.

'Honey, you've got a lifetime to make your first record and five minutes to come up with the second,' one of those brilliant musos said to me at the time. How bloody true that was, though at the time I didn't understand what he was getting at.

*

Unfortunately, the other half of making and selling music is image, look, presentation – whatever you want to call it. I say 'unfortunately' because I'm just a singer, not a clothes horse or a style guru (okay, I do love a good frock and a nice pair of Italian shoes). I'm inspired by music, not image, and I've always wanted to move people with my voice, not my outfit. I knew that my strength came from my voice and its ability to tell stories via song.

I'd learnt the hard way that the visuals or the clothes should rarely speak louder than the person. I knew from all the fuss around 'I Need Your Body' that in the image department it was easy to get attention for all the wrong reasons, *especially* when you're a woman.

This time around, I was determined to have control over all that. I was ready to keep it real, to go for a look and feel that was true to me. I figured I'd be better off looking natural, in jeans and a shirt, whatever, but just being myself.

Instrumental in helping me get there was a Melbourne art director and photographer called Pierre Baroni. Pierre had been art director at Mushroom Records, where he'd started photographing artists. He always says he just tries to capture people's eyes, and the rest takes care of itself. Whatever he does, it works.

Ralph contacted Pierre and asked him whether he'd be interested in creating the album cover art. Pierre said yes. I have no doubt that Sony would have wanted to control the visual marketing, but somehow we managed to convince them to use Pierre. Thank god.

But we needed a title for the album first. Lists were drawn up, and I very quickly settled on 'Don't Ask' as my favourite. It was simple, and was taken from the idea of 'Ask no questions and I'll tell you no lies'. In other words, *just listen to the bloody record and judge it on its merits, without any preconceptions. Please!*

With that title in mind, Pierre came up with a powerful but simple cover idea: just a close-up of my face looking straight at the camera, with very little makeup, simple hair, nothing too contrived.

Now back in Melbourne, we shot the cover image in Pierre's studio, which was above Ralph's new office in a townhouse in Richmond.

A young guy called Michael Angel styled me for the cover shoot and later the clip. He was working for Joe Saba back then. Michael and I had a good time on those shoots and we ended up becoming great friends. Now he's a hot shot designer in New York.

On the surface, the cover idea was hardly revolutionary – a close-up of the artist's face is probably the most common album cover style you'll find. But Pierre knew how to capture a certain something in a face to create a dramatic image.

The result was classic and timeless, a cover of which I'm still proud (well, I'm proud for Pierre). The image was understated, almost soft, but it had a power that was quietly confronting: 'Here I am, this is me, *unchained*. Now sit down and listen!'

Once the cover art was nailed, photographer and director Grant Matthews was charged with directing the film clip for the first single off the album. It hadn't taken us long to decide which song that would be. Of course, it had to be 'Chains'.

In keeping with Pierre's cover, Grant went for a muted palette. There I was, dressed in jeans and a shirt (yay!), cowering in the corner of a darkened room. As the song built, I began to pull the coverings off the windows and managed to let the light in, until I finally started throwing things out the window. The video captured the pain and struggle of the song but had a liberating and empowering mood.

'Chains' was released as a single at the end of August 1994. The B side was 'Standing Up', a song I'd written with Rick and Heather Field when I was in Sydney the year before.

With the record in the stores, the irony didn't escape me that a song about feeling trapped by my past might be the very song that freed me from all that. Fingers crossed.

CHAPTER 10

Chains, the S&M Mix

A month after its release, 'Chains' was still only getting airplay in regional areas. Sales were relatively modest. Without metropolitan radio stations behind it, the song had little chance of charting. It wasn't exactly a great start.

Then someone at Sony mentioned that, for some reason, a popular radio station in Greece had put the song on high rotation, even though it hadn't yet been released over there. That gave me a lift – trust the Europeans to get in first, I thought. But what about my homeland?

Finally, the metropolitan stations in Australia picked it up. By early November the single had taken off and gone gold, reaching number 4 in the charts. I was blown away. I knew 'Chains' was special the day we wrote it, but I also knew that often that's not enough. While I'd hoped the record would strike a chord, after so many obstacles along the way, I had low expectations. So I was genuinely bowled over.

Once I'd scrambled back onto my feet, though, Sony, Ralph and I flew into action. It was back in the days of faxes, and the fax machine chirruped night and day. The album was finally released later that month. By Christmas it had gone gold and 'Chains' had hit platinum.

I felt mainly shock but also relief. I'd put everything I had into *Don't Ask*, and now it was out there for people to discover and enjoy. And they actually were! I remember seeing a record shop window plastered with posters of the album cover and feeling so proud and grateful.

Promoting that record had become the centre of my relationship with Ralph – after all, what had always united us was a shared love and respect for music. Now our lives were intertwined in every way, but it was *Don't Ask* that connected us most and drove us onwards and upwards. Neither of us was scared of hard work, which, it was quickly becoming apparent, was just about all there was time for.

Nevertheless, Ralph and I began to make plans for our wedding. We'd been engaged for two years but had never set a date. We'd just been too busy. But I was ready to commit. Like most women of my generation, I had a dream that somehow I could make it all work, that I'd fall in love and live happily ever after with a caring husband, a successful career *and* a family.

Ralph's and my relationship seemed to tick all the boxes for exactly that reason, even if we were so focused on work that our personal relationship increasingly came second. I was sure we'd find the right time to reverse that, down the track, once we'd put in the hard yards in music. But while we were riding the 'merry-go-round', as I came to call it, being a couple just made sense. After all, I was spending an enormous amount of time away from home and the people I loved – it could be an incredibly lonely existence. I was never going to get into bar hopping in search of company or romance.

I was still living at Keilor East with Silvana – Mum and Dad were at Moonee Ponds running the nursing home, where Mum's total commitment was rewarded with adoration from her clients. Ralph was in a terrace in Richmond which he owned with his brother. We decided I'd buy Ralph's brother out and we'd renovate, and hopefully the house would be finished by the time we were married. Can you believe it? A crazy work schedule, a wedding and now a renovation? We were fucking mad! But that's what we did.

Somehow we remained focused on promoting the record. Almost everything else was on hold – there'd be no trip down to Sorrento this year. I made a string of appearances across the country, sang at Carols by Candlelight, gave interviews and did countless instore signings at which thousands of people turned up. In January I sang 'Waltzing Matilda' before the men's final at the Australian Open. That was fun – I love watching tennis, and seeing the stars battle it out from the baseline at the Australian Open is one of my favourite pastimes.

In February 1995, when we released 'Sorrento Moon' as a single, sales of *Don't Ask* hit platinum (70,000 records in Australia) and were still ticking over well. This time radio immediately got behind the single and 'Sorrento Moon' was soon top ten. My life was getting more hectic by the day. Then 'Chains' was released in the UK and Europe, and things got *really* crazy.

The single was picked up by Capital FM, which had the top breakfast radio show in the UK. I heard later that Sony UK had passed my single to the show's programmer, a woman called Annie. She heard it and loved it, and pressed it onto Chris Tarrant, the show's host, who is a radio and TV legend in the UK. Chris started playing 'Chains' and off it went. Soon it had reached the top ten and I was heading over there to appear on *Top of the Pops*, the BBC's music show that aired on Thursday nights and had been running since the mid-1960s.

The first thing I heard when I arrived at Heathrow airport was 'Chains' on the radio. I heard the song again in the car on the way to the hotel. Seeing my reaction, the driver, a hilarious northerner called Reggie, said: 'You know I only drive stars in my car.' (I found out later he was actually telling the truth – he'd driven countless stars around London in his time.) I couldn't have asked for a better welcome to the UK.

'Chains' had reached number 7 by the time I sang it on *Top of the Pops*. Most artists mimed on the show, but not me – I insisted on singing it live, something I've always preferred. The week after I was on, the song went to number 6. I did the rounds of the media and appeared on a bunch of other TV shows, performing 'Chains' each time. I never grew tired of singing it – I could always throw myself into it, let loose, so to speak, and sing it like I meant it. Because I did.

I toured Britain from bottom to top, working fourteen-hour days, but I didn't care. I believed in that record. So did the Sony team in the UK. Terrie Doherty, Amanda Beale and Jo Headland, a bunch of fabulously strong women, were vital to the success of that record in Britain and I'm forever indebted to them for all their efforts.

After Britain, I was off on a whistlestop tour of Europe. Ralph was with me when he could be, but sometimes we were apart. That's just the way it was. Luckily, I travelled a lot with Mitch Vannoni, who was in charge of international promotions at Sony Music Europe. Thank god for Mitch! She was a brilliant organiser and great team player. But it was her local knowledge that made all the difference. Wherever we were, Mitch knew where to eat, what to drink, how to say it in the local patois, local customs – you name it. She was a woman after my own heart and we drank and ate ourselves under the table on more than one occasion. It's thanks to Mitch that I developed a nose for fine food and wine.

Following the success of 'Chains' in the UK and Europe, I was asked to perform at Sony Music's International product presentation in Rome in May that year. Sony Music boss Tommy Mottola would be there, as well as Sony heads from around the world. This was huge – if you were invited to appear it usually meant the big guns were looking to invest money in you in their territory. I was a bundle of nerves just thinking about it.

Ralph came with me on that trip. We were met at the airport in Rome by Sony Italy's head of promotion, Susan Duncan Smith, a stunning redhead with a winning smile and limitless energy. She took us to our hotel just near the Spanish Steps. Our room was on the top floor and had 360-degree views of Rome.

Italian is my first language – I didn't learn English until I started school at the age of five – and I had an overwhelming desire to hit the streets and converse.

Wandering around that city I felt a profound sense of belonging. As for the Italian men – those Latins are ballsy! Guys on their Vespas would try to pick you up, right there in front of your husband!

We met Susan for dinner at a restaurant. Over a *piccolo aperitivo* Susan explained how the conference worked. When she discussed Tommy Mottola's visit you would be forgiven for thinking the president of the United States was coming. There was no doubt that Tommy was important. On his watch, Sony Music had become a global success. But Tommy wasn't just a numbers man. He'd started out as an artist in the 1960s, before moving into artist management. He took the job at Sony in the late 1980s. Tommy had nurtured the careers of many artists, including Hall & Oates, Celine Dion and his then wife, Mariah Carey. He truly understood and loved music.

I tried to appear calm and professional but I was growing increasingly jittery. I knew there would be no room to mess this one up.

The conference was held at a villa just outside Rome. When we arrived, we were escorted to my improvised dressing-room, an area curtained off from what appeared to be an old schoolroom.

I made myself a cup of tea and had just had one sip when Susan stuck her head through the curtain. 'Tommy will be here in five minutes,' she said. 'He wants to meet you.'

I nodded dumbly. I was so nervous I could hardly speak.

Sure enough, five minutes later Susan was back. 'Can we come in?'

Behind her was Tommy, immaculately dressed in a dark suit, flanked by a couple of bodyguards. Susan introduced us and Tommy held out his hand.

He told me the company worldwide was very excited about what I'd been doing. 'I've been getting some great feedback about you,' he said. 'I know you're gonna knock 'em dead tonight.'

'I'll do my best,' I spluttered.

Tommy nodded and was about to leave. Just before he slipped through the curtain he turned. 'How old are you, Tina?' he asked.

'Twenty-seven,' I said.

'Well you're twenty-two now,' Tommy said. He smiled, turned and disappeared.

I wasn't sure what that was supposed to mean, but I wouldn't be fibbing about my age. After all, I was hardly over the hill. Not yet, anyway. But that was common practice. You could still get away with it back then, unlike today, when everything, including your G-string size, is published on the internet.

My nerves served me well, and the performance brought the house down. I was getting better at this kind of 'showcase' performance. It's certainly an art in itself.

That same month, *Don't Ask* was released in the UK. It reached number 11 on the charts and went silver. By then it had gone double platinum in Australia and was still selling well. In early June 'Heaven Help My Heart' was released in Australia as the third single off the album. *Don't Ask* was now four times platinum.

Frontier Touring were organising a concert tour. We pulled together a backing band that included Rob Parde and began rehearsing. At the same time, Ralph and I decided to set aside a date for our wedding. I figured there would never be a 'right' time to get married – once all this was over I'd be back recording a new record and it would all begin again. What difference would it make, being a little busier, when we were already crazy busy?

But I wanted the wedding to be a secret, if we could swing it. I just wanted one day for myself, for us, and our families and friends, just one day that was private rather than public. I was like so many young women – I wanted the white wedding that said loud and clear to the people who mattered most that this was special and this was forever.

When I gave my family the news they were happy for me – well, some more than others. I know Dad and Mum still had reservations about mixing my business and personal lives, but they knew I was a grown woman and would make my own decisions. Silvana, now in her early twenties, was more vocal. She'd worked for Ralph for a while but it hadn't turned out well. There was not a lot of love lost between them. But, hey, that's families for you.

Mum suggested we make a prenuptial agreement. She, sensibly, was concerned about how entangled my personal life and business arrangements had become. Dad agreed. I talked to my then lawyer, who told me that, in Australia, prenups were rarely worth the paper they were written on. Maybe he was right – I know I believed him. And anyway, why would I need one? Ralph and I were best mates.

Despite their misgivings, Mum, Dad, Nancy and Silvana all agreed to pitch in to organise the big day, which would be 10 December.

'Wasn't It Good', the fourth single from *Don't Ask*, came out in late September. Days later I sang 'Advance Australia Fair' and an a cappella version of 'Waltzing Matilda' at the AFL Grand Final between the Geelong Cats and Carlton Blues. Carlton had been my team since I was conceived in early 1967, so I was thrilled they'd made it through, but I was terrified on the day. I don't know whether it was singing in front of a crowd of almost 100,000 people, or the thought I wouldn't be able to hear myself and I'd stuff it up. Either way, I was sick with anxiety. But it all went to plan on the day, including the game, and the Blues won convincingly by sixty-one points!

Just a few days later I was at the Sydney Convention Centre for the annual Australian music awards, or the ARIAs, as they're known. I'd been nominated for five awards and there was no way I was going to miss it.

Sony were out in full force – Peter Asher, who was by then Sony's vice-president in the US, even flew out for the occasion. I think I performed 'Heaven Help My Heart'. I don't remember relaxing, even for a moment.

It was a huge night. By the end of it, four of the five awards for which I'd been nominated were under my chair: Song of the Year, Best Female Artist, Best Pop Release and Album of the Year. When I climbed the stage to collect Album of the Year, Janet Jackson was waiting by the podium in black leather to hand over the gorgeous silver gong. As I approached, she quickly stepped back in what looked like mortal fear – I think she thought I was going to jump her. Whatever it was, we shook fingertips from a safe distance before I made my little speech. It was a funny moment and at the media gathering afterwards they all grilled me about it.

What was also 'funny' was the fact that I was the first solo female artist to win Album of the Year. I guess I shouldn't have been too surprised – the music business was still a bit of a man's world back then. Yes, there were female artists, and quite a few women working behind the scenes, but the big guns, especially in Australia, were mostly men. It could be intimidating when you were constantly working with blokes – musos, managers, promoters, record execs, you name it. Occasionally I *was* intimidated – even though I love men and get on well with them, straight and gay. You'd have to be Joan of Arc *not* to be intimidated.

Which was where Ralph came in. He was my champion – but not my 'creator'. A few members of the media didn't see it that way, though. If some of their articles were to be believed, Ralph – or some record exec – had virtually created me from some old bits lying about. It was almost as if, after twenty years in the business, I wouldn't have had any ideas of my own or known what music I liked, how to make a record or how to carry myself without some bloke there to tell me.

It was probably just laziness on the media's part, and thanks be to god the world has moved on a bit since then. But the fact was, they had things completely backwards. I'd never felt comfortable with the way I'd been 'packaged' in the 'I Need Your Body' video, for which I'd got a fair bit of stick at the time. When it came to *Don't Ask*, I 'packaged' myself as myself. Like it or lump it. Turns out they liked it. But can I say here, no man did it for me.

Whatever the media made of it, winning four ARIAs that year knocked *me* for six. I felt a mix of pleasure *and* pain (as Chrissy Amphlett said, it's a fine line). I was thrilled and I was grateful, especially to the fans who'd liked my music enough to fork out their hard-earned cash to buy the records. But back then I found it difficult to understand how or why the industry could do such an about-turn after those years when no one would take a punt on me. It was something to keep in the back of my mind, for down the track …

Four days after the ARIAs, the 'You Asked for It' tour kicked off with two shows at the State Theatre in Sydney followed by shows in Melbourne, Canberra, and Sydney again.

It was a terrific tour. All the concerts sold out, except in Geelong – I like to think they still hadn't forgiven me for supporting Carlton in the grand final. The audiences everywhere seemed to enjoy themselves, and there were some hilarious moments. In Melbourne, some joker threw a pair of red undies onstage. 'Who do you think I am?' I deadpanned. 'Tom Jones?'

More dates were added, with the second round called the 'You Asked for More' tour. Then, in late November, *Don't Ask* went to number 1 on the charts and hit seven times platinum – almost half a million records sold in Australia. What's more, I had become the highest-selling female artist of all time in my country. Worldwide, we'd hit at least a million records. Things were definitely looking up.

To top it all off, my wedding day was almost upon us. Due to the extended tour, we'd had to cancel our planned honeymoon. There was just no time. That would have to come later, once all this was done.

But already I was wondering when 'later' might be.

CHAPTER 11

Show Me Heaven

Ralph and I were married at St Marys in West Melbourne, where my sisters and I had been baptised as babies. I wore a cream gown with a long train; there were Rolls-Royces, bridesmaids and matching groomsmen, a flower girl, a matron of honour.

A little more out of the ordinary were the security guards, hired to keep the ceremony private. My decision to turn down a hefty sum on offer from a magazine for exclusive photos had caused a huge barney between Ralph and me. Ralph couldn't understand why I wouldn't want to do it.

But I held my ground. I couldn't put a price on our private life. It was a personal choice – I know some people are happy to have photos published and that's their decision. It was one of the few times I said no to one of Ralph's publicity ideas. Nevertheless, the wedding wasn't quite what I'd envisaged.

After the marriage ceremony the wedding party adjourned to Michael and Sue Gudinski's gorgeous home in Toorak, where photos were taken and we celebrated with champagne. The reception was at 9 Darling Street, South Yarra. It wasn't a huge affair – maybe 100 people or so.

It was the kind of white wedding that girls dream of. But it felt surreal to me – Ralph and I were just two good mates getting hitched. It seemed that what romance there had been between us had fizzled – there was never time. The media reported that I was crying in the car as I arrived at the church. I wasn't, but I did feel overcome. In hindsight, I can honestly say it wasn't with happiness. In fact, my overwhelming memory of that day was of feeling disconnected from my husband-to-be.

My family knew. The mood at Keilor East the night before had been sombre. I think Mum, Dad and my sisters realised I had a hard road ahead of me. So when I nearly fainted in the church vestibule just as I was about to walk down the aisle, Silvana put her arm around me. 'You don't have to go through with it, Peen,' she said. 'We can turn around now – do a Runaway Bride.'

Of course, I did go through with it. It was almost as if I treated it like a work commitment – I just got on with it. After all, how could I not, I reasoned. Even though we'd tried to keep it low-key, I could imagine the uproar if I changed my mind and went home. Every day, people get cold feet when they front up to the altar. In most cases things turn out all right. No doubt I was run-down, exhausted. I'd shrunk to forty-five kilos by then, after months – even years – on the merry-go-round. But I think I knew in my heart that wasn't all of it, and that things wouldn't be all right. I also knew that Ralph and I were friends and colleagues but no longer much more. Missing from our lives together was balance – of work and life, work and play, work and love. Instead, we just had work, work, work.

Don't get me wrong – I absolutely adored my job, and after all the effort and heartache, I felt I'd finally achieved something I could be proud of. But love was also important to me. Even back then I realised I needed that balance between work and my personal life, and that I could only spend a certain time on that merry-go-round. The day would come when I would stop, get off and start a family. I was only twenty-eight but I knew what was important: family, friends and good memories, not money or material things. For me, happiness would be a relationship that balanced business with the personal. So far, however, it hadn't turned out that way.

Would things change once we'd tied the knot? No, if the weeks that followed were anything to go by. In fact, with no honeymoon planned, three days later I was back on tour, giving a concert in Townsville. More shows followed, in Brisbane and Melbourne. I enjoyed every minute of performing – I love singing live to a concert hall full of people – but I had hoped we could squeeze in some private moments together.

Unfortunately, they didn't eventuate. Ralph and I were back on the merry-go-round, and our personal relationship was again on hold.

The US release of 'Chains' and *Don't Ask* was imminent. Back in LA, we shot the US video for 'Chains', which was to be the second single in the States. The director was Randee St Nicholas, a photographer and video director who has snapped everyone from Barbra Streisand and Whitney Houston to Bob Dylan, and made clips for the Bee Gees, Prince and so many more. It was a huge production by Australian standards: trailers, caterers, crew, including best boys and assistant everythings. Wardrobe and makeup worked miracles and Randee was a darling, but, just quietly, I always preferred the Australian video for 'Chains'. It seemed more authentic.

After the clip was in the can we headed off on a ten-city promotional tour in the lead-up to the release of 'Chains' by Epic, the Sony US label. The tour took in Chicago, San Francisco and New York. So the merry-go-round continued.

Of course, there was plenty of fun to be had, which helped take my mind off my private heartache. In New York I performed at an exclusive showcase for the media, radio programmers and music retailers. Then I sang at the opening night of the new Virgin Megastore in Times Square. It was a huge event, with free booze and paparazzi everywhere. It doesn't matter how many times I perform, I still get butterflies, and I sure had them that night in the heart of the Big Apple.

Many in the crowd knew who I was, but some didn't. Still, they seemed to enjoy the show, and when I'd finished my four songs Richard Branson jumped on stage, shouting, 'More! More!' So I sang another one.

One of my heroes was there: Liza Minnelli. I had invited her myself that afternoon, when I'd paid her a quick visit at her Manhattan apartment. She'd shown me through her walk-in closets, which were full of stunning Halston gowns, all hanging in neat rows.

I'd met Liza through a mate, Sarita, who worked in the food industry and seemed to know everyone in music. Having looked up to Liza since I was a kid, it had been gratifying to actually get to know her. But I hadn't expected her to turn up for my show.

Liza made her entrance that evening just after I finished singing. She was swathed in Halston, looking very much the legend she is, smiling and nodding to everyone who turned to see, her big eyes shining. What a beautiful spirit she is!

'Chains' was released in the US in early March 1996, around the same time that the sixth single off the album, 'That's the Way a Woman Feels', was released in Australia. For whatever reason – lack of airplay or promotion, who knows? – 'Chains' reached a respectable but hardly earth-shattering number 38 on the American charts. I was pinching myself anyway: even making the top forty over there felt good. Everyone says it and it's so true: cracking the US market, especially when you're a foreigner, is *tough*.

In May a second single, 'Show Me Heaven', was released in the US to coincide with the album's release there, almost two years after it came out in Australia. 'Show Me Heaven' was a cover. The original version had been part of the soundtrack to the Tom Cruise and Nicole Kidman movie *Days of Thunder*. It had been a huge hit in the UK and elsewhere, although not in the US. My friend and mentor Peter Asher had produced the original version, which was sung and co-written by Maria McKee, and he produced my version, too. I think Peter hoped I might crack the US market this time. It didn't happen. That's life. Still, an appearance on *The Tonight Show with Jay Leno* gave *Don't Ask* a kick along, pushing it to number 1 on the Billboard Top Heatseekers chart.

It was a little disappointing for everyone, but when it came to the US, I was determined to keep my expectations low. The guys at Epic gave it their best shot and I appreciated it.

Meanwhile, the merry-go-round was showing no signs of stopping, and when we headed to Monte Carlo for the World Music Awards I felt like we'd spun off into the stratosphere.

The awards show, which celebrates recording artists from around the world, is televised to a billion or so people and raises money for charity. I was there to accept an award for the World's Best Selling Australian Artist – *Don't Ask* had sold a couple of million copies around the world by that time – and I would be performing 'Chains' live.

I'd been around the block a bit by then, and had my share of rubbing shoulders with celebs, stars and even some of my heroes. But nothing prepared me for the James Bond-style glamour of the event. There was no shortage of potential Bond girls – Laetitia Casta, Naomi Campbell, Claudia Schiffer, Carla Bruni … It seemed like every major pop artist or model had turned up for the show and was staying at the Hermitage, the historic luxury hotel in Monte Carlo.

Each time Ralph and I walked through reception we saw familiar faces everywhere, in that way where you think you've spotted an old friend or acquaintance until you realise you don't know them at all except from TV or a magazine.

We'd arrived a day or two early to attend rehearsals. After my second rehearsal I could see that 'Chains' connected with people – whoever was around would stop what they were doing or would pop their heads in to see who was singing. One person who did, and came over to say hello, was Ricky Martin. He might have been one of the biggest stars in the world, but he was an absolute gentleman. So now there was a James Bond to complete the picture.

When we fronted up at the venue on the evening of the event I realised I'd be a bit out of place in my silver-grey suit – everyone else seemed to be draped in Versace. I was ushered to hair and makeup and the Italian makeup artist, who clearly was used to painting the faces of models at the Milan fashion shows, got started. But I could see she was becoming increasingly nervous.

'What's wrong?' I asked her in Italian. 'Why are you suddenly so nervous?'

'I think Naomi's coming this way,' she hissed. 'She'll be expecting me to do her makeup NOW!'

'I'm not moving,' I said bravely – or possibly stupidly. 'I've got to perform shortly, so I can't wait.' Which was true.

It was left to the poor makeup artist to explain to Naomi Campbell that I was a priority. Naomi was not impressed and didn't even glance at me once. Fair enough.

Diana Ross introduced me to the audience. Michael Jackson was in the front row. Celine Dion was a few rows back. So no pressure! But the song carried me through as it has done so many times before and since.

The official dinner was in the ballroom of the Hôtel Hermitage. An hour or two into the dinner, which was silver (or probably platinum!) service, I was still shovelling caviar and foie gras into my mouth when two magnificent women approached me like a pair of schoolgirls. It was '10' and Honey Ryder – aka Bo Derek and Ursula Andress, the first Bond girl of them all.

'Wow, you brought the house down!' Bo said, directing air kisses my way. Ursula did the same.

I don't think I managed much in the way of conversation – I had grown up adoring these two beauties and here they were generously congratulating me!

A little later I was personally introduced to Miss Diana Ross, another one of my heroes growing up. Now I was the bashful schoolgirl, but Miss Ross was utterly charming, and said she knew who I was. 'You're the girl who sings "Chains"!

What a fine voice you have!' Coming as it did from Miss Ross, it was the greatest compliment I have ever received.

The whole experience was utterly surreal. I was getting better at all this stuff, but somewhere inside I would always be the girl from Moonee Ponds, wondering how the hell I'd ended up there. Sometimes I felt like I was up in the clouds, walking on air. There was no doubt that the merry-go-round was sometimes worth the price of a ticket. It just depended on what that price was, something I was still finding out.

CHAPTER 12

If I Didn't Love You

'You've got five minutes to come up with your second album.'

Back in LA and fronting up for a songwriting session with my old mate Dave Tyson, who'd produced *Don't Ask*, I couldn't help but recall those wise words, which I'd heard when I was making that record. I'd barely had time to blink since *Don't Ask* had been released in Australia almost two years earlier. Now I needed to write and record a whole lot of new material. I could feel the pressure mounting. *Don't Ask* had sold so well, the expectation was that the new record should match or improve on that success.

I didn't have a clear idea of what this record would be – how it would sound, or what direction it might take. But I figured out that the best thing to do was start with the songs, and take it from there. The record would reveal itself and take its own shape.

You have to be in a certain frame of mind to write and it took me a while to get there. Two years of touring and promotion, of hardly ever being home, had left me exhausted. But at least I'd be staying put in LA now for a while. I'd rented an apartment from Australian film director Russell Mulcahy in the Park Wellington building in West Hollywood. Ralph set up an office in the front room and came and went.

Back in Dave's studio with its spectacular views of LA, I knew that this was about as good as it gets. Writing and recording is one of the best things you can do when you're vertical (especially after a glass or two of Dave's red wine). You can let loose, you can cry and, even better, you can laugh.

And once my creative juices were flowing, I did. We had some good times writing 'In Command' and 'Sixteen Years'. After a few sessions together we'd recorded a demo of 'Now I Can Dance'. The song was like a sequel to 'Chains', about the freedom of travelling to new places where no one knows who you are. I'd felt it in LA, and again when I travelled to other parts of the States and to Europe. It's something I had never experienced since I was a little kid, and it did feel good, but I also knew it was a feeling anyone can relate to. That song had a similar kind of free-spirited optimism to 'Sorrento Moon' and was probably also inspired by those glistening LA views from Dave's studio.

Dave's old pal Dean McTaggart was often around, and the two of them would joke continually, trying to make each other laugh. With Dave and Dean I wrote 'Unsung Hero'.

We'd also lined up Pam Reswick and Steve Werfel to help. Pam, Steve and I had written some good songs together in the past, including 'Chains', and I hoped we could recreate the magic.

Songwriting sessions with Pam and Steve were always fun. Sometimes, though, I felt like I was in therapy: Pam would draw me out on what it was I was trying to express, how I felt. She insisted on the detail: who, what, when, how, why. There was no room to be bashful or secretive – I just had to put it out there and trust that my co-writers didn't think I was crazy. It could get intense, but that was what made the process exciting. I wrote a whole bunch of songs with Pam and Steve: 'Best for You', which we wrote early on, 'Wouldn't Change a Thing', 'On the Line' and 'You Make Me Feel Good'. The three of us wrote 'Burn' while I was recording the album. It ended up being the first single.

I had things I wanted to say, feelings I wanted to share in those songs. Nothing momentous – just personal feelings and observations about love, relationships, music. With Pam and Steve I wrote the deeply personal 'If I Didn't Love You'. The idea for the song had come to me when I was in Europe promoting 'Chains'. In many ways it was about my confused feelings for the business I was in. I couldn't imagine doing anything else – music was my life – but often it felt as though it put me through the wringer one time too many. And intricately tied up with that feeling was the growing realisation that the business was the glue holding my relationship with Ralph together, and, day by day, that glue was starting to come unstuck.

Perhaps our shared capacity for hard work had become a rod for our own backs. Whatever the cause, we'd become distant, which was hard, because by nature I'm a communicator – I like to talk things through. My personal life was riven with uncertainty and the ground beneath my feet felt shaky.

But I still had hope we could fix things and I wrote songs about that too. I was an old-fashioned girl who believed that when you get married you stick it out and work at it. Ralph and I had a lot of history and we would always share a love of music.

While I threw myself into writing and recording, things kept ticking over. I bought back the rights to *Strong as Steel* from Mike Brady and Sony re-released the record that year. Five new tracks were added, with only five of the original tracks included.

Country singer Wynonna Judd released a cover of 'Heaven Help My Heart' in the US, which reached number 14 on the Billboard country charts. This was a new experience for me. To have someone cover my song and have success as a songwriter was especially sweet.

Then Ralph rang from Australia with some news. A building in Richmond, Melbourne, was up for sale. Not just any building, though. It was Television House, the big old Victorian place that had once been John Young's YTT headquarters, and where my parents and I had met John and Neville Kent to discuss my joining *Young Talent Time*. Once I *had* joined, I'd spent countless hours in that place during the eight years I was on the show, rehearsing, singing, stuffing up my dance steps, doing homework, mucking around with Johnny Bowles and the others, dreaming. That place had been a huge part of my childhood.

Some years before, John Young had sold the building to the designer Sally Browne. And now it was on the market again.

It was the middle of the night and I was still half-asleep when Ralph called. 'Make an offer,' I said.

'How?' Ralph asked.

I was starting to see some royalties from *Don't Ask*, but whether it would be enough I didn't know.

'I don't care. But I want that building!'

When I got off the phone I was kicking myself. *What had I done?* But I would have hated to see Television House developed, or turned into apartments or something. It was a piece of my history.

In the end, Ralph and I went halves in the building and Ralph set up his office in there.

After months of songwriting, we were ready to begin recording. Dave would be available to produce half the album. For the other five or six songs we'd teed up Mick Jones, guitarist and founding member of Foreigner. I'd had the idea to ask Mick. I loved Foreigner and I was also a fan of Billy Joel's album *Storm Front*, which Mick had co-produced.

A quietly spoken Englishman, Mick had also co-produced all Foreigner's records and wrote or co-wrote most of their songs, including 'I Want to Know What Love Is'. But Mick is more than that – he's rock 'n' roll royalty. He's played with Jimmy Page, George Harrison, Bill Wyman, Eric Clapton and French superstar Johnny Hallyday, to name a few. Mick has just about seen it all.

When Mick and I met at a fancy LA restaurant, Mick was sweet, even shy, but we got on famously, and I think we inspired each other. We were a good mix of youth and experience – I might have been working at it for twenty years but Mick had been at it for almost forty!

Mick was then living in New York with his family, but he and his wife, Ann Dexter-Jones, moved to LA while we made the record. In the end they rented an apartment in the same building as the one I was renting in, so we often hung out together.

Spending time with Mick was an education, and not only in music or production. Mick and Ann had a wide circle of friends, and you never knew who you'd meet at dinner: Ryan O'Neal, Michael Douglas, Rod Stewart …

One night I was seated beside Keanu Reeves. I introduced myself. 'Hi, I'm Tina.' I'd never forgotten my YTT training, and in any case I was certain he had no idea who I was.

Keanu just nodded.

'What did you say your name was?' I asked politely.

Keanu turned to me and with Zen-like composure gave his name.

Once or twice Ann's son, Mark Ronson, spent time with us in the studio, just listening, watching. Already he was making a name for himself as a DJ in New York, but his stellar career as a producer, working with artists such as Christina Aguilera, Robbie Williams and Amy Winehouse, was still over the horizon.

Mick brought in Jeff Jacobs, another member of Foreigner, to play piano and keyboards. And Chris Lord-Alge, who'd mixed *Don't Ask*, did the honours again.

Some brilliant US musicians played on that record, including drummer John Robinson, who is famed for working with Quincy Jones and Michael Jackson on *Off the Wall*. John's also worked with Barbra Streisand, Chaka Khan, Lionel Richie – the list is long – and is one of the greatest session drummers of all time and the biggest groove master on the planet. It was great to work with Rick Price again, too. Rick once more chipped in, playing guitar and singing backing vocals.

We decided to go for a more live sound to give the record a bit more of a rock edge. Drums and bass and some guitar were recorded together to get a feel going, with vocals and other instruments overdubbed later, as usual.

About two thirds into recording the album I took Mick to lunch. I had an idea and I wanted to float it by him. After a wine or two I summoned some Dutch courage. 'Let's record "I Want to Know What Love Is". You know I love that song.'

Mick's power ballad had always been a favourite of mine, but I knew it would be a challenge to sing. The dynamics alone are enough to throw a seasoned vocalist, and then there's the range … It's also a song you've got to *feel* to sing well.

Mick wasn't sure. 'I've never given anyone my blessing to cover that song.' He saw my look of disappointment. 'But Shirley Bassey did a great version,' he said encouragingly.

That comment didn't exactly help. Shirley Bassey was a goddess. But I decided not to give up and spent the rest of the lunch trying to convince him.

Still Mick wasn't sure.

When we got back to the studio there was a fax waiting from Epic, my Sony label in the US. 'How about covering "I Want to Know What Love Is" for the album?' it read.

'It's a sign!' I said to Mick. 'See? We have to do it.'

Mick just laughed, but he let me give it a try. After a couple of run-throughs he gave the all clear. I had his blessing.

In the end, not only did the band's then-keyboard player, Jeff Jacobs, play on the song, but Foreigner's incredible original vocalist, Lou Gramm, also agreed to sing guest backing vocals. Wow. I felt truly honoured. Just weeks later, Lou had surgery to remove a brain tumour.

The guys back at Sony Australia were getting excited about the album. Sony boss Denis Handlin flew over three times and stuck his head in. If he'd turned up again I'd have put him behind a mike. After all, Peter Asher had played percussion on *Don't Ask* (although, admittedly, he was a musician!).

In September 1996, Ralph and I returned to Australia to attend that year's ARIA awards. I'd been nominated for four awards this time: Song of the Year and Single of the Year for

'Wasn't It Good', Highest Selling Album for *Don't Ask* and Best Female Artist.

I won the last two, which was incredibly gratifying. To win Highest Selling Album, in particular, was surreal. That record had exceeded all my hopes and expectations. It had probably exceeded the hopes and expectations of everyone else, too.

While we were in Australia we shot the video for 'Burn', which was to be the first single from the new album. I turned to Pierre Baroni, who had done such a great job with the *Don't Ask* cover. The cover image for the new album was taken during the 'Burn' shoot at Richmond public pool. It was a shot of me, hair wet, submerged up to my shoulders in water the colour of fire. We filmed right through the night because we had to be out of there before the pool opened early in the morning for the locals to do their laps. Thankfully the water was warm, but I looked like a shrivelled prawn by the end.

Naming the new record wasn't so hard – I knew I wanted a two-word title again, and *In Deep* summed up my situation. I was well and truly up to my neck in a long love affair with music. Sometimes it was inspiring and incredible fun. At other times it was just plain scary. Most people didn't realise it, but below the surface I was paddling like a maniac, just to keep my head above water. You have to if you're going to survive in the music business. You can't let bad reviews or interviews get to you. You've got to always sound like you know what you're talking about, even when you don't, and you have to trust that the people around you will help keep you from drowning, people like your family, your manager, your record company.

If I didn't love music so much it would have been simpler to just walk away, to settle down, have a family and sing in the shower. But that wasn't going to be a walk in the park, either. For so long, Ralph and I had been so focused on work that our marriage had been subsumed by it. I just had to accept I was married to music. It could be worse, I figured on my good days.

CHAPTER 13

Master Blaster (Jammin')

It was a week until 'Burn', the first single off *In Deep*, was to be released in Australia. Ralph and I were back in our terrace in Melbourne, getting ready for the next round of interviews and appearances once the record was out, and finalising a tour planned for November.

It was Saturday, and Ralph and I had a rare night out planned. On evenings like this we both made the effort to be a couple rather than business partners, but it was difficult. Still, I wasn't going to let it bother me on this night of nights, because we'd been invited to Stevie Wonder's last of several shows at the dinner-theatre in Melbourne's Crown Casino. The casino had only recently opened but already Elton John, Billy Joel and Whitney Houston had given concerts there. And now one of my all-time musical heroes was booked to perform. What a treat!

Once through the doors, we were ushered towards the stage. Even better, I thought – it looked like we might be given a front-row seat! John Farnham and Glenn Wheatley and their wives Jill and Gaynor were already sitting at a table centre front. We stopped to say hello before taking our seats at a table just to the side. Ralph ordered champagne and we settled back, ready to enjoy what I knew would be an incredible show. I'd only had two sips of my drink, however, when a man appeared from a door near the stage and beckoned us over.

At first I thought it was a case of mistaken identity so I just smiled and nodded.

He beckoned again. 'Ms Arena! Over here!' he called out.

Ralph and I struggled out of our seats and walked over. I felt like I was at school and about to get into trouble. Ridiculous.

But as soon as we reached the man he put out his hand. 'Mr Wonder would like to meet you.'

There had been some talk during the previous couple of weeks about me singing a duet with Stevie. Stevie's management had gone so far as to ask which of his songs I would like to sing. I'd nominated 'Heaven Help Us All'. I was terrified at the whole idea, but had consoled myself that it was unlikely to happen. Now it appeared I might have been wrong about that.

'Are you sure? I spluttered.

'Yep. Mr Wonder is very keen to meet you.'

I pulled myself together. 'Great! I'd love to meet him,' I said confidently. I wasn't kidding. I'd always wanted to meet this brilliant artist.

We followed the man back through the door, down a passageway to Stevie's dressing-room. And there he was, the genius himself. Tall, dark glasses, dreadlocks, a broad smile. It sounds crazy but he seemed to have a glow about him – or was that just the tears in my eyes? I got it together and introduced myself.

'Hi. My name's Tina.'

'I know,' Stevie said, putting out his hand. 'I wanted to meet you.'

I grasped his hand and shook it. 'You did? Why?'

'I'm a fan,' he said. *'Don't Ask* is a great record and "Chains" is a fantastic song.'

Well, he said something like that. I was on the verge of collapse, so I can't be absolutely sure.

'Come and sing with me on stage tonight,' he went on.

'Really? Are you sure?'

'You bet.' He smiled even more broadly.

'Well, it's not an offer I can refuse, right?' The girl from Moonee Ponds had piped up just in time, and she was on the money – I couldn't possibly decline.

Stevie laughed out loud.

'I'd love to,' I said.

And that was that.

So there I was, up on stage *jammin'* with Stevie. After we'd finished singing 'Heaven Help Us All', I bowed. 'Ladies and gentlemen, Stevie Wonder!' I applauded him along with the audience and then made to walk off.

'Where do you think you're going?' he asked.

'To my seat, to watch you,' I said.

'No you're not, you're staying here.'

Stevie must have known I wouldn't need any help with the lyrics of just about any of his songs. I knew so many of them by heart. We sang four songs together in the end, following 'Heaven Help Us All' with 'Signed, Sealed, Delivered I'm Yours', 'Master Blaster (Jammin')' and finally Carole King's classic, made famous by Aretha, '(You Make Me Feel Like) A Natural Woman'. The audience ended up giving me a standing ovation that night, which was pretty damn special.

After the show I was invited backstage again. Over drinks I met Stevie's legendary conductor and arranger, Henry Panion III. A professor of music, Henry is up there in the stratosphere with Stevie, having worked with Aretha, Chaka Khan and countless more, as well as arranging, composing or conducting for many of the great orchestras of the world. Henry actually offered to arrange and orchestrate a song for me if the opportunity arose. We never did manage to collaborate, sadly. Meanwhile, Henry's discography has gone from spectacular to awesome (in the original sense of the word).

Singing with Stevie was a privilege and a reminder once again that the merry-go-round was sometimes a truly incredible ride.

'Burn' hit the airwaves and the shops. It debuted at number 2 and quickly went platinum. *In Deep* came out a month later and debuted at number 1, going gold overnight. I was overjoyed, but more than anything else I was relieved. Even though everyone at Sony had been confident and optimistic, I had kept my expectations low. Never count your chickens – or your hits.

It turned out I was the first female Australian artist to have an album debut at number 1. This was another one of those strange statistics that left me wondering why. Not that I had a lot of time to give it too much thought. Things were busy again: interviews, signings and appearances. And, despite the madness, I was loving it.

After so long in LA, it was great to be home and reconnecting with Aussie fans. Sweet and dedicated, the fans who lined up for hours to get their album signed were such a mix: men, women, kids, grannies, teenagers. Some of these people had watched me since I was a little kid, and they'd grown with me and accepted me for who I'd become. Their ongoing belief in me lifted me up.

Catching up with family and old mates was also wonderful after being out of the country for months. We spent as much time together as we could around Mum's table at Moonee Ponds. There would always be something going on there – someone cooking up a feast, or eating a feast, or dropping by for a chat. The only person missing was Silvana – just when I was so glad to be home she was off on a trip to see the world.

On the evening of my thirtieth birthday, Ralph made plans for just the two of us. He wouldn't tell me where we were going, but promised it would be something special. I would need to put on my glad rags, he insisted.

Dressing up had always been a bone of contention between us. Except when I was working, I was very much a jeans and T-shirt girl (still am), but Ralph always wanted me to look the part of the 'star' twenty-four hours a day. If I popped into the office in my tracky daks he'd freak out. He tried, he really did, but he could never change me.

This time, however, I was touched that he'd made the effort to organise an evening out for just the two for us, so I did as he suggested – nice black satin skirt, my best Gucci stilettos. I even went to a bit of trouble with my hair and makeup, something I rarely do outside of work, as anyone who knows me will tell you.

Ralph drove us to Prahran and parked the car before leading me down a laneway and through a small door into what looked like an abandoned factory. The scene inside was quite beautiful – candles flickered in little niches in the heavy stone walls.

It appeared to be a secret restaurant. A rather handsome gentleman met us, sat us down and brought us a drink while a table was prepared in another room. I ordered champagne. Ralph looked a little jumpy, but he assured me it would be lovely once we got inside.

Suddenly, one of the 'stone' walls slid away. Behind it was a sea of people. There was Tina Turner, Eva Peron, Elvis during his Las Vegas period, a sleazy-looking Santa, at least three

Ralphs, a Sydney Swans player (who let *him* in?) and a couple of Marilyn Monroes.

I glanced at my drink – I actually thought it must have been spiked, the scene was so surreal.

'Surprise!' they shouted at once. 'Happy thirtieth birthday!'

I spotted my mate Michael Angel dressed as a monk. That totally threw me – I burst out laughing. Mum and Dad were there too, looking as confused as I was. Then Nancy and Silvana appeared at my side. They looked like Anne Boleyn and her lady-in-waiting, in stunning gowns, makeup, the lot. When I saw Silvana I collapsed into tears of joy – having been away overseas for months, she'd snuck back into the country without me knowing, just in time for my birthday.

My sisters led me away to a back room where they had a costume ready for me. A shiny gold hoop skirt, a baby-blue satin bustier, an enormous white wig, matching shoes, a fan. When they'd finished, I was Marie Antoinette.

Everywhere I looked that night was like a scene from Peter Sellers' *The Party*. Elvis, sporting the most spectacular cape I've ever seen, was serenading anyone who'd listen. Santa, in particular, was behaving very badly and was last spotted throwing up in the toilet. Eva Peron passed out in a barber's chair. Mum and Dad finally left – I don't think they'd ever seen anything like it, or would again. It was the craziest night of my life. I realised what a fabulous sense of humour my mates had. There's no doubt Ralph had pulled a rabbit out of a hat again.

*

Three weeks later we kicked off a nine-city tour in Perth. The In Deep Live tour was also something that will stay with me forever. Jeff Jacobs, the keyboardist from Foreigner, had agreed to be the musical director as well as play keyboards, and together we'd pulled together a truly brilliant band. Jeff brought in Crystal Taliefero, an incredible multi-instrumentalist and vocalist. Crystal, who had played on *In Deep*, was in Billy Joel's band and had also previously played with John Mellencamp, Bruce Springsteen, Elton John, the Bee Gees – need I go on? Our bassist Schuyler Deale was another great American muso who had also played with Billy Joel. Then we had Virgil Donati and Jack Jones from Southern Sons, and Rod Davies, who'd toured with John Farnham.

My old mate from school, Clare Heasly, with whom I'd had such a good time on the 'I Need Your Body' tour, took on the job of tour manager. It wasn't without its challenges – there were some disagreements behind the scenes, as there often are. But Clare stood up to Ralph in a way I'd never seen any other woman do. They never did see eye to eye. But I always believed in Clare's vision and abilities.

Ralph's assistant, Ann-Marie Meadows, also came on tour with us. A woman who, if required, could have run the country with her hands tied behind her back, Annie had previously worked at Mushroom Records. She turned out to be a lifesaver and fun to have around. Soon she was my right-hand woman.

Pierre Baroni designed the show, which included a sheer backdrop and curtains that glowed various shades of red and orange. I felt like the set of songs we played was strong – there wasn't a weak moment. The audiences were just wonderful – excited, generous, supportive.

Channel Nine produced a documentary of the tour's last concerts at Melbourne Park, where the Australian Open is played. I haven't watched it in years, but I do remember the start included vox pops with fans. As usual, my lips proved popular with the blokes, but, in particular, the kids and their mums and grandmas were gorgeous. Their enthusiasm for the music was inspiring. And being a fan myself of so many artists, including the incredible Stevie Wonder, I could relate. I'm sure Stevie could too. Because, while he might be a genius, when it comes down to it, he's no doubt a fan just like the rest of us. After all, he wrote 'Master Blaster (Jammin')' as a tribute to the late, great Bob Marley.

For me, that was the thing about music that kept me going. It was what I particularly loved about performing live. Because, the truth is, whether we're singing, playing, listening or dancing, in the end, we're all jamming. We're in it together.

CHAPTER 14

Stayin' Alive

It's 7.30 pm on Tuesday, 7 April 1998, and I'm holed up in my dressing-room having my makeup retouched. There's a knock at the door.

'Come in!' I call. I can't turn around – the makeup artist is dabbing gloss on my lips.

'Tina?'

I look up into the mirror and see the reflection of a dark, handsome man. He's clutching a red rose. It's Antonio Banderas.

Antonio hands me the rose. 'Good luck, tonight,' he says.

'Thanks.'

I blow him a kiss. (I know – he's married. But then, so am I. And it's Antonio Banderas!)

He smiles, bows, then is gone.

Wow! What a gentleman!

I take a deep breath. Butterflies the size of cats are making hay in my stomach. Not just because I've been given a rose by Antonio Banderas – although that has something to do with it – but also because tonight is not just any night and it's not just any*where*. Tonight, I'm the opening act at a celebration of Andrew Lloyd Webber's fiftieth birthday. The evening's entertainment includes Antonio singing (and he sure can!) 'The Phantom of the Opera' with Sarah Brightman, and Glenn Close singing (and so can she!) 'With One Look' from *Sunset Boulevard*. There's also Dame Kiri Te Kanawa, Julian Lloyd Webber playing cello, and Bonnie Tyler, to name a few. All at the Royal Albert Hall in London.

The Royal Albert Hall! Its beautiful, vast but strangely intimate interior echoes with the names and sounds of past legends who have performed there (in fact, it is famous for its echo, now reduced by upside-down mushrooms hanging from its dome). I had dreamt about singing there one day. Now that dream had come true.

The song I sang, which was the first of the evening, was 'Whistle Down the Wind' from Andrew Lloyd Webber's musical of the same name. The first time I ever heard the song I cried. It's a monumental composition – sweet with a kind of innocence, and yet emotionally powerful. For that reason, it's a bugger to sing. In fact, it's one of the hardest songs I've ever sung, and that was one of the toughest performances I've ever given. But it was also a beautiful moment.

Ralph told me later people were scrambling for their programs to find out who I was. Hopefully I made a good first impression!

At drinks after the show I met David Gates, a great singer-songwriter who, with his band Bread, had had many hits in the 1970s. I grew up with those songs on the radio – 'Make It with You', 'Everything I Own', 'Diary', 'If'. I'm sure I performed them all under Nancy's tutelage, dancing on a chair, decked out in some ridiculous outfit my sister concocted. And here was the man himself, seemingly oblivious to the effect his music had on a generation of young girls.

Andrew Lloyd Webber's invitation to sing 'Whistle Down the Wind' had come out of the blue. I had just finished the In Deep Live tour in Australia when he rang.

He asked me to record the song for an album of the musical and sing it at his birthday bash. So I'd flown over to LA to record it with producer Simon Franglen, just weeks after the Australian tour finished. Andrew and his wife also flew to LA and popped in while I was recording. We managed to get the vocals down in just two takes, which is not bad going and made a good impression on Mr Musical Theatre, I hope.

The *Whistle Down the Wind* album featured various artists, including Tom Jones, Donny Osmond, Boy George, Meat Loaf, Boyzone and Bonnie Tyler. Around the same time that the show *Whistle Down the Wind* opened in the West End, my version of the title track was released as a single, occasioning another appearance on *Top of the Pops*. But the big hit from the album was Boyzone singing 'No Matter What'. It was huge around the world, especially in Britain. The show ended up running for three years.

The man who wrote the lyrics for *Whistle Down the Wind* was an American composer and producer called Jim Steinman. Jim wrote *Bat Out of Hell* with Meat Loaf and has written or produced countless other hits, including 'Total Eclipse of the Heart' for Bonnie Tyler. The story of *Bat Out of Hell* gives you some idea of the kind of man Jim is. No one in the industry wanted to release that record but Jim and Meat Loaf never gave up. Forty-three million copies later, *Bat Out of Hell* is one of the biggest-selling albums of all time.

Jim was busy producing the musical soundtrack for a new movie starring my favourite Spanish actor – you guessed it, Antonio Banderas. The composer for the *Mask of Zorro* soundtrack was James Horner, whose soundtrack to *Titanic* was then topping the charts around the world, as was the signature song, 'My Heart Will Go On', sung by Celine Dion. Like *Bat Out of Hell*, the *Titanic* soundtrack went on to become another of the biggest-selling albums of all time.

Jim and James were looking for a female vocalist to sing the *Mask of Zorro* signature song, called 'I Want to Spend My Lifetime Loving You'. Apparently Jim heard my version of 'Whistle Down the Wind' and decided I was the woman for the job. He tells the story that he rang James, but when he mentioned my name, James said: 'Who?' Luckily, after James listened to a few of my previous recordings, he gave me the tick. It probably helped that my record company, Sony, would be releasing the soundtrack.

When I got the call I was still in London doing promos and showcases in the lead-up to the release of *In Deep*. It was another one of those can't-say-no opportunities. When asked if I'd do it, I think my actual words were: 'Well, bloody hell, yeah, absolutely!'

The song is a duet, and originally I was to sing it with Ricky Martin. Ricky and I were mates – we'd bonded in various cities on various promo tours – and I was excited to be doing the song with him. But then his track 'The Cup of Life' was released as the theme song for the 1998 FIFA World Cup and suddenly Ricky's schedule went completely *loco*. Overnight, his life became a conveyor belt of appearances, interviews and international flights. I've never seen anyone work so hard. So now they were looking for a male vocalist to replace Ricky.

Regardless, I toddled off to Sarm Studio to meet Jim Steinman. Jim's like a vampire – he only comes out at night – so we recorded my vocals under shadow of darkness. It's a very sensuous song, so I just imagined that a dark handsome man was singing it there beside me and off I went.

James and Jim were gorgeous to work with. James was particularly divine – down to earth, creative, unaffected.

In the end Marc Anthony was teed up to sing the song but Marc and I didn't cross paths until I made the trip to Burbank

Studios in Hollywood to make the video. I dropped in to see him at his home the night before. We got on famously – he was such a funny guy, a natural comedian.

I was back and forth between London, Europe, Australia and the US a lot that year. Ralph was sometimes with me, sometimes not. Things between us went from bad to worse. Now not only our personal relationship but our working relationship had soured. From where I stood, Ralph seemed interested only in work. From where he stood, he probably just didn't get it. When business is going well, what could be the problem? And with both of us on such a crazy schedule, there never seemed to be the time or the place to talk about it.

On the career front, things were going well thanks to my, Ralph's and Sony's efforts (as well as Pierre's, Ann-Marie's and others). Still in London, I fronted up for Capital FM's Party in the Park one warm Sunday in early July. It was only days after the premiere of the show *Whistle Down the Wind* and around the same time the single was released. The event was a fundraiser for the Prince's Trust, Prince Charles's personal charity, which raises funds for youth. Around 150,000 people were in London's Hyde Park that afternoon to see a killer line-up of acts and artists, which included Tom Jones, yours truly and Shania Twain. Natalie Imbruglia was also on the bill. Her album *Left of the Middle* had been a hit around the world the year before, as had 'Torn', the single.

There'd been a time when nothing could have topped performing at the Royal Albert Hall and in London's Hyde

Park. That was until we got a call from the Bee Gees' management. Maybe it was Sony who suggested it to them, but the Bee Gees would have known me as one of John Young's protégés. Barry Gibb and John go way back, to the mid-1960s when they shared a flat in London. Either way, the brothers Gibb were keen for me to support them at their London show, so my next stop that year was the Bee Gees' 'One Show Only' concert at Wembley Stadium.

I'd looked up to the Bee Gees since I was a kid and John Young told me stories about his days living and working with Barry Gibb, who wrote quite a few songs for John back in the day. They were some of the greatest songwriters in the history of pop music. Barry also wrote all the songs on Barbra Streisand's *Guilty* album, which, for me, is a masterpiece. And then there are all their other hits from the 1960s through to the 1990s. Those guys were giants of pop music.

We flew over the band from the In Deep tour as well as my long-time live mixer, Steve Scanlon, to do the show. It was to be in the old Wembley Stadium, which was pulled down five years later in 2003, having stood for eight decades. Old Wembley was often called the Twin Towers, due to the two domed towers that stood on either side of the entrance.

The crowd was near 60,000, so I'm told. But whatever the number, I felt only terror – until I convinced myself I was back at the Grainstore Tavern in Melbourne. And when I thought about it a bit more, I realised that Wembley was actually less intimidating than the Grainstore. For one thing, if there were hecklers at Wembley they were far enough away that I wouldn't be able to hear them. And even if there were 60,000 people out there, they were sure to be considerably more sober than the late-night punters at the Grainstore.

Once I was onstage I was fine. I'd been right – it was a doddle compared to the Grainstore. I didn't hear anyone yell out, 'Show us your tits, Tina,' that night.

In fact, the crowd was great, the place was packed, the band was tight, and it was a truly incredible evening. The Gibb brothers were lovely. Backstage was like one big happy family, with kids running everywhere, wives and dear friends having a quiet drink. They were a close-knit family, a bit like the Arenas.

While we were hanging out backstage, a young Aussie athlete stuck her head in. I'd known Cathy Freeman for quite a while. We saw the same beautician in Richmond – Sarah – and we'd become friendly over the years. I loved Cathy – so warm and modest and yet full of determination and dedication. She was already a great Australian. Cathy was taking a break from running, but I knew she had more to do and would be back with a vengeance. Turns out, I was on the money.

Onstage, the Bee Gees were like they were offstage – open and unpretentious. They performed so many of their hits that night, including 'To Love Somebody', 'Massachusetts', 'Words', 'I've Gotta Get a Message to You', 'I Started a Joke', 'Jive Talkin'' and many more. The One Night Only shows turned out to be the last tour in which the three brothers performed together – Maurice died far too early just four years later.

The set finale was 'Stayin' Alive', from their *Saturday Night Fever* soundtrack. I got down with the best of them to that song. It captured my mood around that time. I was so busy, I was boogieing like there was no tomorrow just to keep it all together. It was working, but only just.

CHAPTER 15

Torn

October 1998. When I look back, I can now see it was a turning point in my life. Talk about sliding doors – so many opened and closed during those four and a half weeks in ways that have played out in my life ever since. Not that I had any idea – I was absolutely oblivious to it. After all, as usual, I was too bloody busy.

My schedule had been punishing all year and it was showing no sign of slowing down. By then I was renting a little flat in London, but I'd spent most of my time crossing the globe from the UK to the US, to Europe, to Australia and back again. On and on it went. It was fun, it was mad, it was draining, lonely, exhausting. At one low point, Nancy dropped everything and flew over to be with me. That's the kind of sister Nancy is: she has never been afraid to speak frankly, and on more than one occasion her wise counsel and support have got me through tough times.

In early October, 'I Want to Spend My Lifetime Loving You', the duet I sang with Marc Anthony as the theme song for the movie *The Mask of Zorro*, was released in Europe. It had come out in the US in July, when the movie was released there, but hadn't charted. Still, Marc and I had done some promotions over there, including an appearance on the national morning show *Live! with Regis and Kathie Lee*.

A week or two after that song came out in Europe, my single 'If I Was a River' hit the stores in the UK. Many Australian readers may have never even heard 'If I Was a River' – it didn't appear on the Australian version of *In Deep* at all. It wasn't one of my own songs and it wasn't recorded at the same time as the rest of *In Deep*.

In fact, the story of 'If I Was a River' began back in 1995, the year I met Sony boss Tommy Mottola in Rome. From then on, Tommy had taken a special interest in my career. I guess after Sony's success with Celine Dion and Mariah Carey, Tommy was on the lookout for another diva to help keep the Sony coffers filled. That's just how the music industry works. But as I mentioned earlier, Tommy was a music lover who had a great ear as well as a great nose for business, and his decisions were usually based on both.

I'd always had a good working relationship with the guys at Epic in the US. Peter Asher, who'd produced so many wonderful female artists, including Linda Ronstadt, Cher and

Diana Ross, had taken an interest in me, producing my version of 'Show Me Heaven' as my follow-up to 'Chains' in the States. So this time around, my Sony friends Stateside were keen to help me crack their territory well and truly.

Tommy had decided to get personally involved, and he commissioned America's top songwriter, Diane Warren, to write a big ballad for me that he hoped would put me on the map in his homeland. Diane had previously written 'Strong as Steel', the song I'd covered all those years ago on that album of the same name, but that was just one among countless hits she'd penned since. Diane's achievements would fill a book, but suffice to say she has written a fair swag of the hits we've all heard on the radio since her first, in 1983 – Laura Branigan's top ten hit 'Solitaire'. The woman behind the names, Diane has written for top artists in every genre.

Diane turned out 'If I Was a River', a power ballad in which the singer professes unconditional eternal love for her *amour*. Tommy gave it the thumbs up – I guess he liked its sweeping, majestic style. To be honest, it was never my favourite song, and I do remember telling the guys at Sony US quite categorically that I didn't believe in the song's sentiment. How could I honestly sing that song when I was struggling with the whole concept of love at that time? Still, sometimes you put up and shut up, especially when you're on someone else's turf. I had to respect that they knew their territory and would do their best. Which I believe to this day they did.

Some time in the first half of 1998 I'd made the trip to the US to record the song at Sony in-house producer Walter Afanasieff's home studio. Walter was another big name on everyone's lips, and Tommy had had the sense to sign him to the company, so Walter only worked for Sony artists. He was Mariah's co-writer and producer, and had gone on to produce just about every hit that Sony had during the 1990s. He's produced songs for Celine Dion, Michael Jackson, Barbra Streisand, Whitney Houston and Lionel Richie, to name but few. He was also an exquisite pianist and crazy Russian genius, a sweet man who lived to produce records.

Walter's place north of San Francisco was a compound, with an enormous garage full of priceless cars and motorcycles. Walter also collected guns and apparently had a shooting range out the back. More up my alley was his immense wine collection. Sony was clearly paying him well, which was fair enough because everything he touched was turning to gold. Nevertheless, Tommy himself sat in on the mixing sessions for 'If I Was a River' and threw in his two bobs' worth.

By hooking me up with the number-one writer and number-one producer in the US, Sony were showing their commitment. It was even more evident when they sent me off with Pierre Baroni and a large budget to Egypt to shoot the video for 'If I Was a River' on the Nile. We travelled there in September 1998, just after the show with the Bee Gees.

The video was shot at three or four different locations. The heat was almost unbearable – 50 degrees Celsius on the ground, and I was barefooted – so we filmed only at sunrise and sunset. I remember one day fronting up to the gate to one of the pyramids with Richard, my UK publicist. We had a photographer in tow, ready to shoot a feature for the UK's *OK!* magazine.

We asked to be let in. After some negotiations, the man on the gate offered Richard 300 camels in exchange for me.

'Keep your camels,' Richard joked. 'You can have her.'

It was extremely generous on Richard's part. For my part, at least I now knew what I was worth! But seriously, it was extraordinary to dip my toes into the Nile. And Pierre created something truly stunning with the video. Somehow I was transformed into an Egyptian goddess with waist-length hair and fluttering scarves. That man could perform miracles!

So with 'If I Was a River' coming out in the UK just days after my duet with Marc Anthony had been released in Europe, October 1998 was a crazy month of interviews, photo shoots, showcase performances and travel, travel, travel. At the same time, what had once been just a nagging whisper of doubt about the relentlessness of it all had grown to a roar. I don't think I'm the first artist to have felt, at some point in their career, that they've become little more than a business asset. Whether it's actually true or not, it's still a terrible feeling, and it causes major damage to your self-esteem. You start to question all your working relationships and begin to believe that everyone wants you for just one thing. It's twisted, I know, but that's the dark side of mainstream success. People tend to assume success must be great for your self-confidence, but so often it's the opposite. Anyway, that was roughly where I was at during those final months of 1998. Where, how and when would it end? I had no idea, but I just knew that something had to give, and soon.

One afternoon I was in London rehearsing with my UK band. I called a halt to proceedings to give a phone interview to an Australian journalist and accidently put my foot in it. When he suggested Natalie Imbruglia and I were 'legends', I made what I thought was a pretty honest and realistic observation about so-called legendary status in music. Neither of us were bona fide legends, not yet, I said. I wasn't having a go at Nat – I'd met her on and off over the years and liked her a lot. She'd just won a bunch of well-deserved ARIAs and had broken into the US market with the song 'Torn', and I was genuinely happy for her. But I knew from experience that in pop music, today's big story can be tomorrow's chip paper.

In the same interview I also may have called the then Australian prime minister 'an uneducated peasant', or something along those lines. Not my finest moment, I'll admit, and I regret it to this day. But from afar I'd been quietly horrified by what appeared to be a rising tide of racism in my own country, as One Nation grabbed the headlines that year, and I thought a prime minister should lead by example and stand up and speak out against divisiveness. As a child of migrant parents growing up in the public eye, I'd encountered a bit of casual racism now and then, but I'd hoped we'd moved on from those days. In hindsight, however, the comment was not only uncalled for but also unbelievably naive on my behalf.

The truth was, I was so burnt out at this point I shouldn't have been doing interviews at all. When I'm exhausted I can't think straight and I tend to blurt things out. Which is exactly what I did. I learnt my lesson: I now never give interviews when I'm tired.

Anyway … needless to say, when the article was printed the proverbial hit the fan back in Australia. According to reports in the media, Nat and I were now sworn enemies. My wading into the political debate caused even more of a fuss. Not long after, I was in Amsterdam getting ready to do a showcase. There I was, dressed to the nines in the makeup chair, when my mobile rang. It was Ralph, explaining in no uncertain terms how he'd spent the entire evening at the ARIAs apologising to Natalie on my behalf and how much I'd screwed up. As if I didn't know! After he said his piece I took the opportunity to inform him I no longer required his services and our marriage was over. We left it at that.

I felt sick with a mixture of pain and relief. Nevertheless, I had a sip of water, took one last look in the mirror then went out to do the show. *That's it,* I said to myself as I stepped onto the stage. *It's done.*

It had been a long time coming. Years of all work and no play had killed both our relationships – business and personal. For too long now, communication between us had been confined to work issues. We'd tried in the early days to keep our personal relationship alive but it had been too hard. So what had seemed a perfect solution to the loneliness and non-existent family life that so many artists experience had turned out to be quite the opposite. It just never worked. And now the house of cards was about to tumble to the ground.

I have no doubt it was a difficult time for Ralph too. He knew things weren't right, but probably didn't know how to begin to fix them. We'd been apart so much over the past couple of years we were like strangers.

From a career point of view it appeared to be terrible timing. Everything was being put in place for a major tilt at the US market. 'If I Was a River' had just been released in the UK in the lead-up to that campaign. And now 'I Want to Spend My Lifetime Loving You' was charting all over Europe. What had seemed like a crazy year just got even crazier in those final weeks of 1998.

'If I Was a River' didn't make much of a mark in the UK, but Sony went ahead with plans to release the album there, and *In Deep* came out in November in Britain. At the same time, 'I Want to Spend My Lifetime Loving You' was sitting in the top ten in France, Belgium and the Netherlands.

I didn't know it then, but the story of those two songs, both released in October 1998, set the path my life was to follow from then on. Ironically, they were both songs about unconditional lifelong love, something I now realised I knew nothing about. My marriage was over. And while Ralph was still acting as my manager – I hadn't had time to organise anyone else to do it –

our days together as artist and manager were also numbered. What had started out as a great team had, over time, become increasingly dysfunctional. It was time to call it quits.

But these things tend to play out in slow motion and that's what happened. Ralph remained my manager for the time being and on paper we were still married. I kept working right up to Christmas, doing promo, then returned home to our little house in Melbourne. Ralph was away. I had just a couple of weeks to recharge my batteries before I was due to start a promotional tour in the US, planned to coincide with the release of 'If I Was a River' over there. *In Deep* was scheduled to come out just after. This time, the Sony guys in America were backing me all the way.

For most artists in the music business, the States is the mountain we want to conquer, because, I guess, it's the tallest and the toughest. So, on paper, everything I had ever dreamed of was at last within my grasp. All I had to do was to hold it all together, keep turning up, reach out and take it.

But while I was incredibly grateful that Sony was prepared to take a serious punt on me in the States, I was also extremely nervous. Now I can look back and think, 'At least nobody died', but back then, with so much going on, it only added to the stress. I was already a nervous wreck, but the prospect of taking on the US was enough to keep me awake all night, tossing and turning in a cold sweat. The pressure was enormous.

In fact, sitting with my family around Mum's table in Moonee Ponds during that summer break, I was ready to give it all up. I'd worked so hard, given it my all. I'd never lost my love for music, for the craft, for singing. But somewhere along the line, my love for my job, for the business of making music, had begun to flicker, then fade. A relentless promotion schedule had taken its toll. I was thirty-one years old and I felt like I was dying inside.

Christmas passed in a blur. After twenty years as a performer I'd become an expert at going through the motions, smiling when required, looking like I was interested. But the truth was I just felt empty.

CHAPTER 16

No More Tears
(Enough is Enough)

Since I was a kid trying to learn my dance steps, I'd always viewed the ups and downs of my life and my career as a necessary part of growing and learning. *If you don't push yourself, if you don't take risks and you never fail, you'll never learn anything from life,* I'd told myself on countless occasions. I'd come to believe that most things happen for a reason, and usually the reason is that you need to learn something.

But during those last months of 1998, I'd begun to question that thinking. *What could I possibly be learning from all this?* I was so exhausted, so overstretched, I was falling apart. I was also struggling to figure out how to properly extricate myself from my relationship with Ralph.

A few weeks later, as I sat on a plane bound for the US, I had turned that thinking right around and was coming at it from an even darker place. Instead of focusing on what I might learn, I was focusing on what it was I must have done *wrong* to deserve such a harsh lesson. With twisted logic I'd turned it all back on me. *I must deserve all this pain for something I've done somewhere in the past. It's all my fault – I'm just a bad person who deserves everything I get.*

In other words, my self-confidence had collapsed. The chains I thought I'd broken seemed to bind me even more tightly. I'd struggled to be free to be myself, free to sing, work and love. And now I felt that that person – Tina, Pina, whatever she called herself – hadn't been worth all the trouble.

Not to put too fine a point on it, I was a basket case. Especially when I had to admit that, on one count, I was right – it *was* my own fault. My capacity for hard work and my desire to keep everybody happy, whatever the price, had taken their toll.

And now, just when I had nothing left to give, I was heading off for a brutal two-month promotional tour of America, the toughest territory on the planet. If I could have prised open the window on that plane I would have jumped right out.

Luckily, the windows on planes are glued in. Also, lucky for me, my job is my addiction. It may have almost destroyed me, but in the months that followed work became my saviour. If it hadn't been for that, I probably *would* have found a way to force open a window on one of the countless planes I took across America and around the globe.

So when I arrived at my apartment in LA, I pulled myself together, had a shower and something to eat, then rang the Sony offices in New York to report for duty. Lee Chesnut, one of the guys in charge of A&R at Epic back then, got on the line.

Lee was a friend and something of a fan. He sounded even more upbeat than usual. After a bit of banter he slipped in nonchalantly: 'What do you think of Donna Summer?'

'She's my hero.' That was putting it mildly. As I mentioned earlier, Donna Summer was one of my touchstones when I was growing up, one of the artists against whom I measured all others. She was brilliant, a woman who, with Giorgio Moroder, had changed the face of popular music. Plus, and this had always inspired me, she'd co-written many of her hits. It was something most people didn't even realise, a state of affairs that had always bugged me.

'How would you like to be Barbra for a night?' Lee was still trying to sound blasé.

I didn't have to ask who Barbra was, not when we were talking about Donna Summer in the same breath. Donna and Barbra Streisand had sung a duet on 'No More Tears (Enough is Enough)', a track that had been a big hit in 1979, back when I was twelve and searching for artists to look up to. I'd certainly found two in Donna and Barbra.

'What do you mean?'

Lee told me his plan. He'd run it past David Massey, who was looking after me at Epic, and David had loved the idea.

'We want you to sing "No More Tears" with Donna, live. What do you think? Could you do it?'

Lee was working with Ms Summer on a live album and TV documentary. She was scheduled to do a show on 4 February at the Hammerstein Ballroom in New York, an elegant, turn-of-the-century concert hall in the heart of Manhattan. Sony was planning to release a live recording to coincide with the launch of a doco of the concert by VH1, a cable TV channel a bit like MTV.

I didn't need to remind myself that I was in this business for moments like these. So often, just when you're down for the count, someone gives you a hand up and you're back on your feet, ready for the next round. That's how you keep going. It's how it works.

'Hell, yeah,' I said. 'I'd love to do it. Just tell me when, where and how and I'll be there.'

Lee sent me a CD of the track overnight, to refresh my memory. Not that I needed it. I already knew the song by heart – I'd probably memorised it as a kid. Still, I listened to that CD over and over and over again.

Wow! What a song! If anything could inspire someone to take a stand, it's 'No More Tears (Enough is Enough)'. Every word in that song hit me like a punch to the heart. I was living it! How strange that the opportunity to sing that particular song, of all songs, came along at that moment. Maybe everything *does* happen for a reason, because there's enough guts and humour in 'No More Tears (Enough is Enough)' to make the most downtrodden, the most heartbroken, lift their eyes to the sky, raise their hands and say: 'That's it! No more!'

I met Donna Summer at the Sony offices in New York the day before the concert. I was horribly nervous – it was such an honour even to meet her. Donna was professional and charming. She seemed genuinely pleased that I would be singing the song with her. I'm guessing she'd heard some of my stuff – Lee would have filled her in.

We rehearsed the next day, the same day as the concert. Everyone was edgy and it was pretty intense, because the whole thing was going to be committed to video. We couldn't stuff this up!

I was singing Streisand's part. We ran through it a couple of times. Donna tweaked things as we went and that was it. Sink or swim.

That very evening there I was, watching from the wings at the Hammerstein, waiting for my cue. Donna looked and sounded spectacular. Slim and statuesque (I'd be playing the part of the mushroom again, as I'd done with my mate Julie Field), she sang with poise and grace, filling that room with her stunning voice. After a few songs, she introduced me to the audience as her 'little sister from Australia'. That worked for me.

I think we both enjoyed singing the song. I don't think I let her down. Halfway through, the song turns into a big disco anthem, at which point we just let rip.

Anyone who saw that performance would vouch that we both sang our hearts out. I know I did. I don't usually read or quote reviews, but *Billboard* described it as 'the genius pairing of the year'. It certainly was in my book.

A week after my duet with Donna Summer, 'If I Was a River' was released in America. I was on the road, crisscrossing that great land, meeting radio jocks and programmers, TV hosts, journos, retailers and, most importantly, fans, shaking hands, making small talk, performing. We went just about everywhere, from Minneapolis in the north to Kansas City in the centre and Houston and Miami in the south. In those days, when the music business relied so much on radio, and sales depended so heavily on bricks-and-mortar retail, it was the only way to do it. But it was a mammoth task. During the entire tour, I barely communicated with Ralph, who was back in Melbourne. It was left to one of Ralph's offsiders who was travelling with me to keep him informed.

I was running on empty, but singing 'No More Tears' with Donna Summer in New York had given me the extra little *oomph* I needed to keep going. And as each day passed my determination was growing. The pain had to end. Things had to change.

I kept it together and turned up smiling each day. Somewhere inside, though, I just knew 'If I Was a River' wasn't going to work. But when you're in a territory other than your own, you have to trust the locals. You also have to accept that music is an art, not a science – no one gets it right all of the time. Still, the fact was, I never connected with that song, not when I recorded it and not when I was on the road performing it and trying to sell it. And if I couldn't connect with it, why would listeners? It's a lovely song, but at that time in my life it was the *wrong* song. In retrospect, if they'd sent me out with a song like 'No More Tears (Enough is Enough)', then maybe the story would have been different.

As it was, for whatever reason – and the variables are as difficult to read as tea-leaves – 'If I Was a River' didn't chart in the US. Nevertheless, Epic pressed ahead and released *In Deep* in the second week of March. They'd given it their best shot, and for that I am eternally grateful. Working with those guys had been a fantastically positive collaboration. I met so many interesting people and, despite increasingly difficult circumstances, had many good times.

After a detour to Europe, I returned to Australia, exhausted in a way I'd never felt before. On top of the collapse of my marriage and my business partnership with Ralph, I had to deal with my own disappointment and an overwhelming feeling that I'd let my American friends down. But, while I felt like a wreck both physically and emotionally, I had developed new resolve. Things couldn't go on the way they had been. I wasn't ready to give up but I *was* ready to make some changes. The question was, though, what would happen to Ralph and me? Without the other, could either of us survive, personally or professionally?

I now knew that I could and I would. A bit of good news had helped me come to that conclusion. 'I Want to Spend My Lifetime Loving You' had stayed in the top ten in France, Belgium and the Netherlands for weeks after it charted in October, and was still in the charts five months later. Not only that, but my version of 'I Want to Know What Love Is' was climbing the charts in France. Ultimately it hit number 13. Suddenly just about everyone in France had heard of Tina Arena. Sony still hadn't released *In Deep* over there but were keen to get it out. France would be my next stop.

First, though, I had a few things to do in Australia. Ann-Marie, Ralph's assistant, had recently resigned. I rang Annie and asked her to work exclusively for me. I knew I couldn't take the next step without her. Thankfully, she agreed. Then I moved out of the house Ralph and I had shared. Finally I contacted my lawyers, who drafted a legal letter informing him it was over between us.

It was time to take the next step. It had been a good partnership while it lasted, but as Donna and Barbra said, enough is enough.

CHAPTER 17

Aller Plus Haut

Suddenly my working life seemed to be full of women. After Ralph and I parted ways, I'd been on the lookout for a new manager. An old friend, Belinda Lewoshko, was in New York working in artist management with Wendy Laister. Wendy may have been sweet and polite in that English way, but she was a hardened veteran of the music business and had previously run a PR company that looked after the Rolling Stones, Paul McCartney, Janet Jackson and Guns N' Roses, among others. Wendy had recently set up her own management company and was looking after Aerosmith. She and Belinda agreed to take me on.

As well, I still had the wonderful Ann-Marie Meadows in my corner. A woman of integrity and depth, she saw me through some tough times, including the three years it took for the divorce to be settled, and she saved my arse on too many occasions to mention. Ann-Marie was based in Melbourne, but she travelled with me a lot, despite her fear of flying. One of the first things she did for me was find me a house in Melbourne so I had somewhere to live when I was there, which turned out to be not often that year. Instead, I travelled between London, which was my base, and Paris.

Then, in France, I began working closely with two inspiring women. Virginie Auclair was in charge of international marketing at Columbia. A year later she became boss of the label in France. Virginie was one of the smartest women I've ever met. Typically French, she was extremely cultured, plus she spoke great English (thank god). Virginie seemed to take a shine to me, and I liked her too. She was quite reserved – she was never a show-off – but was deeply committed to her job. We just clicked. Virginie was very senior, and back then Columbia France was buzzing with a full roster of local and international artists, but she spent a bit of time with me, which was extremely generous under the circumstances.

The other woman I worked closely with at Columbia France was Valérie Michelin. Valérie was tall, blonde, imposing and gutsy. She loved her rock 'n' roll, and was a force to be reckoned with. I liked her a lot. Like Virginie, Valérie spoke English with an alluring accent. Valérie eventually took over from Virginie as Columbia boss in France.

It was a nice change to be working with so many women at that time in my life. Somehow the dynamic changed in a positive way, and those women supported me just when I needed it. They were all such strong, interesting characters, and their humour got me laughing again.

Virginie and I worked closely together to put the plans in place to release *In Deep* in France. One afternoon, at a meeting to discuss those arrangements, she said to me: 'Tina, I know the record is going to be great, but we'd like to add a couple of tracks.'

That wasn't out of the ordinary. The US and UK versions of the album included 'If I Was a River' and 'Whistle Down the Wind'. I knew the French would want to include 'I Want to Spend My Lifetime Loving You'.

'Sure,' I said.

Then Virginie threw me a curve ball. 'In French,' she said.

'Wha-a-a-a-a …?' I responded.

Virginie must have thought I was making a pathetic attempt to say 'yes' in French. 'Great,' she said. 'I just figured, you can speak Italian, and you did a Spanish version of "Sorrento Moon", so why not do a song or two in French?'

'Wha-a-a-a?' I said again.

Virginie smiled. 'Well, that's settled, then. Let's listen to some demos and see if we can find a couple of good songs.'

I just nodded. But on the inside I was terrified. What was I getting myself into? Spanish and Italian were one thing. French, while it might be a Latin language, was another world altogether. I need to connect with a song to sing it well. I need to understand what it says, believe in it and be able to sing it with conviction. Otherwise I feel like I'm just going through the motions, and the listener will feel the same. I couldn't speak or understand French, so I had no idea whether I'd be able to connect with a song in that language. I do like a challenge, though, so I agreed to give it a go.

Valérie Michelin began trawling through demos, looking for something that would speak to us, even if, for me, it was in a foreign language. One evening, we were having an aperitif at her place. She pulled out another pile of demos and popped one into the player. As the song began she passed me the handwritten case. It was a fairly ordinary recording, and the song had virtually no arrangement, but something about the melody caught my attention, and in a strange way I connected with the chorus, even though I didn't understand the words.

'What does it mean?' I asked Val.

'*Aller plus haut* means "to go higher",' she said. 'If you like the song, why don't we get the songwriter in and you can ask him about it. His name's Robert Goldman.'

I looked at the CD case in my hand. 'No, it's not,' I said. 'It says here it's J. Kapler.'

'Ah, that's just a pseudonym,' Valérie said. 'Robert is Jean-Jacques' brother and manager. Robert also used to manage Obispo.'

English-language readers may be unfamiliar with the music of Jean-Jacques Goldman or Pascal Obispo, but in France they're universally known as celebrated singer-songwriters.

It turned out that 'Aller Plus Haut' was the first song Robert had ever penned solo. It had never been recorded or released. Robert had come to songwriting after years in music management. He'd collaborated with his brother on a couple of tracks for Celine Dion and Florent Pagny (another French singer-songwriter) that had been released a few years earlier. Robert has also been credited as 'Jimmy Kapler', 'Jeannot Kapler' and, in the Eurovision Song Contest, as 'Jill Kapler'.

Robert and I met to talk through the song. The more we talked the more I loved 'Aller Plus Haut' and the more I connected with it. As with all great songs, the lyrics are something of a puzzle and it takes time to piece them together. Even then, the words and the song will mean different things to different people. For me at that time, the song was about being true to yourself, about accepting the past and looking to the future, *pour aller plus haut* – so you can go higher. It was exactly how I needed to think and feel at that point in my life and it was an inspiration. I needed to get out of the hole I was in emotionally and go higher. Once I understood the meaning of the lyrics, I could visualise what I was singing about. In the end, the French words weren't too hard to learn and my accent wasn't too bad.

Valérie wanted one more song in French for the album and asked me whether I had any ideas. As a matter of fact I did, but when I told her and her colleagues they were aghast.

My idea was to do the French classic 'Les Trois Cloches' (The Three Bells). It had been a huge hit for Edith Piaf, and I had loved it since I heard it back in Aunty Gisella's sitting room when I was four. I wanted to pay tribute to that great chanteuse who had made such a big impression on me as a little girl.

But Valérie and her colleagues thought it was a daggy idea. Maybe they just didn't have the distance I had to see the song for what it is: a brilliant classic that has struck a chord with people all over the world.

'What if we did an updated version?' I suggested.

'If it's a flop, remember it was your idea!' was their response, which was fair enough.

When we went into the studio to record those songs, I had zero expectations. We'd agreed that if one of us wasn't happy with how the songs turned out, we'd can them. Robert Goldman produced alongside a songwriter and producer called Christophe Battaglia. It was great to have Robert, the writer of 'Aller Plus Haut', producing that song. He was able to instil his sensibility and help us stay true to the mood and meaning. Somehow it all just came together.

In Deep and 'Aller Plus Haut' were finally released in France in July 1999. *In Deep* charted quickly but 'Aller Plus Haut' took a little longer. By early November, though, the song was number 2 on the French charts, and number 1 in Belgium. Having gone into that project with no expectations, it came as a huge shock. Like me, listeners fell in love with 'Aller Plus Haut'. It was just that kind of song.

Suddenly, in the second half of that year, everyone wanted to talk to me. Though my French was still virtually non-existent, I was popping up on French television shows regularly. Usually someone would translate live on the spot, but it was pretty scary.

Slowly, however, I was beginning to pick up a bit of the language. Despite the French's reputation for intolerance of people who won't speak their tongue, everyone was extremely patient as I blundered through with my dreadful French.

In fact, I was treated like royalty. In those heady days, before digital distribution and market forces halved the music industry's profits, an artist with a hit record was pampered. Sony France were putting me up in the swish Hôtel Costes, favoured by supermodels and movie stars. I had a chauffeur, ate in the best restaurants and was given clothes and jewellery by top designers.

One day Ann-Marie and I wandered out of the Hôtel Costes to get something to eat. Halfway along the street I glanced back. There was a crowd following behind.

'I wonder what they're doing?' I said to Ann-Marie, pointing.

Annie looked over her shoulder. 'Are they a tour group or something?' she said.

A second later she elbowed me. 'They're following you, you bloody idiot!' she hissed. 'They're fans.' My profile had risen so quickly in France I was unprepared.

We decided it was time to do a real concert in Paris. For me there could be only one venue. The Olympia is a landmark in Paris's ninth arrondissement. Built in the late nineteenth century, it survived World War II and Nazi occupation only to almost be knocked down for a car park in the 1990s. It was saved, thankfully, and has been fully restored to its former glory. But what I love most about it is who has performed there. Edith Piaf made her name there. Jacques Brel, Marlene Dietrich, Charles Aznavour, Dalida, Johnny Hallyday – they all performed on the Olympia's stage. More recent names include just about everyone from the Grateful Dead to Madonna and Christina Aguilera.

When the show quickly sold out we scheduled another one, this time at the Palais des Sports. We flew over a band of Australian musicians – Nick Sinclair on bass, Chris Kamzelas on guitar, Kere Buchanan on drums and Diana Rouvas and Chrissy Thomas on backing vocals and acoustic guitar. Then there was Paul Gray, once the frontman for eighties band Wa Wa Nee and a singer-songwriter himself. Paul was my musical director and played keyboards.

I don't know why, but performing to a French crowd was incredibly intimidating and I was sick with nerves before I went on stage at the Olympia. When I got out there, though, it was fine. For one thing, the acoustics are just lovely in that hall, and when the acoustics are good, it always boosts my confidence. Plus the Aussie musos gave a knockout performance. But the French crowd was great, too. Lively, responsive and fun, they were not much different to the crowds back home. Many were young and they were very vocal, singing along and clapping. The place came alive. It was a fabulous night.

I will be forever indebted to Virginie Auclair (who, sadly, we lost to cancer a few years ago), Valérie Michelin and Robert Goldman. Thanks to their vision and effort, I found a new audience in France, and a whole new chapter of my life began. It was something I had never planned or expected, but as things unfolded, I found I was able to start getting on with my life, to spread my wings and go that little bit higher.

CHAPTER 18

I Want to Know
What Love Is

The success of 'Aller Plus Haut' was only half the story that year. Other events in 1999 also changed me in ways I was not aware of.

First I met a tall, dark and handsome Belgian. His name was Jeremy, and he was the assistant engineer on the 'Aller Plus Haut' recording sessions. Jeremy and I struck up a friendship and began to see more and more of each other. We shared a love of music, but also a love of hanging out at home, cooking, eating, just being together. I was in and out of France that year, but whenever I was in Paris we met up, usually at his place. We were both working through stuff, and so were great companions for each other. Jeremy was an absolute sweetheart, but more than that, he helped me realise that I had worth. It sounds terrible, but I'd lost sight of that. He was a lot younger than me – eight or nine years younger – and maybe he found my lack of self-confidence strange, given my age and successful career. Whatever it was, he gave me the confidence to start believing in myself and my own judgement. He also helped me realise that someone could love me and I could love them back. I'd been living on barren land without any idea what to do about it. I think I'd forgotten what love was, or how you give and receive it.

Jeremy also introduced me to some of his family. His uncle David McNeil, a songwriter, is the son of the Russian painter Marc Chagall, and he and Jeremy's aunt Leslie would invite us over on Sundays to their beautiful home in a secluded part of Paris (their neighbours were Carla Bruni and Nicolas Sarkozy). Jeremy, Leslie and I would make a trip to the local markets. Back at their place, Leslie and I would get to work in the kitchen, then we'd all sit around for a long, leisurely lunch. It was so familiar and *familial*, something I realised I had been missing out on for the last few years. I hadn't seen enough of my family. Jeremy, Leslie and David and their son, Dylan, who was around Jeremy's age, became my French family and reminded me that family and love make the world go round.

Something else happened in 1999 which, while it seemed like a little thing, gave me confidence and opened my eyes. It happened out of the blue. While I was in Australia for a quick visit, I got a call from an Italian singer-songwriter called Luca Barbarossa. Luca was recording an album that he'd licensed to Sony and he wanted me to sing a duet with him on the first single, a song called 'Segnali di Fumo' (Smoke Signals).

To be honest, I didn't even know who he was, but of course I found out. It turned out he was a beautiful songwriter and a great singer and storyteller.

Following a bit of discussion with Wendy and Belinda, and after I'd heard the song, I agreed to do the duet with him. But he needed my vocals done quickly and I didn't have time to make the trip to Italy.

'Why don't I send you the files and you can record the vocals in Australia,' he suggested. 'Do it how you want. I trust you.'

I was terrified at the thought. How on earth could I produce my vocals on my own? Usually I had someone there to get the right sound, and then decide how my voice should be in the mix. But I didn't have a choice, so I talked to Steve Scanlon, the engineer who had mixed my live shows for years, and he agreed to record my vocals in his home studio.

With Luca's blessing and Steve engineering, I produced all my vocals and backing vocals myself. There was no one there to direct me or tell me what to do. It sounds like a little thing, but it made me realise that I could create music on my own, that I didn't always need someone there to call the shots. I actually had it in me to call the shots myself.

When I sent the files back to Luca he was thrilled, which was great, and of course the song was then finished over there. But doing that little bit of recording without a producer there to direct was a minor revelation. If the need or opportunity arose, I could produce as well as write and sing.

Then there was a chance meeting on the set of one of the many French TV shows on which I appeared that year. This time it was a popular variety show called *Tapis Rouge* (Red Carpet). The show was hosted by the French equivalent of Michael Parkinson, a TV legend called Michel Drucker. That particular episode of *Tapis Rouge* also featured an interview with the writers and main cast of a musical called *Notre-Dame de Paris*, as well as songs from the show.

Based on Victor Hugo's novel of the same name (the English translation is called *The Hunchback of Notre-Dame*), the music for the show was written by a famous Italian singer-songwriter Richard (or Riccardo) Cocciante. Mum, being a fan of Italian music, knew Richard's work well. The French lyricist was French–Canadian Luc Plamondon, who had previously written the lyrics for *Starmania*, a musical that is probably as famous in France and Canada as *Jesus Christ Superstar* is in Australia or the UK.

Notre-Dame de Paris is a tragic love story set in harsh and unjust times. Quasimodo, a hunchback who lives in the belltower of Notre-Dame, falls in love with Esmeralda, a gypsy girl. Also lusting after Esmeralda is Frollo, the priest. Esmeralda, however, is in love with the highborn and handsome Phoebus, who is engaged to Fleur-de-Lys but fancies a night with Esmeralda. Unfortunately, things do not turn out well for the beautiful gypsy girl.

The Paris production of the show, which had been running since September 1998, had been enormously popular and had made it into the *Guinness Book of Records* for having the most successful first year of any musical production, ever, anywhere. The album was the highest selling French record that year and had just won an award at the World Music Awards in Monte Carlo.

I sang two songs on *Tapis Rouge* that day: 'I Want to Know What Love Is' and 'Memories', in a duet with Patrick Fiori, who was playing Phoebus in *Notre-Dame de Paris*. I always sing live when I perform on TV shows or at showcases, but not everyone does – some people opt to mime.

When my performances were over, I joined the other guests on the couch to have a chat with Michel. The other people sitting there were, of course, the writers and lead cast of *Notre-Dame de Paris*. I was beginning to understand French, more or less, so Michel would question me in French and I would answer, mostly in English, which he would then translate for the live audience. It wasn't *too* nerve-racking but I was glad when it was all over and I could kick back with a glass of wine in my dressing-room. Those were the days when divas had an entourage, so there with me were Ann-Marie, various Sony people, my makeup artist, a stylist and my chauffeur. We were having a laugh together – I've never been one of those nightmare artists who cause trouble for everyone. I want to have fun myself, which I do ninety-eight per cent of the time.

Then Sabine from Columbia popped her head around the door. Sabine Feutrel was Heckle to Valérie Michelin's Jeckle. 'Luc Plamondon wants to meet you,' she said.

'Sure,' I said. I didn't know much about Luc or Richard. All I knew was that they were big writers and *Notre-Dame de Paris* the musical was their creation.

A minute later there was a knock.

'*Entrez*,' I called.

The door opened and there were Luc and Richard. After much kissing and hugging, European style, they sat down.

I began chatting with Richard in Italian. 'Where did you learn the language?' he asked after a minute or two.

I told him about my heritage.

'Ah!' We kept chatting. Meanwhile, I could see that Luc was itching to say something.

Finally he butted in. 'We'll keep it brief,' he said in English. 'We'd like to arrange a meeting with you as soon as possible to discuss an idea.'

'Of course,' I said. 'Talk to Ann-Marie here and tee something up with her.'

Annie gave them her number and a meeting was arranged.

When I met Luc and Richard a couple of weeks later, Luc was again straight to the point. (I found out later that Luc was *always* to the point, something I absolutely adore about him.) 'We'd like you to sing a song for the *Notre-Dame* soundtrack,' he said.

I liked the idea and said so – I love the music.

Luc blurted out his next request. 'And we'd like you to play Esmeralda in the London production. Will Jennings is doing the translation. The show opens over there in May next year.' Esmeralda was the leading female role. Will Jennings had, among other things, written the lyrics for the *Titanic* theme song, 'My Heart Will Go On'.

Luc's offer took me by surprise. Singing a track on the studio album was one thing. Committing to a musical production in London's West End was another thing altogether. 'Can I get back to you?' I said.

'But you'll give it some thought?' I suspect they were hoping I'd say yes on the spot. 'Please, *please*, give it serious consideration,' Luc said. 'We just know you're the next Esmeralda.' It turned out that when they'd heard me sing on *Tapis Rouge* they decided there and then that they wanted me to do it. I guess they could see that I was able to sing live, and when I sang with Patrick they saw there was a bit of chemistry.

In the end I flew to Montreal to see the Canadian production, which opened in June. That was when I made up my mind. The music was beautiful and the production inventive. Esmeralda, the young gypsy dancer, was such a strong character – it was clear that Victor Hugo felt a lot of compassion for her.

Accepting the part of Esmeralda was perhaps the first career decision I made completely on my own. I just followed my heart and said yes. I had never lost my love for musical theatre and so often, when I needed a taste, an opportunity seemed to pop up. This time, I loved the music, and I loved the character. And to be a leading lady in London's West End was one of those dreams I'd had as a kid, one I never thought would come true. I just had to do it. How could I possibly say no?

There was something else that helped me decide. Taking the part would mean I'd be forced to more or less stay in one place for a while. With eight performances a week, there was no way I could be away from London for any length of time. I could still pop across to France for a day or two if Sony needed me to, but otherwise I'd have to stay put. London had been my base off and on for a couple of years by then, and I liked it there, mostly because I was rarely recognised. I could live a low-key, independent life in London, without attracting too much attention. It made things just that little bit easier and more relaxing.

The only down side was that Jeremy and I would be apart. But we so often were, anyway. He knew what my job entailed and we were both used to my comings and goings.

Once the deal was done, Michel Drucker invited me and the French cast of *Notre-Dame* back on *Tapis Rouge* for a kind of handover. Many of the cast and crew who were there that night would later be heading to London to be part of the UK production, including Garou, the French–Canadian singer who played Quasimodo. But some, like Hélène Ségara, who had played Esmeralda in the French production, wouldn't be crossing the channel.

It was a big thing – the show had been huge in France and the cast were much loved. On *Tapis Rouge* that night I performed the theme song from the show: 'Live (for the One

I Love)'. When I finished, the audience and the guests on the couch gave me a standing ovation. I then did something I have rarely done on camera. I cried. It's such a powerful, sad song, and it was an emotional moment.

Of course, I immediately felt like a complete drongo. I still don't know what came over me. It had been a long day, perhaps. In fact, it had been a long few years. Perhaps it was the unconditional acceptance and love I felt in that room. The French revere their singers and I was lucky enough to be accorded a little of that reverence. Particularly sweet was the fact that they'd neither seen nor heard of Tiny Tina. I'd started virtually from scratch in France and the French had accepted me as I was and on my own terms. It was incredibly liberating – in France I could just be me. My French was still pretty dreadful, but the French people didn't seem to mind. France had taken me under its wing.

Connecting with the French and their music that year had opened my eyes and my heart to a whole new world. It seemed to have happened by accident – although I'm sure Virginie Auclair and Valérie Michelin at Columbia would have told you there was nothing accidental about it. I'd simply followed my heart in France, with no expectations, and yet 1999 turned out to be hugely rewarding. I found an audience who took me as I was, even when I mangled their precious language. I also found comfort and friendship with Jeremy and his lovely family, and was able to begin healing my heart. Jeremy, David and Leslie, Dylan, Virginie, Valérie, Sabine, Michel Drucker, and, most importantly, the French people – I owed them all big-time!

CHAPTER 19

Vivre

In the final months of the millennium I returned to Australia. Ralph and I did not cross paths. Our divorce settlement was dragging out – unfortunately, it wouldn't be resolved for more than two years.

I appeared at the opening of Fox Studios in Sydney in November, with Kylie Minogue, Marcia Hines, Shirley Jones (from *The Partridge Family*) and Hugh Jackman (that guy is so multi-talented!) then headed back to Melbourne. On New Year's Eve, I performed at Crown Casino in Melbourne at a VIP ball, along with John Farnham, Kate Ceberano and Rod Stewart.

But my sojourn in Australia was short. Soon after Christmas I was on a plane bound for Montreal to record the vocals and shoot the video clip for my version of 'Live (for the One I Love)', the song from *Notre-Dame de Paris* that Esmeralda sings as she awaits her fate. The single was due to be released around the same time the show opened in the West End.

When I arrived it was minus 35 degrees, which came as a bit of a shock after Melbourne's 35-degree heat. We shot the clip in a warehouse outside Montreal. All the crew were Québécois. My hopeless French combined with their accent meant I couldn't understand a single word they said.

When I returned to Paris, my sister Silvana was there to meet me. She'd taken three weeks' holiday from her job at Mushroom Records and flown over to celebrate her twenty-seventh birthday in the city of love. A visit from one of my sisters was always a pick-me-up and reminded me just how much I missed my family when I was away. Silvana stayed with me at the quaintly French Hôtel Victor Hugo in the sixteenth arrondissement, where Sony often put me up.

On the night of her birthday, we went out to the Buddha-Bar, an opulent up-market restaurant bedecked with enormous gold buddhas, latticework, candles and chandeliers. It was back in its early days when it was one of *the* places to eat in Paris. Jeremy and his cousin Dylan came, too, along with Jeremy's partner in music, Rémi Lacroix, and Sabine from Columbia. We ate and drank like kings that evening. Afterwards we went to a little jazz bar and ended up drinking tequila and dancing on the tables. The plan was to make Silvana's birthday a memorable one, but our recollections the next morning were foggy.

Three days later, Silvana, Jeremy, Ann-Marie and I were in Cannes for the inaugural NRJ Music Awards, sponsored by NRJ, a radio station in Paris, and French TV network TF1. The awards were handed out the night before the first day of Midem, the Cannes music trade fair where the world music industry gathers once a year to swap gossip and ideas, showcase artists and products and buy and sell rights. Oh, and party – mustn't forget that! I'd been nominated for an award for 'International Breakthrough of the Year'.

The stars were out in full force: Tina Turner, Mariah Carey, Bono, Jean-Jacques Goldman and Hélène Ségara (Esmeralda in the French production), who ended up winning 'Francophone Breakthrough of the Year'. It was a night of nights. I won the award, which was incredibly gratifying and humbling. Then we partied on, dancing till the wee hours.

I arrived in London to start rehearsals for *Notre-Dame de Paris* with a diamond ring on my finger. It had been a gift, from myself to me. I'd bought it at Boucheron in the Place Vendôme in Paris. The manager, Thierry, had asked me in to give me a gift. I had accepted the invitation, although I was hesitant. Thierry presented me with the most beautiful watch – Art Deco in design, with diamonds.

'I can't accept it,' I said.

But Thierry insisted. I was shocked that someone would give me such a beautiful present. Then something came over me, and when I spotted a stunning platinum ring encircled with diamonds, I decided to buy it. It was a *Pretty Woman* moment, minus Richard Gere. I had to tell myself to stop being a peasant and thinking I wasn't worth it. When I got my credit card statement later I choked on my Coco Pops but I never regretted it. It gave me the little boost of confidence I needed.

I set up camp in a house just off Walton Street in Knightsbridge, which belonged to Wendy's family. For the next six months or so I would be working in one place, which, after years of traipsing around, would be quite a novelty. I already knew I liked living in London. I could recharge my batteries when I was in England. It made things easier – I could just go about my business without having to worry about whether I was having a bad-hair day.

Jeremy was back in Paris. We'd decided to call it quits, but we remained friends. The truth was, our age difference worked against us – at twenty-four he was eight years younger than I and at a different stage in his life. I was thirty-two, and while I wasn't ready to settle down, I knew I wanted to some time soon. It was the last thing Jeremy was thinking of. He still had too much to do – while he worked as an engineer, he was also a musician and songwriter. He'd helped me get over my marriage break-up, but when I talked of babies he made it clear that wasn't on his immediate agenda and I agreed. He still had a bit of growing to do.

I would be making the odd lightning visit across the channel, though – 'Les Trois Cloches' had been released and was climbing the charts in France and Belgium. It was a good feeling. I hadn't been sure how the French would take to a foreigner singing a classic by one of their greatest artists in an Aussie accent, but they embraced it just as they'd embraced me.

I had a wake-up call once rehearsals for *Notre-Dame* started. It had been eight years since I'd worked in musical theatre and it took a while to get up to speed. It's always an incredibly physically and mentally demanding job, and you've got to be super fit to last the distance every night. But *Notre-Dame* was more than that: it was *emotionally* draining. The show ran for two and a half hours, and during that time I sang in around twenty songs, each one of which packed a punch. The songs are powerful and moving, and you can't fake the emotion when you're singing them.

Another challenge was the cultural differences. The French approach a stage production differently, and it took a while to get my head around that. One thing that got up the Brits' noses was the producers' decision to use backing tracks rather than an orchestra. I can understand why they made that choice – musical theatre is such a financial risk at the best of times – but it didn't go down well with the musicians' union and things got complicated.

It sometimes seemed like a classic example of the French–English divide. The French like to do things their way and they didn't like the English telling them how to suck eggs. But of course, we were in English territory: we quite rightly had to abide by their protocols and rules. As an Australian of European heritage, I guess I could see both sides. Needless to say, there were some interesting moments.

But it was fantastic to be part of such a large team of performers. Most of the cast, which included dancers and acrobats, were French–Canadian. An exception was Steve Balsamo, an English singer-songwriter who, as a relative unknown, had famously won the part of Jesus in the 1996 London production of *Jesus Christ Superstar* in a tough audition process. With a Venetian dad and a Welsh mum, Steve has music in his blood.

Then there was Garou, who is now a superstar in both Canada and France. Garou's story was similar to Steve's: Luc Plamondon heard him singing in a bar in Quebec and asked him to play Quasimodo in his then unstaged French production of *Notre-Dame de Paris*.

It was a brilliant decision on Luc's part: when Garou was on stage he *became* Quasimodo, expressing all the pain and heartache Quasimodo lives and breathes. It was a privilege to work with him – we got on so well, and we remain good friends.

I also loved working with Bruno Pelletier, who played the poet Gringoire, the narrator in the show. Fleur-de-Lys was played by yet another French–Canadian, Natasha St-Pier, who has also become a big star in France and Canada. Natasha was one of the few cast members who spoke English fluently, and we instantly clicked.

As well as a troupe of dancers, there was a troupe of acrobats brought over from the French production. The acrobatic work in the show was truly spectacular.

Two weeks before the show's premiere I flew to Monte Carlo to accept the World Music award for the Best Australian Solo Artist. I don't remember seeing any Bond girls this time, although Elle Macpherson was there to present me with the award, as well as yet another opportunity to play the short guy. I sang 'Live (for the One I Love)', called simply 'Vivre' in French. It had been released in the UK as a single just days earlier. I would never get blasé about awards – and this one meant a lot. Many of the *Notre-Dame* cast were there, because they had once again won the French award. Bravo to them!

The UK production of *Notre-Dame de Paris* premiered on 23 May 2000. Of course, it was scary – it was my first performance in London's West End and the pressure was on – but being surrounded by so many great performers who knew the production backwards helped. The audience's response was fantastic: we got a standing ovation, which, after all the work, was gratifying.

Mum and Dad had flown over to attend opening night. Also attending was Sophia Loren, to whom my parents were introduced. It was already a night they'd never forget – meeting Ms Loren made it legendary. I don't know where I was, but I missed out on the pleasure. The folks have been telling me about it ever since.

Some reviews of the show published in the days that followed didn't quite match the audience's reaction. In fact, one or two verged on nasty. One reviewer hated the music but liked the production; another liked the music but hated the production. It was disappointing but not particularly surprising. Once again it seemed like a classic case of the English–French divide: the music and the whole mood of the production were so European, so Latin – dark, emotional, expressive. The script or 'book' was also very modern, a series of vignettes built around songs – the narrative was not spelt out in black and white. I think that the things the Europeans loved about *Notre-Dame de Paris* were exactly the things that the English reviewers didn't love: the two sensibilities are just so different.

But, strangely enough, the English punters did love the show. They filled the house every night, and every night bar one, they gave us a standing ovation. After a few nights of that kind of reception we knew something was going right.

Another bit of good news was that 'Segnali di Fumo', my duet with Luca Barbarossa, had been picked up by Italian radio and put on high rotation. The song had been released there on the same day as the *Notre-Dame* premiere. According to Luca, everywhere he went it was playing. It was always great when you sent a song out into the world and people responded. I never tired of that feeling.

Mum and Dad stayed three weeks. It was the first time in years we'd spent real time together and it was wonderful. We'd do the grocery shopping at Harrods, which wasn't cheap but sure was good! That was one downside of living around the corner from the famous department store – I spent an absolute fortune on food and wine.

A month after the show opened, I took a night off from *Notre-Dame* to perform at the Prince's Foundation Gala Dinner at Buckingham Palace. With an extraordinary band put together by brilliant muso Lewis Taylor, I performed 'Chains', 'Sorrento Moon' and 'Live (for the One I Love)'.

It was a fabulous evening and took me back to those first World Music Awards at Monte Carlo, although this time I had the sense to wear a frock, thank god! The place was heaving with European royalty as well as celebs. I caught up with Elle Macpherson again; Donatella Versace, Lauren Bacall and Joan Rivers were also there. I'd met His Royal Highness the Prince of Wales a couple of years before at his 'Party in the Park', but I seem to remember that, after quickly shaking my hand, he'd made a beeline for the lovely Nat Imbruglia. It was a priceless moment, bless him!

But the next night was even more astonishing in a way, when I attended an intimate dinner with Prince Charles and Camilla Parker Bowles, as she was then known. Surprisingly the dinner would not be at the cheap Indian restaurant around the corner from their place. No, I would be going to dinner at Buckingham Palace. Who would have thought a girl from Moonee Ponds would ever end up there? (Come to think of it, Dame Edna Everage, Moonee Ponds' most famous resident, had probably already beaten me to it.)

The invite was a way of saying thank you for my performance the night before. I was delighted but terrified. For one thing, what do you wear to dinner at Buckingham Palace?

There are protocols to follow and traditions to be observed, surely? Luckily, the invite came with all the information I would need.

There were to be no toes showing, nor leg skin. It had to be closed-toe shoes and sheer stockings. Then the gloves: above the elbow if your gown was strapless; to the elbow otherwise. Finally, the gown had to be 'structured'. I think that meant no floaty sacks, which was lucky because, being vertically challenged, I tend to get lost in them.

I managed to get my outfit sorted, and ended up having a lovely time. Charles and Camilla met us personally and we chatted for a while. He actually knew my work, as did Camilla. They seemed like a happy couple, very comfortable in each other's company – while they'd been together for many years by this time, they had not yet married. Then, after a tour of the palace (oh, the art, just for starters!), we had a three-course meal. It was an ultimate London experience to tick off my bucket list. I think I have to thank Esmeralda for the opportunity, though: Camilla liked musicals and she loved *Notre-Dame de Paris*.

Performing in the West End of London was another ultimate London experience to tick off the list. And leading an ordinary life in London for so many months – buying the groceries, cleaning the house, cooking the dinner (even if I was treading the boards every night) – was probably just what I needed at that time in my life. But it wasn't the beginning of a quieter life for me. Far from it. Because things were hotting up again, this time in my homeland.

CHAPTER 20

The Flame

It was a media scrum. Just about every news outlet in the country was represented, from the *Wangaratta Chronicle* to Mackay's *Bush Telegraph* to Channel Ten, as well as reporters covering for international news.

We were hustled into the room in order: John Williamson, Julie Anthony, John Farnham, Olivia Newton-John, Vanessa Amorosi and, finally, yours truly.

The announcement of the line-up for the Sydney Olympics opening ceremony was made at the Melbourne Cricket Ground. We answered a few questions, the cameras flashed. It was a standard media conference, but with a difference — because, for all of us, it was a truly special day, and we were absolutely chuffed to be there.

I'd arrived from London two days earlier, having taken a short break from *Notre-Dame de Paris* to be there for the announcement. Before returning to the UK, I recorded the song I'd be singing at the ceremony with the Melbourne Symphony Orchestra and the Australian Youth Choir. Called 'The Flame', it was written by John Foreman, a young Australian composer who went on to work as musical director on several TV shows, including *Australian Idol* and the new *Young Talent Time*.

A month later I was back in Australia, this time in Sydney for the opening of the Olympics. The atmosphere was electric. Daylight saving had been brought forward especially for the Games and, as if in response, summer had come early. Long sunny days were followed by balmy evenings. The entire city was decked out in its best clobber – there were flags and flowers everywhere.

On the day of the ceremony we were bussed to the stadium in Homebush, western Sydney. I know I'm always saying how nervous I get, but this one took the cake. The audience would be upwards of three billion people, give or take, and that freaked me out. I think it freaked everyone out. I just hoped I wouldn't trip over mid-chorus.

My old workmate and friend David Atkins was the artistic director for both the opening and closing ceremonies and, together with Ric Birch as executive producer and director of ceremonies, what a brilliant job he did. I was watching the event unfold on a big screen backstage – security was unbelievably tight.

It was a stunning spectacle that told the story of Australia, from ancient times to the present. Everyone remembers little Nikki Webster, the thirteen-year-old girl with blonde curls who represented the young nation. John Williamson sang 'Waltzing Matilda'. Human Nature and Julie Anthony sang the Australian national anthem, 'Advance Australia Fair'. Then Aussie icons John Farnham and Olivia Newton-John sang 'Dare to Dream' as they strolled among the athletes. After Vanessa Amorosi's 'Heroes Live Forever' it was my turn.

'The Flame' was the song that preceded the lighting of the Olympic flame by Australian athlete Cathy Freeman. They'd dressed me in a shiny bronze-gold dress by fashion designer Fiona Scanlan. The Sydney Children's Choir also sang. Up on that stage, looking out at the enormous crowd, I wanted to pinch myself. I felt like I was part of history in the making. And, despite all my fears, I didn't trip once.

Dad and Nancy had flown up especially for the occasion. Mum couldn't make it because she was working at the nursing home in Moonee Ponds, but I'm sure she and all her clients were glued to the telly that night.

Watching Cathy light the flame was a supreme moment. To share it with her was an honour, and I will treasure the memory forever. It felt so right: she, a great and true Australian, up there holding the Olympic torch high; while down below, there was I, the child of migrants but nevertheless an Aussie just like Cathy. As we waited for the flame to reach the cauldron my heart missed a beat. But when the flame finally burst forth, tears were streaming down my cheeks.

*

It had been an unforgettable evening, starting with a call on my mobile while I was backstage getting my makeup retouched.

'Hi, Tina.' The voice had a strong French accent and sounded far away. '*C'est Vince.*'

'*Ça va?* How are you?' I said. Here I was, about to trot out onto the stage at the Olympics and perform for a few billion people, and now Vince was calling me.

It wasn't that I didn't want to hear from this particular guy – quite the opposite. But just thinking about him put me in a state, even though I'd only met him once. What was wrong with me?

Vince wished me luck and told me he'd be watching. Which was lovely, but now, with a worldwide audience to worry about, all I could think of was him. It was ridiculous.

We'd met a few weeks before, in August, on the eve of my trip to Australia for the Olympics announcement. I'd gone with a bunch of the *Notre-Dame* cast and crew to get some dinner between the Saturday matinee and evening shows. We were wolfing down our sushi in the local Wagamama when a tall, tanned blond man dressed all in white came down the stairs. As soon as I saw him I thought I knew him. After a second glance I spotted his bright blue eyes. *It's Brad Pitt!* I thought to myself.

I turned to a dancer next to me and said quietly: 'Look who's just walked down the stairs.' He clocked this blond Viking and blurted out: 'Holy shit!'

Now Brad was coming towards us. It was then I realised it wasn't the movie star at all. But the guy was so handsome I didn't want to have to talk to him. Then he began chatting to my colleagues in French. Obviously he knew some of them.

I couldn't take my eyes off him, but I didn't want to meet him. So I quickly paid for my meal and snuck away.

I was skulking back in my dressing-room when the principal dancer, Cynthia, popped in. Strong and brave and a great listener, Cynthia had become a true friend during our time together in *Notre-Dame*.

'Darling, don't forget we're having drinks tonight!' she cooed.

'I won't,' I said. I could hardly forget – I'd arranged them myself. I'd booked the bar upstairs for the cast and crew after the show. We were saying goodbye to the wonderful Garou and Bruno Pelletier, who were finishing up on *Notre-Dame* that week after almost a year performing in the French and now British productions. It would be my last night with them, because I was headed to Australia in the morning.

'Good,' Cynthia said, 'because I want you to meet someone.'

'Not that tall guy with the long blond hair.'

'As a matter of fact, yes. His name is Vince. He's staying to see the show tonight.'

'No, no, you're not going to do that to me. I don't want to meet him.' And I didn't. He was too good-looking for me. It was intimidating. And anyway, Jeremy and I had parted only relatively recently.

Cynthia just raised her eyebrows and smiled knowingly, then disappeared like a naughty fairy.

Now I was *really* in a state. The thought that this man would be in the audience tipped me over the edge. And once I was onstage, all I wanted to do was get off and go home. Vince, whoever he was, had rattled my cage.

Back in my dressing-room after the show I opened a bottle of champagne to soothe my nerves. Just as the cork popped, Cynthia appeared in the doorway. 'Nearly ready?' she asked.

'Here, sit down and have a drink with me,' I said.

Cynthia would never say no to a glass of French bubbles, so I poured her one.

I inhaled my drink then started pouring myself another.

'Come on,' she said, pulling the bottle out of my hand. 'We're going upstairs. We've got to say goodbye to Garou and Bruno. You organised these drinks.'

I protested as loudly as I could but she wouldn't let me get out of it.

'Well, just don't introduce me to that guy,' I said as we climbed the stairs. 'I won't know what to say, my French is poor and he probably doesn't speak English. It's pointless.'

Cynthia turned around and gave me the eye. 'You are so full of shit, Tina,' she said. 'Stop being a child and grow up.' Cynthia was not one to mince her words.

It sounds crazy, but I'd only seen this man once and I was in an absolute tizz. I'd never felt anything like that before.

We walked into the bar. Everyone was already there, drinking, talking. Someone ordered me another champagne. I'd just taken my first sip when I felt a hand on my back.

Cynthia was pushing me forward towards the tall blond guy. 'Vincent, Tina. Tina, Vincent,' she said.

It was then I finally remembered my manners. I smiled at him, said hello and put out my hand.

He kissed me once on each cheek. Then we began to talk.

Vince was so unpretentious and genuine, all my nerves immediately disappeared. His English was worse than my bad French, but it didn't matter. Somehow we were managing to communicate.

Vince said he'd loved the show and my interpretation of Esmeralda, which was sweet of him. It turned out he was an actor and had worked on the French production of *Notre-Dame*. Since then he'd been acting in a travelling theatre company production of a famous French comedy by the eighteenth-century dramatist Pierre de Marivaux, called *L'Île des Esclaves* (Slave Island). He'd just had a holiday in the south of France where his family lived – hence the suntan.

Despite the language barrier we talked and talked, and before we knew it, it was closing time.

Garou organised the troops to kick on. 'Come on, we're going to a club.' I call Garou a young Tom Jones. He loves his poker games at the casino, loves girls, loves life. He's always fun to be around.

We set off behind Garou. 'It's not far,' he said encouragingly. Half an hour later we finally stumbled into the bar.

Once we were settled in a corner with a couple of drinks in front of us, Vince and I began talking again. Looking into his handsome face I realised there was a lot more behind it – an intellect and an interesting man. I also liked the fact that he didn't know anything about me at all – he had little interest in popular culture. That was refreshing.

Finally I glanced at my watch. It was after 3 am. *Shit*, I thought. *I've got to be on a plane in the morning and I haven't even finished packing.* And then I remembered that my poor driver was still parked outside. He'd followed us to the bar and had been waiting there ever since. I felt terrible about that. Usually I'd just send the driver home and get a cab. But on this night I'd forgotten.

So it was like Cinderella at the ball – suddenly I had to leave. But goodbyes, French style, are never speedy. I did the rounds, which probably took another half an hour. It would be the last time I saw Garou and Bruno for some time so they got extra hugs and kisses. Everyone wished me luck for the Olympics and they all promised to watch. Then I said goodbye to Vince. 'I have to catch a plane in the morning,' I told him.

'Where are you going?' he asked.

When I told him about the Olympics, he said: 'Wow! I'll be watching.'

I gave him my number. 'Call me.' And I left.

Just as I was climbing into the car, I heard my name. Vince was there behind me.

'What's up?' I asked.

'It was great to meet you tonight,' he said in broken English.

'I'm so sorry I have to go,' I said, which was true. I would have stayed up all night to talk to him if I could.

We agreed to catch up and he promised to stay in touch.

As the car drove off I thought to myself: *I'll probably never see him again.* But we did stay in touch over the following weeks, texting and phoning when we could.

And then he'd called me just before I was due to go on to sing 'The Flame' at the opening of the Sydney Olympics. 'I'm ringing to tell you I'm watching,' he'd said. *'Bon courage.'*

'Merci,' I'd said. And that was that. But when I walked out into the stadium to sing, there had been an added spring in my step. To then see my friend from the beauty parlour, the great Cathy Freeman, light the flame – it would go down in my book as one of the most memorable nights of my life.

CHAPTER 21

Good Times

In the end, due to my *Notre-Dame* commitments, I missed seeing Cathy win her 400-metre race and a gold medal. Thirteen years later I'm still kicking myself. Instead, I returned to London. Vince paid me a visit while I was there. Nothing happened but it was nice to know he considered me a friend. There was something about that Frenchman I couldn't put my finger on. For some reason I couldn't get him out of my head. But it was time to move on to the next chapter of my life, and I knew I'd be spending less time in Europe in the coming months.

When I finally finished on *Notre-Dame* I felt mixed emotions. Performing a lead role in London's West End had been tough and tremendous in equal measure, but I was keen to get back to my other job. I had managed to get some writing done while I was in London but now I was itching to do more. One thing that inspired me around that time was a bit of a win in the US.

A cover of 'Burn' by American country singer Jo Dee Messina had reached number 2 on the Billboard country charts, while her album, also called *Burn*, went to number 1. It reminded me that not only did I love songwriting, I was actually not too bad at it.

But first I headed back to Australia to appear as a guest presenter at the ARIA awards in Sydney. At the same time, Sony released *Souvenirs*, a compilation of my songs and recordings that had not been previously available in Australia. The album included 'Show Me Heaven' and 'If I Was a River', the French singles, some live recordings from the Olympia in Paris, plus my live duet with Donna Summer, 'No More Tears (Enough is Enough)'. That performance had also appeared on Donna's live album *Live & More Encore*, something I'm still proud of.

The ARIAs were the usual palaver. My good mate Michael Angel accompanied me, which caused a bit of chatter. Killing Heidi took out the Album of the Year and a few other awards, and dance house duo Madison Avenue won Single of the Year.

I hadn't been nominated for any awards – I hadn't even had a single out in Australia that year – but along with Slim Dusty I received an Outstanding Achievement Award, for my success in Europe. It sounds like a cliché, but to receive an award like that in my own country felt like a great honour – for some reason, recognition in Australia will for me always be the sweetest. Maybe I still hadn't recovered from those early rejections when I was starting out as an adult performer. Either way, it was the icing on the cake following the Olympics, and a fantastic way to end a good year, during which I had at last begun to move on after the split from Ralph. I was starting to feel like a whole person again.

On Christmas Eve I sang at Carols by Candlelight at the Myer Music Bowl in Melbourne. I'd done a few Carols by Candlelight over the years and it was always a magical night. The atmosphere was joyful, and seeing that galaxy of candle lights and smiling faces was a wondrous experience each time.

Then, after a family Christmas involving more food and drink than the recommended yearly intake, I headed for the Sandcastle in Miami. The Sandcastle sounds like a fancy hotel, but in fact it was a songwriting retreat organised by the songwriter Desmond Child. Desmond's success began with 'I Was Made for Loving You', which he wrote with Kiss. From there he wrote songs with Jon Bon Jovi, including 'You Give Love a Bad Name' and 'Livin' on a Prayer'. Since then he'd written hits for Cher, Bonnie Tyler, Aerosmith and many more. He'd co-written 'Livin' la Vida Loca' for Ricky Martin.

It was the second songwriting retreat Desmond had organised – he'd run a similar one the year before. He'd taken the idea from a legendary songwriter's retreat, Printemps des Troubadours, held by Miles Copeland, Sting's manager, in his medieval castle in France.

Attendance at both retreats was by invitation only – somehow my manager Wendy had scored me an invite to the one in Miami.

More than thirty songwriters turned up for the five-day fest. We started with a dinner at Desmond's grand old home, which was like an English gentlemen's club, right there in the middle of Miami. Desmond was larger than life, bright and hilarious, but demanding. I liked him straight away. Some of the other writers there included Richie Sambora, Mark Hudson and Julio Iglesias Jr.

After breakfast the following day, we were each told where we'd be writing that day. I'd be in the studio. When I got there I found Desmond and songwriter Peter Amato waiting for me. By the end of that first day, we'd written 'Soul Mate #9'. The song was tongue-in-cheek and we had a lot of laughs writing it. I loved the idea – how many soul mates can a person have in one lifetime? Working with those two pros, the lyrics and music just seemed to flow.

Three other songs I wrote in those five days at Sandcastle made it onto my new album, which was good going. A lot had happened since I wrote *In Deep* and I was ready to get it all out. This record would be about love and pain, growing up the hard way and learning how to stand on my own two feet. I had consciously decided to freshen the palette and write and record with new people. I wanted this record to be a break from the past. I wanted to experiment a little, to create something exciting and new.

I wrote 'Tangled' with Randy Cantor and Robbie Nevil (remember 'C'est la Vie' from 1986?) and it was an intense session. That song captured something about my heart at that time, my state of confusion. Meeting Vince had thrown me in more ways than one.

I wrote 'You Made Me Find Myself' with Desmond and Ty Lacy on the second last day. It was another song that seemed to be just waiting to be put down on paper. The lyrics attracted quite a bit of attention when the album was finally released – everyone decided it was written about Ralph – but I wrote that song for me.

I'd had those songs in me for too long, but at last they were out.

On the last evening of the retreat we all headed down to Cafe Nostalgia in Miami Beach. Cafe Nostalgia was a nightclub that had started out as a home to Cuban music in Miami but had lately become a bit of an industry hangout. The place was vintage Miami, with worn 1970s decor and some colourful characters gracing the bar. We were there as the entertainment, performing our new songs. After five days of hard work it was great to have a drink and enjoy the show. Mark Hudson played MC and he had us all laughing.

Desmond, Victoria Shaw and Gary Burr performed a song they had written at the previous Sandcastle, and which Ricky Martin had just released as a single, 'Nobody Wants to Be Lonely'. Everyone else got up and did their stuff. Finally it was my turn, and I sang 'You Made Me Find Myself'. I'm not sure why I decided to sing that one, but it encapsulated how I felt about my previous life and where I was at now. Whatever it was, it brought the house down. I guess everyone in that room could relate to it in some way.

When the Sandcastle wrapped up I flew to LA. There I caught up with some other songwriters and wrote 'But I Lied' and 'Woman'. Next stop was New York, where I wrote 'Something's Gotta Change' with Russ DeSalvo and Arnie Roman. I was quickly getting enough songs together for the new album. Now I just needed a producer.

One night while I was in New York I was having dinner with Wendy, and we were talking generally about the music we loved and whose work we admired. Nile Rodgers' name came up. Now, if you don't know who he is, that's okay – but let me give you a quick run-down. With his co-writer Bernard Edwards, Nile is one of the original architects of contemporary dance music. His 'chucking' guitar style has been copied or sampled on probably every dance song you've ever heard. His hits began with his 1970s band Chic, songs that are now part of popular music's DNA: 'Le Freak', 'Everybody Dance', 'I Want Your Love', 'Good Times', Sister Sledge's 'We are Family' and 'He's the Greatest Dancer', Diana Ross's 'Upside Down' and 'I'm Coming Out'. His production credits include David Bowie's *Let's Dance* album and Madonna's *Like a Virgin*. He produced INXS's 'Original Sin'. More recently he did some co-writing with Daft Punk and appeared on their hit album *Random Access Memories*. In short, the man is a musical god.

It so happened that Wendy knew Nile – her cousin Nick Rhodes is in Duran Duran and Nile produced their album

Notorious. So when I wondered aloud what it would be like to work with the Godfather of Dance, she said: 'Do you want to meet him?'

Of course I wanted to meet him, regardless of whether we worked together or not. So Wendy teed up a meeting while I was there in New York.

Meeting Nile was a thrill and we seemed to get on well together. He's a lovely guy: friendly, funny and cultured. He'd spent quite a bit of time in Europe back in the days of Chic, who were huge in France, and he knew I'd spent a lot of time there recently, so we talked about that. By the end of the meeting we'd agreed to give some thought to working together, but nothing was definite.

Then he said, 'What are you doing tonight?'

'Not much,' I responded.

'Well, my old mates Duran Duran are playing. Do you want to come?'

'Sure,' I said.

So I went with Nile to see Duran Duran at the Beacon Theater on Broadway. Nile joined them for the encore. He'd brought along his famous Fender Strat guitar that he calls 'the Hitmaker', and seeing him on stage playing in his utterly distinctive style was inspiring. Nile's mother was fourteen when she had him and both his parents had drug problems (Nile had struggled with his own addiction, too), but I got the sense that nothing was ever going to hold back this brilliant mind and musical genius.

After the show we hung out for a while, then went back to his Manhattan apartment to keep talking. We ended up riffing in his kitchen and later he told me that was when he made his decision. He wanted to work with me. By the end of the night, it was almost all arranged. Nile would produce songs for my new record.

First, though, I was set to do some writing and recording with Peter-John Vettese, a mad Italian–Scottish musician and producer who had an abiding interest in quantum physics. Pete had played keyboard in Jethro Tull in the 1980s and had since worked with all kinds of artists. I'd loved his work on Annie Lennox's *Diva*, and he'd recently co-produced the Bee Gees' new album, which ended up being their last one together.

Pete's studio was in Parsons Green in London. So I headed back to London and the house in Knightsbridge. Not long after, though, I sold my apartment in LA and bought a little house in Fulham (well, the bank did). It was back in the days when a British pound was worth three Australian dollars, so I was mortgaged to the hilt. But it was great to have a house of my own, and being able to write and record around the corner with Pete was so easy and convenient it felt like a luxury. For a while at least, I would no longer be the girl from Moonee Ponds. Now I was a Fulham girl. I was back within cooee of Paris, and Vince, too, although I still had no idea whether that was going anywhere …

CHAPTER 22

Dare You to Be Happy

I've never laughed so much. I wasn't joking when I said that
the guy who would be co-producing my new album, Peter
Vettese, was mad. It must have been in his genes – his Italian
dad was a saxophone player who brought gelato to Scotland,
which sounds like a good idea until you remember that up
there it's freezing for eleven months of the year. Pete had a way
of looking at the world that cracked me up – his Scottish side
clicked with my Aussie side while the Italians in us understood
each other.

Pete was a bit like me, considerably louder than he was
tall. In the studio he'd get up to all kinds of crazy things – we
danced a lot, he'd be jumping off the walls (it was his studio,
so I guess he could do what he liked). He once said that when
it came to making records, people came first and the music
second. It was a refreshing way to approach it, and it meant

he got the best out of people – happy and comfortable musos make for better music (industry types take note!).

The mad Scot may have been fun but he challenged me every day, tearing away my safety net and constantly pushing me to take leaps of faith. Together we wrote a couple of songs. 'Dare You to Be Happy' summed up how I was feeling at that time. Pete had come up with the line and I'd embraced it as a challenge to myself – get it together, start enjoying yourself. I did and I was. I'd rediscovered my mojo and was determined to have fun, which was easy when Pete was around.

We demoed 'Dare You to Be Happy', but when I suggested we start working on the track he refused. 'No, no, no. I can't do that one. That one's for Nile.' It turned out he was right: when I listened to it again I realised the song had disco anthem written all over it, and if anyone knew how to create a disco anthem it was the songwriter from Chic. So I put that one in the back pocket to take to Mr Rodgers later. That Pete had so easily relinquished a song he'd co-written was typical of his approach – he always wanted what was best for the music.

The other song I wrote with Pete was 'Symphony of Life'. It was a special song to me, because it expressed my feelings about having Vince come into my life.

My relationship with the handsome blue-eyed Frenchman had started out as a friendship. But recently it had developed into something stronger and deeper. Despite a considerable language barrier – his English was poor, and my French was ordinary – we had no trouble communicating. We talked for days at a time, thumbing through dictionaries to find the right word. We seemed to have a lot to share, and we shared it, in two languages. I felt a real spiritual connection to Vince, and 'Symphony of Life' was about that.

Not surprisingly, 'Symphony of Life' was one of my favourite songs on the new album. After we'd recorded the vocals, Pete went away to play with the instrumentation and arrangement. A few days later, he played me what he'd done. I listened to it but didn't say much. I wasn't sure at first. But as I'm always telling other people, forget your preconceptions – just listen to the bloody song! And when he played it to me again, I just loved it. It has an ambient Europop feel that moves from dark to light and literally 'takes you higher', as the song says.

Another song I worked on with Pete was 'God Only Knows', which I'd co-written with Jeremy and his friend and musical collaborator, Rémi Lacroix. We'd written it one Sunday afternoon at Jeremy's place in Paris. They played me a piece of music they'd been working on and I started singing a melody. Later, I penned the lyrics. In retrospect, the song was a true and honest account of my relationship with Jeremy. We'd been in it together, but we had no idea where it would lead, if anywhere. It was about living in the moment, without any guarantee of a future. Because 'god only knows'.

Both songs feature live strings – recording a string orchestra rather than using synthesised or sampled strings – which always adds something rich and lush to a song. Pete was keen on live strings, and so was I. One day he said to me, 'I want to introduce you to a mate of mine, a bloke called Simon Hale.'

'Who's he?' I asked.

'He's a string arranger. He's worked on loads of things. He does all the strings for Jamiroquai,' Pete said.

Jamiroquai, who had ingested their fair share of Chic pills and Nile Rodgers licks (who hasn't?), featured stunning disco strings on their records, which, coincidentally, charted all over the world.

'Great, I'd love to meet him,' I said to Pete. But I was in and out of the studio a lot so I still hadn't been introduced to Simon weeks later. One day we were working on 'Symphony of Life' when the doorbell rang. I went to get it – Pete was too busy groovin' out, as usual.

I peered through the window and saw a guy in head-to-toe cycling gear standing there with something in his hand. I opened the door.

'Hi, you must be the courier,' I said.

'And you must be the artist,' Simon said. 'Hi, Tina, my name's Simon Hale.'

Ouch. 'Fuck! I'm so sorry, Simon.'

While it was not exactly the reception he'd been hoping for, in true Simon Hale style he burst out laughing.

Simon went on to create some beautifully memorable string arrangements for the record and we've been working together ever since.

*

Nile Rodgers' studio was at his house in Connecticut, which overlooked a little bay. I spent eight days at Nile's place, staying in the guest quarters. With rolling lawns, a private jetty and a view, it was very different to Pete's studio in the middle of London.

Also working on the project was Richard Hilton, who played keyboards for Nile's projects, as well as engineering and programming. Richard and I struck up a friendship – he was a lovely guy and great musician and more than a decade later we're still friends. What a talent he is!

Nile produced, but he also played all the guitar on the songs we did together. I still pinch myself when I think about it – thousands of records feature Nile-*like* guitar, but mine had the real thing.

Pete had been right – Nile knew exactly what to do with 'Dare You to Be Happy'. And when it came to 'Soul Mate #9' he tinkered with the arrangement and put the chorus right up front, an old trick he'd perfected in his Chic days.

After I finished at Nile's, I flew to Paris to record a handful of French tracks for their version of the new album: 'Coeur de Pierre' (Heart of Stone), 'Tu Es Toujours Là' (You Are Always There) and 'Si Je Ne T'Aimais Pas' (If I Didn't Love You). French legend David Hallyday was lined up to produce 'Coeur de Pierre' and singer-songwriter Pascal Obispo would produce 'Si Je Ne T'Aimais Pas'.

Jacques Veneruso, who wrote 'Tu Es Toujours Là', produced that song.

Valérie Michelin and I decided 'Tu Es Toujours Là' would be the first French single, but when I heard the mixes I wasn't happy. It had such a different sound to the album; to my ears it lacked a certain pizzazz I was looking for.

During that period the French–African singer Kelly Joyce, daughter of chanteuse Emmanuelle Vidal de Fonseca, had a smash hit in Italy with a song called 'Vivre la Vie'. It had a fantastic retro sixties sound, à la Amy Winehouse's *Back to Black*, which came out five years later. (And which, of course, had been produced by Mark Ronson, the stepson of my mate Mick Jones, who co-produced *In Deep*. Talk about six degrees of separation …) When I heard 'Vivre la Vie' I had to find out who had produced it. It turned out to be an Englishman called Paul Manners. Paul was a bass player who had travelled to Italy for a two-week gig decades earlier and had never returned to his homeland. He had a studio near Rimini and had produced this brilliant record.

I convinced Valérie to let me demo 'Tu Es Toujours Là' with Paul. So off I went to Falcon Valley, Paul's studio in Italy, and we quickly put together a demo of the song. But when I played it to Valérie later she didn't like it and they ended up canning it. I was devastated, but one good thing came out of it: I had made a connection with Paul.

In fact, I recorded a song for the new record while I was there – 'I'm Gone' – and I made a mental note in my head that I wanted to work with Paul again.

*

I called the new album *Just Me*. It represented the past two years of my life, and the songs on the record covered the full gamut of emotions. *Just Me* was about my experiences as a survivor determined to move on and grow. The title was pathetically obvious, really – I wrote the album for me, and no one else.

The album was slated for release in Australia and France in November. The first single was to be 'Soul Mate #9'.

But when the guys at Sony Australia heard the mixes they were confused. I'm not sure what they expected, but often record companies hope beyond hope for more of the same, in this case more of *Don't Ask* and *In Deep*. When it's not more of the same, they scratch their heads. (And when it is, they're just as likely to tell you it's too much like the previous albums!)

I said what I always say: 'Listen to the bloody songs before you make up your minds.'

But at that time, the local artists who were selling well tended to be indie rock or pop: Killing Heidi, Powderfinger, Regurgitator. Having spent a few years in the UK and Europe, my musical tastes had moved towards dance and Europop. And anyway, those who knew me would know I'd always been a fan of R & B and dance music. It was in my blood. For this record I'd chosen to move away from big ballads and had gone for more of a pop vocal style. To me, it seemed like an exciting but natural progression.

Having had such a ball making *Just Me*, Sony's reaction was a disappointing start. Nevertheless, they gave it their best shot and released 'Soul Mate #9' in September. I returned to Australia to do the usual promo stuff: instore signings, TV appearances, interviews and so on. The fans were as numerous, friendly and supportive as ever. But when it came to radio, I felt like I was in a time warp and it was 1994, when no metro station would play 'Chains'.

Other things were challenging my plan to stay happy. Two years on, my divorce settlement seemed no closer to being finalised, with things becoming extremely protracted. Ann-Marie, who was back in Melbourne with a new baby, had been looking after it all on a day-to-day basis. But it now seemed like it would end up in court. The whole thing had become an incredibly expensive and heavy exercise, for both Ralph and myself.

And to top it off, Vince and I had called it quits. Now, 'daring' myself to be happy seemed like nothing more than a stupid joke.

CHAPTER 23

Symphony of Life

All my plans to be happy, follow my dreams, move on and enjoy life had fallen apart halfway through 2001. It seemed that in the end I just wasn't ready for it. I guess I thought I was getting better only to find myself miserable again. So one day I woke up and looked at Vince and thought: *I don't deserve a man like this. He's too good for me.* I ended it, just like that. I think I actually said to him: 'What are you doing with me? You could do so much better.'

Wrapped up in my misery, I genuinely didn't know how to deal with a man who was so kind, gentle, generous and respectful. I felt like I was out of my depth, and I truly believed I didn't deserve it. Have you ever heard of anything more pathetic?

The other thing in the back of my mind was the ongoing tussle with Ralph. With the divorce turning into a shit fight, I didn't want to drag Vince through it. It wouldn't have been fair.

216

Vince was hurt. He also thought I was nuts, and looking back, he was right. I was still a mess. Nothing is ever simple, least of all love, and getting my life back together was proving to be two steps forward, one step back. So we parted, although we promised to keep in touch.

In the end, I began to see more of Jeremy again. He'd always been there, a familiar friend I could rely on. And in October I brought him out to Australia, not long before the launch of *Just Me*. He was a trooper, escorting me to the ARIAs and the launch party. Whatever I had to do, he'd be there.

When *Just Me* came out in mid-November, 'Soul Mate #9' hadn't made much of a dent in the charts, having had minimal airplay on radio following its release a month or so earlier. *Just Me* debuted at number 7 and went gold immediately, but compared to *Don't Ask* and *In Deep*, sales were disappointing.

As you have probably gathered by now, the life of a singer is a lot like the Big Dipper at Luna Park. So, while I might have been chugging around a corner at the foot of a mountain at this point, suddenly I was atop a little rise with the news that, in the States, Pam Reswick, Steve Werfel and I had won a BMI songwriting award for 'Burn'. (BMI stands for Broadcast Music Inc, which is an American performance rights organisation, like Australia's APRA.) It was nice to be recognised over there for one of my songs. It had won thanks in part to Jo Dee Messina's version, based on the number of times it had been played or performed that year.

*

In January 'Dare You to be Happy' was released as a single. With little airplay, it sank like a stone. A month later, Ann-Marie and I went shopping for clothes to wear to my divorce settlement, which was due to be heard in the Victorian Supreme Court. In the end, the case was settled out of court. The details of the settlement were confidential, but I felt that I'd lost much of what I had worked so hard for.

Nevertheless, it was a relief it was all over. At last I was truly free of the past. Free to be me. Free to move on.

One piece of good news around the time of my divorce settlement was that Nancy was pregnant. Mum, Dad, Silvana and I were thrilled when she told us. We Arena girls had been a bit slow when it came to motherhood, but at last one of us was taking the plunge. I was overjoyed for Nancy – she had a wonderful husband who loved her and soon she'd have a beautiful baby. It reminded me that happiness in a relationship was possible, and that sometimes you've got to get out there and grab it by the horns.

Another piece of news came through that also gave me a lift. My manager, Wendy Laister, rang to say she'd had a call from the management company IMG, wanting to know whether I'd be interested in playing the lead role of Sally Bowles in an Australian production of *Cabaret* based on Sam

Mendes' acclaimed 1993 Covent Garden revival, which later ran on Broadway for several years.

Wendy asked me what I thought.

'Sure … maybe,' I said. 'I love *Cabaret*.' I knew it well enough, being a fan of Liza Minnelli, who played Sally Bowles in the film. But Sally's a complex character and I did wonder how they saw me in the role. I also wondered whether I'd be up to the task. Unlike *Notre-Dame*, *Cabaret* had a lot of spoken dialogue, which would be a huge challenge for a singer like me. I heard later that Toni Collette was originally slated for the role of Sally but had been unavailable. Hers would be big shoes to fill.

'Great. Sam Mendes wants to meet you.'

I was speechless for a moment. 'Pardon?'

'He wants to meet you before they make a decision.'

I was ready to get my teeth into something new and now this opportunity had presented itself. And, having just finalised the divorce settlement, the thought of a regular income was appealing.

Soon I was on a plane bound for LA, my old stamping ground. Sam, who had shot to fame as the writer and director of *American Beauty*, which won a truckload of Oscars, BAFTAs and Golden Globes, was there working on his next film, *Road to Perdition*.

I met him at Fox Studios and we got chatting. Sam cross-examined me in a polite, relaxed fashion and seemed genuinely happy to meet me. I heard soon after that the gig was mine if I wanted it. In the end I could only do the Sydney shows, because I had commitments lined up in France later that year, including some live concerts.

Once I'd signed on, I found myself in New York being fitted for Sally's famous corset. It had become synonymous with Sam's production and I could see why. A stunning creation of intricate black lace, when teamed with thigh-high black boots and suspenders it was something of an attention grabber, to put it mildly. It would be a brave new look for Tina Arena, let alone Pina!

After a trip back to France to do some promotional stuff for 'Tu Es Toujours Là', I set up camp in Sydney by myself. Jeremy and I had well and truly gone our separate ways by then, so I was on my own. It gave me time to think, and anyway, I'd be so busy with the show there'd be no time for anything else.

Former soccer star Craig Johnston rented me his apartment. It had a stunning view of Woolloomooloo, but I barely saw it – once the show started, I virtually lived, ate and slept in my dressing-room at the State Theatre.

Cabaret is the story of Sally Bowles, an English cabaret performer, and her relationship with a young American writer called Cliff Bradshaw. Set in Berlin's seedy Kit Kat Club in 1931 just as the Nazis are rising to power, it's a dark tale of decadence and terror, of people living on the edge.

Every day I was becoming a little more Sally and a little less Tina. Sally was already a complex character, but in Sam's production her complexities and idiosyncrasies were magnified. I could relate to her. Like me, she was resilient – an eternal optimist. Also like me at this point in my life, Sally wanted to be a performer on the one hand, while on the other, she wanted the white picket fence, two and a half kids and to live happily ever after. I could definitely empathise with that. But like Sally, I was no closer to achieving the latter. I was thirty-four and a single woman. I'd recently said goodbye to two good men, one because he was at a different stage in his life to me, and the other because I thought he was too good for me. There were no new prospects on the horizon. That's just the way it was.

An American crew travelled out to stage the show, starting with the director, BT McNicholl, who had assisted Sam on the Broadway production. We rehearsed for weeks in the studios at NIDA in Sydney's Kensington. The songs were challenging enough, but then there was the dancing and on top of that dialogue and *acting*. It stretched me in every way – it was incredibly challenging but wonderful, invigorating, exciting! I was working with brilliant actors – people such as Ian Stenlake, who played Cliff, Henri Szeps (Herr Schultz), Judi Connelli (Fräulein Schneider) and Nadine Garner (Fräulein Kost) – and I learnt an enormous amount from them all.

Ian and I, being lovers in the play, had to work closely together. Doing love scenes was a brand-new experience for me – there was quite a bit of pretend snogging involved –but thank god Ian was not only a total pro but an absolute darling. We laughed and laughed.

Opening night was 22 August. As the date approached I became more and more beside myself. Since I was a kid, every time I'd performed a song on stage I felt like I was taking a risk, that something might go wrong, that people would hate it, that I was *exposing* myself. But that was nothing compared to playing Sally Bowles, let alone in my own country. I think it would have been easier to do it in Paris or London. But in Australia, I knew the locals would be tough on me. I had no illusions – I was sticking my neck out in this role and just asking for my head to be lopped off. I was terrified.

In the end, things turned out okay, as they do. It was such a powerful production, and a brilliant cast and crew. After it was all over that first night I cried with relief. Mum and Dad had come up for the show and I fell into their arms.

Cabaret was the standard eight shows a week, so I never did see much of Craig Johnston's lovely apartment. But I know Sydney's State Theatre like the back of my hand, and still think of it as my second home.

While I trod the boards at the State, 'Symphony of Life' was released in Australia and France. This single got some traction and debuted at number 8 in Australia. That felt good – the song was a personal favourite. Every time I heard it I was reminded of Vince, although the feelings were bittersweet. I was beginning to realise that leaving him had been a big mistake and that I might never find myself in his arms again.

My final *Cabaret* performance was on 15 September. Just days later, Mum rang. Nancy had had her baby, a little girl they called Sofia. We were over the moon. Sofia was my family's first grandchild and niece, so her arrival was particularly special for all of us.

I hopped on the first plane to Melbourne, but it didn't get in until after 10 pm. I took a cab straight to the hospital. Walter had managed to butter up the nurses so they agreed to let me in. It was after 11 o'clock at night when I finally saw Nancy. There was Sofia, wide awake, wrapped up like a bug in a rug. She was like a little messenger, sent to remind us what was important in life. And with her bright eyes and head of dark hair, what a darling cupid she was!

I couldn't stay in Australia to enjoy Sofia's arrival for long, sadly. I was scheduled to play three concerts at the Olympia the following month – 'Tu Es Toujours Là' had charted well when it came out in France in February, and 'Symphony of Life' was getting plenty of airplay. Soon I was on a plane bound for Paris.

My Australian band flew over to accompany me. Once again they did me proud and we put on three cracking shows at my favourite French venue.

I stayed on in Paris to do promo. One evening, feeling at a bit of a loose end, I rang Vince. That wasn't so out of the ordinary – as agreed, we'd kept in touch. Often we texted and occasionally we talked.

'What are you doing tonight?' he said after we'd chatted in our Franglish.

'Not much. I've got something on between five and seven pm and then I'm done.'

'Do you want to catch up?' he said.

'Sure.' I hadn't seen Vince in a year, probably. But we were still friends, and I had nothing else on. It would be great to see him – no, to be honest, I was *dying* to see him.

'Where are you?'

I was staying at a gorgeous little hotel in the seventeenth arrondissement called Villa Alessandra. So I met him there.

As soon as he walked through the door I fell in love with him again. We gave each other a big hug and that was that. We ended up staying up until three o'clock in the morning, talking and talking, sometimes in French, sometimes in English. Vince's English had improved since I'd seen him last, and my French was coming along too. Not that we'd ever had trouble communicating. Vince and I just seemed to understand each other, in any language.

It's true that my life that year felt like a roller-coaster ride. Sally Bowles would have said it was a cabaret. But with Vince back in my life, it suddenly felt more like a symphony, in which highs and lows, beauty and pain, laughter and tears come together to create something powerful and beautiful, something lasting. A symphony of life.

CHAPTER 24

Never (Past Tense)

Vince and I had barely been apart since we fell into each other's arms that night in Paris. I'd never really been able to get him out of my head. Now I realised that was because, in my heart of hearts, I knew he was the man for me (my soul mate number one!). I think he was coming around to that idea too.

When I wasn't travelling we lived at my apartment in Fulham. Together, Vince and I were learning two languages – he English, I French. Learning French, *really* learning French, opened my heart and mind to a whole new world. Until then I'd felt like I was peering through a frosted window. Now, slowly, the window became clearer, until one day (it took a few years!) I realised I was no longer looking in – I was right there. I had to work at it, though. It was like going to uni – I listened carefully, made notes, practised. But it was worth it. Vince did the same thing, and being able to converse in the other's language brought us even closer.

Valérie Michelin had suggested we record the Olympia shows with a view to releasing a live album. I thought it was great idea – I'd always wanted to do a live album. I love performing on stage and had always preferred my voice live to my voice in the studio. But there'd been a few obstacles. For one thing, the budget was tight, which meant there was virtually no money for post-production. We'd have to go with whatever we got from the front-of-house mixing desk. Thank god the engineer Chris Ridgway had golden hands!

Often vocals are redubbed later on live recordings, but the quality of the recording was so good (and the budget so tight) we kept the original live vocals. Valérie wanted a single for the album, and after much discussion we decided I'd record a duet in the studio with a gorgeous R & B singer called Jay. Previously a member of French boy band Poetic Lover, Jay has a stunning voice (later, Luc Plamondon cast him in his musical *Cindy*). The song was called 'Je Te Retrouve un Peu' (Little by Little I Find You).

It's a charming song, but I also loved the video clip – shot in the streets of Paris, it was nothing more than me dressed in an overcoat just being me, and Jay looking handsome. I guess it helps when you have Paris as the backdrop, but in France I never felt any pressure to dress up (or down) like a pop star, or to show too much skin, or look a certain way. Simple and classic is their approach, which kept things uncomplicated for me.

It was true, that, over there, being Tina Arena sometimes felt easier. But at the same time, after so many years, I needed a break from her. Maybe, having found love, my focus was shifting. Whatever it was, I wanted to let go of it all a bit. So one day, when I was on the phone to Wendy, checking in, I said: 'I'd love to be a guest vocalist on something, and not be "Tina Arena" for a change. I just want to do something different.' I would have been happy if I'd been credited as Fanny Fedora.

Wendy put the word out. It turned out a New York outfit called the Roc Project, which was made up of DJ Ray Roc and singer Tina Novak, were looking for a vocalist for their song 'Never (Past Tense)'. It was an odd situation: because Tina (now there's a coincidence!) was signed to a different label to Ray, she wasn't allowed to sing on the song.

Wendy asked me over the phone what I thought.

'Well, what does the track sound like?' I asked her.

'I don't know. I can't tell.'

'Send it to me.'

When I heard it, I loved it straight away. I've always liked dance music and it had smash written all over it: irresistible beat, irresistible hook line.

Ray flew over to London and we recorded the vocal and shot the video clip there. It was terrific to be part of something different, and refreshing to not be the main focus – Ray Roc was the focus, and the song even more so.

When 'Never' was released in April it quickly became a huge hit on dance floors around the world, and ended up being a top 5 hit on the Billboard dance charts. Then Dutch DJ Tiësto remixed it, and it featured regularly on *Queer as Folk*, a hugely popular American TV drama about five gay guys, based on the UK show of the same name. Tiësto's version turned up on the soundtrack for season three of the show.

We included the song as a bonus CD with *Vous Êtes Toujours Là* (You Are Always There), which was the name of my first live album.

It had been two years since I'd written and recorded an English-language album and I was ready to get back into it. Things were tricky, though. Sony had slashed budgets – well, they'd slashed mine – so the budget allocated to writing was extremely tight. The fact was, *Just Me* had ended up being costly to make. Because we'd come off the back of two very successful albums, some big bucks had been thrown around. The album hadn't recouped its costs, and two years later, the industry was on the slide.

I was keen to write and record with Paul Manners, the guy who had helped create that retro sound for Kelly Joyce and who had recorded a version of 'Tu Es Toujours Là' and produced 'I'm Gone', the track I'd ended up including on *Just Me*. I always want to start afresh with each album, an approach, it must be said, that the Sony guys were never particularly comfortable with.

Despite the tight budget, Paul was keen. So in mid-2003 I found myself in a gorgeous little village called Montefiore Conca outside of Rimini in the Emilia–Romagna region of north-east Italy. Paul's studio was just out of town, in a magnificent old farmhouse set in a stunning valley.

On Paul's recommendation I booked myself into the Villa Leri. When I arrived, I discovered that it was also a retreat for kids with drug problems. The place was associated with the Catholic Church, and the idea was that the kids would heal and recover by expressing themselves via theatre and the arts, as well as growing all their own food. They grew everything – vegetables, wheat for bread, grapes for organic wine, olives for oil – and also produced their own meat, and milk for cheese. The villa was set against a vista of rolling green hills, ancient fortifications, cobbled streets and medieval houses clinging to the hillsides. All in all, it was an inspirational place to record.

Everyone was so friendly – being able to speak the language no doubt helped. They knew I was a singer, and they seemed to like having me there.

While I was there, the kids at Villa Leri staged a beautiful musical called *Chiara di Dio* (Clare of God), the story of Saint Francis of Assisi and his chaste love for his follower Chiara, who went on to set up an order of nuns called the Poor Clares. On occasion I'd get up and sing a song with them. It was just great to get back to basics. Nature, music, good food.

I made two or three trips to Montefiore Conca and Falcon Valley Studios that year, staying a week or so at a time. Paul and I had a ball. Paul was impossibly talented and yet a warm and open individual who was fun to be around. We were on the same wavelength and we recorded some great demos: 'Talk to Me', 'Peel Me (Like an Orange)', 'Doesn't It Feel Good', 'No Apology', 'Italian Love Song' and 'Take Me Apart'. We wanted to create a sound that paid tribute to 1960s legends like Petula Clark and Dusty Springfield, two inspirations for me over the years. To get a warm vintage sound we recorded in analogue rather than digital and we went back to basics, with the voice smack in the middle.

When the demos were done, we sent them off to Sony. This would be the last album of my contract. At the same time, three dates in November were locked in for concerts in Australia – two in Melbourne and one at my home away from home, the State Theatre in Sydney. It was a joy to get home and touch base with my Australian fans.

It had been a good year. I was head over heels, which always adds a glow to life, and I'd slowed down, just a little, to try and learn how to smell the roses again. It had been so long. And I was excited about the new album. On a tiny budget Paul and I had created something I was proud of, some good songs, beautiful melodies, heartfelt lyrics. I couldn't wait to get into the studio to work on them.

Soon after Christmas, I was back in London for a gig at Shepherds Bush. It had been lined up by Penelope Young, who was based in the UK and had temporarily taken over from Wendy Laister as my manager. Now that I was living in the UK and working so much across the Channel it made sense for my manager to be based there, rather than in New York. Penelope was looking after me until I found someone permanent.

An Australian bloke called Bruce Pawsey had organised the Shepherds Bush show to celebrate Australia Day. I knew Bruce, who had started out as a drummer in Melbourne working with the Ceberanos. He'd been my UK tour manager back in the 1990s when I was promoting 'Chains' and *Don't Ask* over there. I'd always liked him, a clever, warm and generous bloke who was tall and good-looking to boot. They'd been tough tours and he'd done a great job.

Penelope also liked Bruce when she met him and thought he might be the man to take over my management. When we put it to him, he agreed. Penelope was relieved and I was, too.

I was gearing up to record the album with Paul. Bruce and I were just waiting for the go-ahead from Sony. But we hadn't heard anything in a while. Then, in a phone conversation, it was made clear to us that they didn't like the demos – that they weren't commercial enough, or something. Whatever Sony were looking for, it apparently wasn't there.

Not long after, Bruce received a letter. Sony were not prepared to record or release my new album. Instead, they'd like to release a Greatest Hits instead.

I'd been dropped. Sony and I were, as the song says, past tense.

I'd been retrenched, lost my job. It was devastating. I just kept thinking, *How can they sack me?* The usual worries that everyone has when they suddenly find themselves unemployed kept me awake at night, not least the fact that I had only recently mortgaged myself to the hilt. I wandered around in a daze for two weeks, not knowing what had hit me or what to do.

Finally, I sat down and wrote Sony boss Denis Handlin a letter. I thanked him for giving me a chance, and for all their support over the years. I said that, while I didn't understand their decision, I was grateful for everything they'd done for me. It seemed the right thing to do and I've never regretted it.

It was true that I didn't understand it back then, but I do now. They wanted to cut their losses, and had found a way out. That was why they'd given me so little to make the demos with. Back then, recording music was still an extremely expensive business and now the industry was in trouble.

My only consolation was that so many artists before me have found themselves without a contract at various points in their careers. Now I'd joined the list. It was a bizarre feeling, like I'd been thrown overboard in the middle of the ocean with no land in sight. Maybe, if I could only swim to shore, I could go back and study for that law degree …

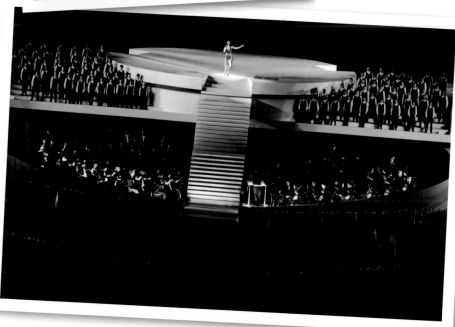

On 15 September 2000, I sang 'The Flame' with the Sydney Children's Choir at the Sydney Olympics opening ceremony. Soon after, Cathy Freeman lit the Olympic flame, and the Games were officially open. It was an incredible moment and an evening I'll never forget. *Getty Images*

To sing at the Olympics I had to take time out from my role as Esmeralda in the London production of *Notre-Dame de Paris*. The show had broken all records in France, and some of the French cast crossed the Channel, including Canadian star Garou, who played Quasimodo. It was my first show in London's West End; I returned seven years later to play Roxie Hart in *Chicago*. *Robbie Jack/Corbis*

With a poster for Sam Mendes's 2002 Australian production of *Cabaret*, in which I played Sally Bowles. The corset I wore in the show certainly grabbed people's attention. It still hangs in my wardrobe. *Getty Images*

On the red carpet with my dear friend, fashion designer Michael Angel, attending the ARIAs in October 2000. That night I received an Outstanding Achievement Award for my success in Europe. *Getty Images*

I was five months pregnant with Gab in July 2005 when I appeared at the Paris Live 8 concert, held in the grounds of the palace at Versailles. Here I am with British R & B star Craig David singing the Beatles' 'Come Together'. It was great to be part of such an inspiring event. *Bertrand Guay/AFP/Getty Images*

Above & opposite: Gab with his brand new parents in late 2005. Thank god Vince had some idea about how to look after a baby, because I didn't have a clue!

Christmas 2005 in our apartment in Paris with my sisters and Mum and Dad. Gab had just been born and the folks paid a surprise visit. It was the best Christmas present I've ever had.

Life on Place du Docteur Félix Lobligeois in Batignolles, Paris. We had some great parties in the square, and made many friends.

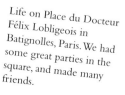

Two weeks after Gab was born in November 2005 my first French album, *Un Autre Univers*, was released. A month after that, Vince and I attended the NRJ awards in Cannes as I'd been nominated for Best Female French Artist. Motherhood wasn't going to slow this girl down! *Getty Images*

I've been performing at Carols by Candlelight since I was a kid. It's always a magical night, whether at the Myer Music Bowl or Sydney's Domain, as shown here in 2007. *damianwhite.com*

On the set of the video for 'Entends–Tu le Monde', which was filmed in Sydney in January 2007. Vince came for the ride and appeared in the clip as well. *Fabien Dufils*

Performing at the Hamer Hall in Melbourne in December 2007 as part of the *Songs of Love and Loss* tour. Nicholas Buc is conducting the 35-piece orchestra with Kelly and Talei Wolfgramm on backing vocals (left). *Getty Images*

I have always loved performing with other artists. Here I am with Italian legend 'Zucchero' in Australia in 2008. I sang a duet with Zucchero on his album *Zu & Co*, and appeared with him at the Royal Albert Hall in 2004, along with some amazing artists, including Eric Clapton and Pavarotti. *Getty Images*

And with Andrea Bocelli on his tour of Australia in the same year. Andrea was lots of fun – he could do the best Australian accent I've ever heard. *Getty Images*

Dressed as Tinkerbell, backstage at a 2009 annual Les Enfoirés charity concert in Paris with Pinocchio, aka Pascal Obispo. The concerts are a huge production and lots of fun, while raising funds to help feed 600,000 hungry people in France every week. *Joanne Azoubel*

In 2010 I toured Australia with Ronan Keating. We'd sung the odd duet before, but never toured together. We had a ball, playing concert halls and wineries. *Naomi Rahim*

With my mentor and good friend John Young in October 2010 when I had the honour of inducting him into the ARIA Hall of Fame. I sang his song 'Here Comes the Star', which was a hit for Herman's Hermits in 1969. *Rohan Kelly/Newspix*

On *Hey Hey It's Saturday* in 2010 with two people I admire and respect enormously: David Atkins, with whom I appeared in his show *Dynamite* back in 1990, and the ever lovely Olivia Newton-John. I sang a duet with Olivia on her 2002 album *(2)*.

With Troy Cassar Daley, Kasey Chambers and David Campbell at the Flood Relief Appeal in Brisbane in early 2011. Along with many others we were there to raise money for those affected by Queensland's biblical floods. *Peter Wallis / Newspix*

On stage in Dunkerque, northern France. Every year the local council stages a free concert in the park of the beautiful Château Coquelle. In June 2011 it was my turn.

In 2011, with the then French Minister of Culture and Communications, Frédéric Mitterrand, who officially awarded me the Chevalier of the Order of National Merit, France's second highest honour. I feel, well, honoured, to say the least! *Getty Images*

It was a Sunday in August 2011 and I was still in my pyjamas when I heard that Cadel Evans had won the Tour de France. In the end I sang the national anthem at the prize giving. I figured a live a capella version would have more impact than an instrumental recording. *Picture Media/Reuters*

Below: Gab is already showing an interest in music. Here he is jamming with his cousin Sofia. Gab might look like his dad (right), but I think I got a bit of a look-in with my niece, whom some people say resembles me when I was little. God help us all!

With Silvana's darling boy Louis in 2012. I love being an aunty, but what my nieces and nephews make of me is anyone's guess, especially once they're old enough to read this book!

With Gab in Montpellier
for the Les Enfoirés concerts
in 2011. Gab takes it all in
his stride.

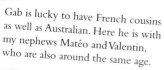

Gab is lucky to have French cousins
as well as Australian. Here he is with
my nephews Matéo and Valentin,
who are also around the same age.

Making pancakes in our house in Paris before the builders moved in. I love cooking almost as
much as I love music – even when the sous-chef keeps licking the spoon.

All dressed up with somewhere to go. Backstage while on tour in 2012 – just me and my date, the double bass. My real date, Vince, was behind the camera, taking far too long to get this snap.

Above: Recording a demo in Paris in 2012. And below, at Sing Sing Studios in Melbourne in August 2013, putting the finishing touches to my new album, *Reset.*

CHAPTER 25

Un Autre Univers

In Australia, Sony released my *Greatest Hits 1994 – 2004* album in October 2004. To justify the '2004' bit, they included one new song on the album, which was released as a single a few days later. 'Italian Love Song' was written and recorded with Paul Manners. It was a tongue-in-cheek song about a love affair with a certain type of Italian man (the kind who might chat up his best friend's mum), a man who needs forgiveness, probably because he's been up to no good.

It was witty and fun, but what I liked best about it was the video clip, because it featured my favourite non-Italian man – Vince (though in fact, his great-grandmother was Italian). Australian director Anthony Rose made it on a slim budget with just a couple of crew. We filmed it in the stunningly picturesque seaside village of Collioure, in the south of France, not far from the border with Spain.

Vince played the handsome, mysterious Italian to a T. The fact he is French and looks Scandinavian didn't matter. It was the first time Vince and I really collaborated creatively. Following my experience with Ralph, I'd been wary of mixing business and pleasure, but working creatively with Vince was a different proposition and we've done it many times since.

To promote the album, which went gold and made it into the top ten, I toured Australia at the end of 2004. It was a huge tour of sixteen concerts, across every state, from Hobart in the south up to Cairns in the far north, and Perth in the west. Vince came with me, and we had a blast. The band – Paul Gray, Kere Buchanan, Chrissy Thomas, Nick Sinclair and Chris Kamzelas – were not only musos at the top of their game but also a great bunch of people, and everyone got on brilliantly.

In Queensland we went to places that artists rarely go, such as Rockhampton and Townsville, and it was wonderful to connect with all those people. I don't know whether the fans realised, but to me it felt like a farewell tour. I had no idea if I'd ever be back working in Australia, so it seemed right to be getting out there, performing my songs and bringing that chapter to a close. It was the end of an era.

My home would now be in London, although I had no idea what I'd be doing over there, either. Without a recording contract in Australia, I had no contract anywhere, including France.

One thing that *was* working out was Vince and me – we never tired of each other and we were just getting started.

There was still so much to find out about each other. And with no record contract, I actually had the time to get to know him.

Vince was still doing a lot of theatre work and a few months prior to the Australian tour I'd gone on the road with him for ten days of shows in the north of France. We stayed in B & Bs and for once I wasn't the one getting up on stage. It was fun.

When we'd returned to Paris, Vince's god-sister, Nathalie, had rung to say she was organising a surprise party for Vince's thirtieth birthday. I'd been touched that they considered me enough of a friend to share the secret with.

The party at Nathalie and Laurent's studio just outside of Paris was fabulous. The theme was the circus, and I dressed as a contortionist, with a pair of fake legs around my neck like a stole. Vince got the shock of his life when he saw us all, a bunch of circus freaks ready to party.

So Vince was family, now, and to have my nearest and dearest by my side felt so right after years of being apart from my loved ones and so often feeling alone.

But having lost my job, it seemed like my life would be forever swings and roundabouts. Trying to get a balance between family and work still seemed to be eluding me.

In early March 2005 I flew back to Sydney to perform at the Gay and Lesbian Mardi Gras after-party. I had never forgotten my last Mardi Gras experience, when I sang 'I Need Your Body' and the crowd were so supportive and generous. This one was going to be good, too, I could just feel it in my bones.

As usual, the costumes were fabulous and so were the dancers. With big sixties-style hair and wearing a skimpy little outfit teamed with white stockings and suspenders, I sang 'Never (Past Tense)' followed by 'Dare You to Be Happy'. It was another great night to remember.

But now that was it. My recording career had come to a big loud full stop. I had no idea what I was going to do from here on. The one thing I did know was I had a mortgage payment to make the following month. And another one the month after that.

Back home in London, I'd barely unpacked my bags when I got a call from Valérie Michelin. That was hardly extraordinary. I was still doing the odd bit of promo in France and popping over there on and off, doing shows or performing on television.

'I'd like to sign you for three albums,' Valérie said after a brief exchange of pleasantries. 'Now I can have you all to myself and I don't have to talk to those *bloody Aussies* anymore,' she joked. In fact, Valérie adored Australians. I think she found our forthright honesty endearing. But on previous records, Valérie had had to negotiate everything we did in France with Sony Australia, and it had often been tricky. Now she would have the reins, and she was obviously delighted by the prospect.

I was delighted she'd offered. In fact, I was overjoyed. 'Wow,' was all I could say to begin with.

What I learnt that day is, never underestimate the universe. Have faith, always. Not that this was going to be a walk in the park. Singing the odd song in French was one thing. Signing up for three French-language albums was another altogether. It was not only the language issue – in fact, my French was improving every day. But anyone who has tried to work in another country knows how confusing and foreign it can be. The language is different, sure, but so are the rules, the practices, the politics, the people. My experience on *Notre-Dame de Paris* and my previous work in France had already opened my eyes to the cultural divide that exists between the Anglo and French approaches to just about everything.

But, hey, nothing ventured, nothing gained, so I said yes. How could I say no? Valérie had thrown me a lifeline, but not only that, I loved working in France. The French had been unbelievably good to me and I had enormous respect for their music and their culture.

Very quickly, though, my excitement turned to terror as I began to contemplate how on earth I'd navigate that new world with the most basic of maps. My terror was amped up to eleven two weeks later when I found out I was pregnant.

We hadn't planned it, especially since I'd just taken on a mortgage you'd need mountaineering gear to scale. But funnily enough, despite those worries, when I'd come home to London after Mardi Gras I'd felt relaxed in a way I hadn't in years. It had helped that when I arrived my two dear old friends Mel Harris and Tim Page had come to stay – Tim's mother had recently died and they had flown over to attend her funeral. Tim is a much-celebrated Vietnam War photographer. He covered the war along with his friend Sean Flynn, Errol Flynn's son, who went missing in Vietnam in 1970. Tim has been searching for Sean's remains ever since, which led him to jointly produce a book and then a travelling exhibition in memory of photographers and journalists killed during the Vietnam War. Mel, a documentary producer, is one of my best mates.

Tim speaks good French and he and Vince were having a fine old time. Coming home to find Vince and my darling friends enjoying each other's company had cheered me enormously. We hung out, ate, drank, ate, talked, and ate and drank and argued and talked some more. After the events of the previous year, it was such a happy and relaxing time. And it was just before or during Tim and Mel's visit that it must have happened. It was as if the baby decided we were ready and chose us.

When the pregnancy was confirmed I went into shock. I'd always known I wanted to have children, but right now? Vince, on the other hand, was thrilled. Once I was through the shock, so was I. It suddenly seemed exactly right. Soon we were ecstatic.

Now I just had to tell Valérie, who had already leapt into action and was busily getting contracts drawn up, song demos sent over and marketing plans mapped out.

When I broke the news to her I think her words were, 'Even better!' Which was very supportive on her part. I guess it didn't hurt that the father was French.

Valérie took the opportunity to ask where I planned to live – London or Paris.

I'd thought about it and already decided I wanted to stay in London. My manager, Bruce, was based there, plus I had my little structure set up – my stuff, my neighbourhood, my friends, my bearings.

'Fine,' Valérie said. 'But we'd like to get you an apartment over here. It'll be cheaper than putting you up in a hotel all the time.'

That made sense. So in May, Vince and I flew to Paris in search of an apartment. Valérie had given us a budget, and it sounded very generous. But when we began to view properties it quickly became apparent that all we'd be able to afford was a dump or a dog box. Space is at a premium in Paris, and everything we looked at was either too small to swing a poodle or grungy or noisy or out of the way – or all three.

Virginie Couarc'h came to the rescue. Virginie was working at Columbia, and she got in touch with some real estate agents in the seventeenth arrondissement.

One morning she rang with information on yet another place for rent. 'Check it out. It sounds like it has potential,' she said breezily.

'Where is it?' I asked doubtfully. We'd seen so many shockers I'd just about given up.

'Batignolles,' she said. 'Place du Docteur Félix Lobligeois.'

'You're kidding?' I said.

Virginie was taken aback. 'No-o-o-o … Why? Do you know it?'

'I'll fill you in later. I've got to tell Vince.'

The universe was clearly working overtime. Paris is a big city but I knew Place du Docteur Félix Lobligeois well. In fact, I'd fallen in love with it many months earlier, when Vince and I had strolled through there one day, hand in hand. It was a classic Parisian square with a pretty church, stunning old apartment blocks with balconies, little shops and a park at one end. With stars in my eyes, I'd said to Vince, 'Wouldn't it be heaven to live here on this square one day. It's so beautiful!'

'*Putain!* And expensive!' Vince had responded, deflating my fantasy with good old French frankness.

But now that dream might just become a reality – unless the apartment was another dog box.

It wasn't. It was a lovely place, roomy and bright, on the fifth floor of the best building, and we took it.

A month or so later Vince and I were ensconced there while preparations were in train to record my first all-French-language album. My pregnancy was going well. Once I got through the first trimester, my energy had bounced back with a vengeance. In fact, I couldn't be stopped – I was like a woman on a mission. Which was lucky, because I was beginning to feel like I'd fallen out of the sky onto another planet in another universe. The French music world was just so different to what I was used to in Australia, the UK or America, and for the first time I was finding out *how* different.

For starters, while the French revere their singers – which is a wonderful thing to see and experience – they revere their

240

lyricists and composers even more. Most highly esteemed is the lyricist, or *auteur* (author); the *compositeur* who writes the music comes second; and the singer, known as the *interprète* (interpreter), is third. So the song rather than the singer is at the heart of the *chanson Française*. French people will argue endlessly about whose version of a particular song is best, that is, who best *interprets* a song.

If I'd known all this when I had the idea to sing 'Les Trois Cloches' I'd have probably packed up my mike and gone home. But as it turned out, my efforts were recognised and rewarded, I guess because I paid tribute not only to an extraordinary singer but to a great song.

So songwriters are the genuine and lasting stars in that firmament. It's fantastic, really – in Australia we often don't have a clue or care who writes the songs. On a practical level, though, because the French so keenly guard their history and culture and support and protect their artistic community, it meant there'd be fewer opportunities for me to write. Columbia would take a much greater role in choosing the songs for my album, most of which would be written by known and revered French songwriters. Creatively, I would have to take more of a back seat. It would be frustrating, no doubt about it, but that was just the way it was.

When you're in not just another universe but *another's* universe, if you've got any sense you show respect, go with the flow and look and learn. And that's what I did. The fact that I was now five months pregnant focused my mind. Sure,

I was excited about making the album, and ready to promote its socks off. But stepping back from the songwriting might just give me the space I needed.

And anyway, I couldn't risk messing up this project by making demands or insisting things should be one way or another. Because I now had a child to think of. This other universe was about to become something else again.

CHAPTER 26

Aimer Jusqu'à l'Impossible

In the end I collaborated on the writing of half the songs for my first French album, which I decided to call *Un Autre Univers* (Another Universe) for obvious reasons. The title was also the name of one of the songs on the album. For that track I had the idea to take the music from 'Woman', which was a song on *Just Me*, and translate or rewrite the lyrics. But my translation skills were never going to cut it, I knew. So I threw it at Vince. 'You need to do this for me,' I said.

He tried to get out of it – he has never imposed himself on my work – but I wouldn't let him. Vince had written quite a bit of poetry in his time, and I knew he was good, even if he didn't. He finally agreed and wrote entirely new lyrics, changing the name and the sentiment of the song. It remains one of the most extraordinary lyrics I'll ever sing, and my partner wrote it.

Vince also helped me navigate the new and strange universe of French music. I relied on him to explain things from a French point of view and to understand the nuances of the language and the politics.

Robert Goldman, still writing under the pen name of J. Kapler, wrote two of the tracks – 'Tu Aurais Dû Me Dire' (You Should Have Told Me) and 'S'Il Faut Prier' (Pray). Jacques Veneruso, who wrote 'Tu Es Toujours Là' contributed 'Changer' (To Change).

Then there were the songwriters Elodie Hesme and David Gategno. They wrote the track that became the first single off the album, 'Aimer Jusqu'à l'Impossible' (Love to the Impossible). That song spoke to all of us – it had the same indefinable quality that made 'Aller Plus Haut' so irresistible. It was a song about loving unconditionally, loving beyond reason, in the face of anything or everything, no matter what happens.

But when I heard the finished track, I wasn't happy. I adored the strings, which had been arranged by Stanislas Renoult, but I didn't feel the production fully captured the anthemic power of the song.

Bruce suggested I fling it to a couple of friends of his, Mark 'Duck' Blackwell and Paul Guardiani. Like me, Paul was an expat originally from Melbourne of Italian origin. Duck had come from the Bristol music scene around Massive Attack and

Tricky, and he'd been a member of the band Straw. They'd since teamed up as a writing and production duo.

So Bruce sent Paul and Duck the files. A few days later they came back with a pumping track, lush and full with a rich and round bottom end. It was exactly what I was looking for. All I had to do now was convince Valérie, which I did by telling her in no uncertain terms how much I loved it.

While we were still in the middle of drawing up a short list of songs, Elodie and David had approached me directly to discuss a song they hadn't completed writing.

'We'd love you to have a listen and see what you think. We haven't shown it to any record company yet,' Elodie explained.

'Why not?' I asked.

'Because it's a bit political and we're not sure they'd go for it,' she said.

When I listened to it I fell in love with the song immediately, but I could see why they were nervous. Called 'Je M'Appelle Bagdad' (My Name is Baghdad), it was about the destruction of that beautiful city during the invasion of Iraq two years earlier. Unlike Britain and Australia, most European countries, France included, did *not* declare war on Iraq, and like many people all over the world the French had watched events unfold in horror.

But the song was about more than that – it was about how humankind creates beautiful things and then tears them down, and how time transforms everything. The first verse spoke about what Baghdad used to be, an enlightened city of jewelled pavilions, but how so much had been lost and now bombs rained down.

For me the song wasn't political, it was reality, and it moved me. And anyway, I wanted to push the boundaries a bit. I hate doing anything that's too obvious. The way I saw it, as a foreign singer I was out of the box anyway, so why not take a few risks?

So the next time I saw Valérie I put my case for including the song on the album. I had expected her to say no, but she got it. We never imagined it could be single material, but once we heard the produced track and how the poetry of the lyrics meshed with the emotional power of the music we were blown away. In the end 'Bagdad' was slated as the second single.

During one of our many boxing matches as we drew up a short list of songs, Valérie had asked me whether I'd like to do a duet.

'I'd love to do one with Henri Salvador,' I said. I absolutely idolised this great French singer-songwriter, but he was nearly ninety years old and I knew it would be a long shot. Henri was a classic all-round entertainer. As well as being a true crooner in the original sense, he'd been on television and in the movies. His music always put a smile on my face.

'Well, it just so happens I know his wife, Catherine,' Valérie said. 'I'll ask her to put it to him.'

Trust Valérie. She always seemed to make things happen with a quick wave of her Gallic wand.

Henri said yes straight up. Apparently he knew and liked my work and thought I did what I did well. Coming from him it felt like a great compliment – I'd figured Henri, being old school, wouldn't be easily moved by contemporary music.

Henri proposed the song 'Et Puis Après', which he'd written with singer-songwriter Lydia Martinico. It was just perfect – charming, witty, romantic.

On our day in the studio together, Henri turned up with a killer bottle of red wine. I don't know what it was, but it was delicious, and so we drank and we sang and laughed.

We recorded the album quickly. I was like a woman possessed, full of energy, going at a hundred miles an hour. I was in love, I adored being pregnant and I was as happy as I'd ever been. Singing while pregnant was a new sensation. I was at ease, chilled, and I did most of the vocals in two or three takes.

The fact I was working so late into my pregnancy, especially given it was all in the public eye, came as a shock to many of the French people I encountered. I remember turning up for a fundraiser for Pièces Jaunes, a charity that helps children in hospital and which is championed by Bernadette Chirac, the then president's wife. Madame Chirac looked me up and down in trepidation. '*Tu vas bien?*' she asked. 'You're not about to give birth right here, right now, are you?'

'Don't worry, I'm fine,' I assured her. And I was. I felt great.

So when I was asked whether I'd like to perform at the Paris Live 8 concert I said yes straight away. Bob Geldof had announced the Live 8 initiative on the last day of May and the concerts took place just over a month later, on 2 July. I have no idea how they pulled that off. It was a huge event – more than 1000 musicians performed at the eleven concerts, which were broadcast around the world. The shows took place just prior to the G8 summit and were put on in support of the Make Poverty History campaign and to pressure the G8 to pledge more aid to poor nations.

The French Live 8 concert was staged at the Château de Versailles, just outside of Paris. The palace of Louis XIV has always represented the opulence of the French monarchy prior to the Revolution. The Live 8 organisers chose it for that reason – the place was a symbol of the wealth of the world's eight richest nations, the participants in the G8 summit.

Over 150,000 people turned out for the concert on an extremely hot summer's day. I'd been slated to sing 'The Prayer' with Andrea Bocelli, but he was running late. Instead I did an impromptu duet with English R & B star Craig David. We practised the Beatles song 'Come Together' in the car half an hour before we went on. I was five months pregnant and thought I was going to collapse in the heat. But we got through it and later I appeared again to sing 'Aller Plus Haut'.

Live 8 was a fantastic and worthwhile event to be a part of, and less than a week later the G8 nations pledged to double their aid to poor nations. (A year later, however, things were moving slowly, and no doubt the global financial crisis also had an impact on those pledges. Nevertheless, the

Live 8 concerts raised awareness and focused attention on world poverty.)

About a month later we made the video for 'Aimer Jusqu'à l'Impossible', the first single off *Un Autre Univers*, with wonderful French video director Thierry Vergnes. I was six months pregnant. The clip was filmed off the Champs-Élysées and in the Institut du Monde Arabe. I was wearing a gorgeous black Dior dress that was cut on the bias. From behind you couldn't tell I was pregnant, but from the front it looked like I'd swallowed a basketball. Thierry did a fantastic job. For most of the clip, which was stunning, you wouldn't have known I was pregnant, but occasionally there'd be glimpses of my belly or silhouette. It was great – they didn't hide it but they didn't emphasise it either. It just seemed so natural and so normal. After all, singers get pregnant too.

'Aimer' was released on 14 November and debuted at number 3 on the French charts. Two days later I was hanging out with Vince and our friends Jacques and Gilles at Jacques' atelier downstairs in our building. It was 10.30 at night and what had started out as a quiet aperitif had turned into a party, as usual. We were always having little soirees around the square – someone would bring the wine, someone the bread (I was famous for my prawns!), and this was no different. Now the boys were onto their hundredth bottle of red.

I interrupted proceedings with an announcement. 'My waters have broken.'

Vince, Jacques and Gilles nodded, then kept talking. Suddenly they all stopped and stared at me. They looked like the living dead – all the blood had drained from their faces.

Then it was on for young and old. Gilles rushed around the corner to retrieve his work van. Gilles is an interior designer and the inside of his van always looked like a grenade had exploded in there. Five flights up, I changed for the fourth time, adding my previous outfit to the growing pile of wet clothes in the corner. Vince attempted to pack a bag, but that last glass of wine wasn't helping. Still, being a very capable guy, he managed to get the job done with his trademark cool.

My contractions started around 11.30 pm and an hour later I was in Gilles' van and on the way to the American Hospital in Neuilly-sur-Seine.

Vince and I had originally planned to have the baby in Australia. We were still technically living in London, travelling back and forth on the train as need be. But finally, my doctor had told me I had to stop and stay put in Paris. In the same breath she told me I'd be mad to fly back to Melbourne to have the baby. As she so delicately pointed out, I wasn't twenty-five anymore.

When we arrived at the hospital it seemed to be deserted. A nurse finally appeared and I was wheeled to a room. When the contractions grew stronger I was taken down to the delivery suite. Still I saw not another soul. It was quite surreal. My doctor was called. She lived some distance away and it would be a while before she arrived.

In the meantime, they discovered that the umbilical cord had wrapped around the baby's neck. The doctor on duty made the call to perform an emergency caesarian.

Our little boy was born in the early hours of 17 November 2005. But after a quick kiss and cuddle, he was bundled up and whipped away and I was wheeled into recovery.

I'd had an epidural and couldn't feel a thing from the waist down, but I was determined to get upstairs to see my baby.

The nurse would have none of it. 'You must stay here to rest, Mlle Arena,' he said. 'You're not going anywhere.'

It's one of the few times in my life they've been able to hold me down. I guess an epidural will have that effect.

Our little man ended up spending the first three hours of his life with his father and godfather, Stéphane Dumontier, who'd rushed over when he heard the news.

Finally I was wheeled upstairs to see the boys. My brand-new baby was just perfect. There wasn't a mark on him – he was beautiful. In fact, he was a carbon copy of his beautiful father.

CHAPTER 27

The Look of Love

When I looked into my darling baby's eyes I fell instantly in love. We named him Gabriel Joseph. We both liked 'Gabriel' plus, being the same name in French, English and Italian, it would keep things simple for our son. As well, Vince's great-grandmother had been a Gabrielle. We called him Joseph after my father, Giuseppe (Joe).

I don't remember getting much sleep during the first couple of months after Gab's birth. In fact, I don't remember much at all. I was a stunned mullet, terrified. I had no idea what I was doing – I didn't have a clue.

Luckily, Vince was a natural. He just rolled up his sleeves and got in there. He could bath Gab, burp him, rock him off to sleep, change his nappy – whatever needed to be done. Vince had had more experience with children than I had. He'd always helped friends out if they needed someone to look after their kids. He just wasn't fazed.

About two weeks after Gab was born my new album *Un Autre Univers* was released and I went back to work, doing promo. Morgane, my makeup artist, was working overtime to make me presentable and disguise the dark circles under my eyes. But I'm sure I had a vacant stare most of the time. I'd give an interview or do a TV appearance in between breastfeeds. Thank god for Vince.

Christmas was approaching but this year I wouldn't be going home. Gab was just too little and I was exhausted. Then, through the fog, I began to notice that Vince was acting strangely. He was popping out all the time, giving odd little excuses. He seemed distracted, busy with other things, although I wasn't sure what.

I asked him if anything was wrong.

'*Non,*' he said, putting an end to the discussion.

Then, one afternoon, he told me that he had to go out and he might be some time.

'Okay,' I said. I figured the poor guy needed a break. So did I, truth be told. Gab was a gorgeous little thing, but as any parent knows, your first baby is always a shock to the system.

Before I could say anything else, Vince was gone, the door slamming behind him.

'I don't know what's wrong with your old man,' I said to Gab, 'but it's just you and me now, kid.'

I swear Gab's eyes widened with fear.

But we managed. A couple of hours later Vince still wasn't home. Clearly he needed some time out.

Finally he called me. 'I'm at the door but I can't find my keys,' he said. 'Can you come and open up?'

I was in the middle of changing yet another pooey nappy. 'You'll have to wait,' I said. 'I'll be there in a minute.'

When I was done I grabbed Gab and headed for the front door. I wrestled with the lock with one hand and pulled it open.

'Hi, darling.' Mum and Dad were standing in the doorway, huge smiles on their faces.

I was so shocked I nearly dropped the baby. Last I'd heard, Mum and Dad were going to try and get over to visit in the new year. Now here they were on my doorstep clutching a big fluffy teddy.

Vince had organised everything in secret. What a champion. It was a divine thing to do.

Mum and Dad had rarely been able to visit me for all the years I'd lived away. They were too busy with the nursing home, and just couldn't leave it. But this time, Mum had somehow found someone to hold the fort for four weeks.

Days later, Silvana arrived from London, where she was now working as Sharon Osbourne's personal assistant. Silvana and Mum and Dad stayed in friends' apartments on the square. It was perfect – we saw each other every day, and Mum, Dad and Silvana helped out with Gab. Vince and I actually got some sleep! We felt blessed.

We had a truly beautiful Christmas, there in our Paris apartment on beautiful Place du Docteur Félix Lobligeois. Vince's parents came up from the south of France and his sister

Sophie also came with little Matéo and her husband. Vince's Uncle Alain and his wife, Chantal, were there too. Mum and Vince's mum, Jeannick, did the cooking.

Not long after Christmas, Nancy arrived with her husband, Walter, and little Sofia, who was now three and full of ideas she just had to tell you immediately. After Gab, seeing everyone all together was the best Christmas present ever.

In January Vince and I attended the NRJ Music Awards down in Cannes. Gab came with us and Vince's parents minded him while we attended the event. I'd been nominated for 'Best French Female Artist'. I sang 'Aimer' with six other French female artists, including Natasha St-Pier, who I'd performed alongside in *Notre-Dame de Paris*. For the record, pop singer Jenifer won the award that night.

In February, also in between breastfeeds, I participated in my first Les Enfoirés concert. 'Les Enfoirés', which can be translated variously as the Tossers, the Bastards or the Arseholes (I think you get the idea), is the name given to the artists and celebrities who perform in a yearly charity concert for the 'Restos du Cœur' (Restaurants of the Heart), of which there are around 2500 in France, feeding 600,000 hungry people every day.

The idea to set up a charity to feed the hungry came from French comedian Coluche in 1985. But not long after he launched it, he was killed in a motorbike accident (earlier that week he'd broken the world speed motorbike record of 252 kilometres per hour).

Coluche had given Jean-Jacques Goldman a week to write a song for a concert he wanted to put on to raise money for the charity. Jean-Jacques had come up with 'La Chanson des Restos' (The Restos' Song), the chorus of which is now sung at the end of every concert.

Les Enfoirés has since become an annual event. There's a different theme every year and each concert is released as an album. It's a brilliant concept.

None of the artists or crew is paid a fee, but you wouldn't know it judging by the magnitude of the production. The concert is now bigger than a Baz film, and it's televised all round the country.

For me, doing Les Enfoirés was second nature. It was like *Young Talent Time* on steroids, with elaborate sets, a cast and crew of hundreds, crazy costumes, dancing, music, the whole shebang. It's enormous fun for everyone, including the cast, the crew and the audience, and it raises vital funds for the restaurants.

That first time I participated, I sang 'Highway to Hell' with Hélène Ségara. It was a dream come true, believe it or not. I'd always wanted to cover that song since I heard it as a little girl and it was great to pay tribute to AC/DC, who are much adored in France. I let my inner rock chick out and hollered the house down. Since then I've been part of many Les Enfoirés concerts and have loved every minute.

The same month, I went to Tunisia to film the video clip for 'Je M'Appelle Bagdad', which Valérie was hoping to release soon after as the second single off the album. By now you've probably gathered that motherhood wasn't exactly slowing me down, but it was difficult. In fact, that was the toughest shoot I've ever been on. We'd decided it would be best if Gab stayed at home with his dad – I'd be working fifteen-hour days and Gab was too young to fly, anyway.

But I was still breastfeeding, so there I was, in between takes, expressing milk. It was bloody awful and I spent most of my time off-camera sobbing. The makeup artist must have thought I was completely insane, plus he had to constantly touch me up – the tears were playing havoc with my mascara.

Nevertheless, I squeezed into the gorgeous gold dress and got on with it. And the result was something special, thanks again to Thierry Vergnes.

Between March and August I appeared at Night of the Proms concerts in France, Belgium, Morocco and Germany. Night of the Proms shows feature a mix of classical and pop artists. 'Aimer' was still in the top ten and radio everywhere continued to play it. In fact, the music programmers made it very clear to Columbia that they didn't want a new single, not yet. In the end 'Bagdad' wasn't released until June, a full seven months later. It also made the top ten.

In July, 'Aimer' was declared 'La Chanson de l'Année' (Song of the Year) on the French TV show of the same name.

So things were as busy as ever. What *had* changed was my view of the world and my focus. Now I had Gab to think of. He came first and he was the reason I got up in the morning. Suddenly I had a different perspective on things – on everything, in fact. In a funny way, now that my job was no longer my raison d'être, I loved it all the more and had a renewed respect for what I did. Juggling parenthood with a career was turning out to be incredibly challenging, but that's what made it so rewarding.

Vince and I kept it as simple as we could. There were no nannies. Either Gab came with me or he stayed with Vince. Sometimes we'd call on our friends to babysit. We did our best to be together as much as possible. Gab was growing up already, into a gorgeous bouncing baby who was interested in everything going on around him. He was a joy, and I was like a pig in mud.

By midyear we were once more moving back and forth between London and Paris. When we were in Paris it was work, work, work. Everyone knew me over there so it could be full-on. In London, we could chill out, spend time together, just the three of us, or hang out with friends.

Working on *Un Autre Univers* with Valérie and her crew had been fabulous fun and very successful, and I was looking forward to starting on the next French record. Now, though, I had the urge to sing in English. For one thing, it was easier – when I sang in English I didn't have to think about my pronunciation. English was my first (well, my second) language, and I couldn't walk away from it indefinitely.

But it was a testing time for the business. Since 1999, revenue in the music industry had plummeted. By 2009, three years in the future, it would have halved. To write and record an album of new material without a record company behind me would be too risky. Plus, as ever, I was looking to do something new.

One day I was cooking lunch in my kitchen in London, listening to an old Dusty Springfield record, when an idea came to me. I decided I wanted to do an album of covers, paying tribute to songwriters and artists who had inspired me during my career, singers like Dusty.

I trawled through my collection and half an hour later I had a long list of songs. Then Vince and I sat around the table and whittled it down, arguing, throwing around ideas. I love collaborating creatively with Vince and once again he was the perfect foil. He's very objective and on this occasion he questioned each one of my choices, playing the devil's advocate and throwing up alternative suggestions.

In the end we had a bunch of songs we both felt had broad appeal and yet were still personal favourites. High on the list was 'The Look of Love', a song by Burt Bacharach and Hal David. Dusty Springfield made it famous and it had to be one of the greatest love songs ever written. I'd wanted to do a Dusty tribute album for ages but had given up on the idea eventually, realising the parameters were too limiting. There was no reason I couldn't include a handful of Dusty songs in this collection, however.

Once we had a list I talked to my manager, Bruce, about what to do next. Bruce suggested we control as much of the process as possible and then license the recording to a record company. That was music to my ears.

So we decided to get on with it. It was a risk, though. There was a good chance no record company would want to take it on. Nevertheless, I was determined to forge ahead. If necessary, I could always release the album through my website. I just knew in my waters that people would get it and love it. I never doubted for a moment.

Now all I needed were some like-minded types to help me make it happen, people like Duck Blackwell, Paul Guardiani and Mr Strings himself, alias the bike courier, Simon Hale.

It was incredibly exciting. It was also very scary to take on a big project like that without backing. But by my side I had Vince and now Gab. I was surrounded by love, and I felt strong enough to move mountains.

CHAPTER 28

I Only Want to Be With You

Things were busy in the flat in Fulham. Silvana had moved in, so my in-house family had grown. Having one of my sisters on tap was fantastic – it was just how I liked it – and Gab had an aunty around to spoil him rotten.

It was late 2006 and there were a few projects underway. The most important was Gab's first haircut – his soft blond baby locks had grown and now they needed a little tidying up. I'd asked my stylist from the salon around the corner if he'd come over and do the honours. Matt was French like Vince and we'd become friendly.

Scissors in hand, Matt was chasing Gab around the kitchen – having just learnt to walk, Gab now refused to stay in his chair and he was lurching around like a drunken sailor.

It was hilarious, and we were all laughing our heads off when Silvana came home. She thought we'd lost our minds. In the end even Matt, a truly gifted hairstylist who was great with kids, gave up in defeat. Gab's hair stayed wispy for a few months more.

Two other projects were on the agenda. One was my second French album. We were planning to record it sometime the following year, so I'd put that temporarily on the backburner. Then there was my album of covers, which I'd named *Songs of Love and Loss*. I'd started with the title 'Torch Songs', but I didn't feel it was quite evocative enough. The dictionary definition of a torch song is something like 'a song about love or loss'. Now *that* was perfect.

The song list was eclectic. I'd chosen what I considered *real* songs or real songwriting, songs that told stories, songs with beautiful and memorable melodies, songs that made you *feel*. It seemed to me that many of the songs on the radio at the time were disposable, lacking in emotion, intelligence, storytelling or art.

In addition to 'The Look of Love', I picked two more songs made famous by Dusty. 'I Only Want to Be With You', by Mike Hawker and Ivor Raymonde, was her first single. 'I Just Don't Know What to Do with Myself', like 'The Look of Love', was by the stellar songwriting team Burt Bacharach and Hal David. I had to pay tribute to Burt Bacharach – back around the time 'Chains' was released in the US, Burt had called me in LA one day and asked me to lunch. I thought it was a hoax at first, but we did get together. Burt was hilarious and yet such a gentleman. He was very complimentary, telling me I should never stop interpreting great songs because I had something people wanted to hear. I'd always remembered his words and now I could honour them by doing just that.

Another songwriter I'd always admired was Carole King. Her song 'So Far Away' was particularly poignant for me, having spent so many years travelling and apart from my family.

Then there was 'The Man with the Child in His Eyes', written by Kate Bush when she was thirteen or fourteen. I'd always found that song extraordinary. I'd never forgotten the time I'd met Kate Bush at the King of Pop Awards in 1978 when I was ten years old. She was tiny, only nineteen herself, wearing purple velvet jeans and clutching a pack of Marlboro. To my eyes she was the coolest and most beautiful looking girl I'd ever seen.

I had to include a Lulu song, and it had to be 'To Sir with Love'. I'd adored the movie and the sentiment of the song.

The REM song 'Everybody Hurts' had always resonated with me. I figured it was a song that would resonate with everybody.

Two originals were included: 'Woman', which was on *Just Me* and which I'd always loved, and 'Until', which I'd written with Duck Blackwell and Paul Guardiani.

All the songs in the list were special to me for one reason or another. But they called for a vocal style quite different to that of my 'Chains' days. Starting with *Just Me*, I'd begun to move away from the big notes towards more subtle dynamics.

Singing these songs was about nuance as well as power. The aim was to retell these great stories in a fresh way.

Now we had finalised the tracks for *Songs of Love and Loss*, Duck and Paul came on board, and we started work on the arrangements. I was determined the strings be live – sampled or synthesised strings wouldn't cut it – and I wanted Simon Hale to do the arrangements. But hiring a string orchestra would be expensive, so we needed a record company to step in if it was going to work.

By then Bruce had talked about the project to various record companies. John O'Donnell at EMI jumped at the idea. He got it straight away and was happy to let us run the show our way. 'I trust you, Teen,' he said. 'Just go away and do it. I know it will be good.' John's a one-off. He's incredibly personable and what drives him is a passion for the arts. We couldn't have had a better supporter. So that was that. We had a licensing deal with EMI. It was exciting but also a huge relief. We wouldn't be living in the park after all.

Simon got stuck into the string arrangements, booked the London Studio Orchestra and managed that side of the recording. We recorded the album over several days. Duck and Paul were at the wheel, and Duck, especially, played several of the instruments on the album. We had a fantastic time, and what made it even better was we did exactly as we wanted. I was executive producer, so I could call the shots. It was heaven!

Vince, Gab and I made the trip to Australia for Christmas. Mum and Dad were over the moon to see Gab, who had well and truly found his feet by then. He kept them on their toes, toddling around Dad's garden, trying to climb the fig tree, picking the tomatoes and fava beans before they were ready. He was given tools and a workbench for Christmas and he looked quite the part, banging 'nails' in with his little hammer. He'd started talking too, and could make himself understood in both English and French. When he was tired he'd mix both together. Mum soon had him speaking Italian as well. He had us all laughing every minute of every day.

Going home to Australia for Christmas always felt like being let out into the sunshine after being trapped in a freezer. I could warm my bones and relax. Having Mediterranean blood, I *need* the heat. But soon we were back in the freezer of London in winter. There was still work to do on the album, and then I'd be starting rehearsals.

Yep, I would be treading the boards again in London's West End. I know – I hadn't exactly slowed down since Gab's birth. But I was so enjoying my work now, and when an opportunity arises, why not jump on it?

In actual fact, this one had fallen in my lap. The Broadway musical *Chicago* had been running for almost ten years in London and showed no signs of closing any time soon. (It finally closed in 2012, after a season of fifteen years.)

By John Kander and Fred Ebb, the same songwriting team who gave us *Cabaret*, *Chicago* is one of the great musicals, with an irresistible setting, powerful story, colourful characters, great music and *loads* of dancing. Like *Cabaret*, it's dark, which

I love, and the female characters are strong and meaty. It's a cautionary tale about the hollowness and fleeting nature of celebrity – in this case, the celebrity of big-time criminals in Chicago during prohibition. I'd be playing the female lead of Roxie Hart, a chorus girl who becomes an overnight star when she murders her lover.

It was a role that turned over frequently, in part, as I soon found out, because it was so demanding. Anyway, I met the producers and director and they gave me the job.

Vince and I had a night out to see the show, and what a show it was! Afterwards, though, Vince seriously suggested I go into training. As I may have mentioned, *Chicago* is full of dancing, never my strong suit.

'Nah,' I said. 'I'll get fit during the rehearsals.'

Well, I sure did get fit. It was hardcore for a woman on the cusp of forty. Those rehearsals were a crash-course in Fosse-style choreography, so called after Bob Fosse, who wrote the book for *Chicago* and was the director and choreographer of the original production. (Among many other things, Fosse also directed the film of *Cabaret* starring Liza Minnelli.) His jazz dance style has been borrowed ever since.

Have I mentioned that in *Chicago* there's a lot of dancing? That it's *full* of dancing? And every high kick has to be spot-on. Looking back now, it was funny, but at the time, it was torture. I was dancing for hours at a time and cried every day for the first week. Dean the choreographer must have thought I was demented.

When I finally hit the stage for my first public performance on 2 April 2007, every last cell of fat on my body had been burnt to a cinder – my legs were concrete toothpicks. Three days in and I was ready to curl up in a ball and sleep for a thousand years.

But once I struggled through that, I loved every minute of it. It's hot entertainment, in every sense. And the story, like the best stories, is as relevant now as it was in the 1920s, when it was set, or the 1970s, when the musical was first staged. It's all about celebrity and media spin, something I'd experienced firsthand, having lived in the public eye for more than thirty years.

In a funny way, though, unlike Roxie, I had avoided many of the pitfalls of celebrity, particularly since my divorce. That had been very public and I'd since taken steps to avoid that kind of attention. Maybe I was just too normal now – I wasn't out doing crazy things or behaving badly in public. In France I was often recognised, no doubt about it, but in that country I could be myself, pretty much. I didn't have to try to be someone I wasn't. In Australia, people had known me for so long, I think they thought of me as a second cousin, the kind whose photo sits on the mantelpiece, just part of the furniture. Plus I'd always tried to treat others the way I'd like to be treated, so I was never really put on any kind of pedestal, which meant they couldn't tear me down.

The fact was, however, I'd been dealing with the media for almost my entire life, so I was well acquainted with the spin. It was just part of my work. But now that my personal life had become so important to me, I was determined to keep it relatively private. Vince understood the role the media played but he wasn't seduced by notoriety at all. And Gab was too young. Luckily, in London, even when I was starring in a big West End production, the media more or less left me alone. When it comes to celebrities, they do seem to love a train wreck over there, and I didn't fit the bill, thank god.

I played Roxie Hart for six weeks, which sounds short compared to my previous efforts, but it was more or less standard for that part. Ironically, while the show was a critique of celebrity, it depended on an ever-changing rollcall of 'stars' in the lead roles to put bums on seats.

By the time I finished, I could have run a marathon or climbed Mount Everest. I didn't – I went back to my other work. *Songs of Love and Loss* was nearly finished, but my next French album was barely started. There'd be the inevitable boxing rounds with Valérie over which songs to include (I'd enjoyed those in a perverse way, and we both gave as good as we got), and then some writing and recording.

On the home front, we'd sold the apartment and bought a house in Clapham. Gab might have been just two feet tall but he seemed to take up an awful lot of space. Once we moved into the new place, things quickly began to take shape. Very soon it felt like home, a *family* home, and I had beside me the two people I wanted to be with more than anything in the world. Things were good.

CHAPTER 29

7 Vies

Added to my list of things to do in 2007 was an event I couldn't get out of even if I wanted to: my fortieth birthday. I wasn't scared – in fact, I was looking forward to it. My life to this point had been an amazing ride. I'd been lucky enough to be born into a supportive and loving family, I had two of the best sisters in the world, I'd had a fantastic childhood doing what I loved, I'd worked hard, had success in my homeland and abroad, seen the world and had enough ups and downs to learn a helluva lot the hard way, which I've realised is the best way. And now, with Gab and Vince beside me, my journey had taken a new turn. Despite dramatic changes in the music industry, which was my world and my livelihood, I was feeling optimistic and excited about the future. I was sure the next decade would be an interesting one.

In my usual style I ended up celebrating in four places on different sides of the globe. Also in my usual style, I was working on the day of my actual birthday, in Australia doing a quick promo tour prior to the release of *Songs of Love and Loss*. But it gave me a chance to celebrate with Mum, Dad, Nancy, Walter and Sofia.

Nancy also suggested that she and I catch up for a few quiet drinks on Sunday afternoon at the Grace Darling Hotel in Collingwood. When I arrived there were a bunch of old friends already there – Julie Field, Morena Miceli and Danielle Bernardo. I joined them and we had a lovely afternoon chatting and laughing. With Vince and Gab back in London, it was great to have dear family and friends around me.

My other parties included a beautiful soiree at Clapham in London with Silvana and our London mates, involving vintage champagne and a box full of the most extraordinary cupcakes I'd ever seen, courtesy of my little sister.

In Paris we had a shindig in Batignolles. We had let the apartment on the square go, so we went to Jacques and Val's, who were like family. If it was anything like previous dinners at Jacques and Val's, the celebration probably involved an aperitif followed by dinner, which was always an event, especially because there would be quite a wait in between. No doubt there was more champagne involved, as well as a good French red or two – those bon vivants would never serve up a bad wine.

And finally, we had a few days with friends in Corsica. We hired four or five villas and chilled out, eating, drinking, talking, reading, doing nothing. I'd fallen in love with that place the first time I went there with Vince a few years earlier.

It felt like one of my spiritual homes, not least because it's a lot like Sicily. The landscape is rugged mountains one minute, Mediterranean island paradise the next. The ancient towns and villages are picture-postcard, with stone villas, cobbled streets and red-tiled roofs. And the island is populated with some *extremely* interesting characters – stubborn and passionate people (sound familiar?), who, despite the economic realities, are still determined to win their independence after almost 250 years under French rule.

In fact, one of Corsica's most famous musicians had featured on my new French album, which we recorded after my *Chicago* stint. With his brother Alain, Jean-François Bernardini fronts the Corsican folk music band I Muvrini. They sing in Corsican, melding traditional polyphonic vocals with traditional and contemporary instruments, and are astonishing live. They've recorded with many well-known artists, including Sting.

Vince and I made the trip to Bastia in Corsica to ask Jean-François whether he'd recite some poetry over a track I'd originally written with Peter-John Vettese. Pete had come up with the fabulous 1960s-style music and I'd written a melody and my first-ever French lyric, which at that stage was just a chorus. Jean-François agreed, and wrote and recited some beautiful poetry, which for me captured everything I love about Corsica.

That song, called 'Dis-Moi' (Tell Me), was left-of-field but Valérie liked it. Unfortunately, however, she and I didn't always see eye to eye when it came to song choices for the new French album. In fact, we seemed to come up against one obstacle after another during the making of that album, which was recorded in both Paris and London. I found out later a lot was going on at Sony behind closed doors. With the music industry experiencing major changes, the big companies were suffering. Sony France wasn't immune, and many people there feared for their jobs. Valérie, who was head of Columbia in France, was under major pressure at work, even though the label was actually doing very well. Everyone was running for cover and had less time or patience to collaborate on things. They seemed to just want to drive things through and move on.

Still, there were some interesting songs on the album, which was chiefly produced by Duck and Paul. 'Entends-Tu le Monde?' (Can You Hear the World?) featured a sample by the Senegalese singer Thione Seck and was produced by DJ Molecule. I co-wrote several of the tracks, which was satisfying, and Vince wrote lyrics for quite a few.

I called the album after the song '7 Vies', which I co-wrote with Elodie Hesme, one of the writers on 'Je M'Appelle Bagdad'. The song is about how women, whoever or wherever they are, need seven lives to survive (it's a play on the seven lives of French cats – of course, in English, cats have nine lives). I loved the lyric and it resonated with me personally. I'd just turned forty and yet I felt like I'd lived at least seven lives, give or take. What's more, I'd survived them all.

The first single off the album ended up being 'Entends-Tu le Monde?' I wasn't sure that song was the best choice for a single but Valérie was. Maybe she was right – it reached number 10 on the French charts, although sales were down, as they were across the board.

I didn't know the detail of the changes going on at Sony France, but I'd been around long enough to know the instability would affect my album. And I think it probably did. As well, despite Valérie's achievements and great success with Columbia, she was ultimately retrenched, along with many others. Things would never be quite the same.

Songs of Love and Loss, the album I'd dreamt up in the kitchen and which had been a labour of love, was released in Australia in early December 2007. My second French album, *7 Vies*, was scheduled to come out a month or so later. Making two records back to back had been full on and I swore I'd never do it again. It was crazy, and now I'd be promoting them both!

Vince and Gab travelled with me to Australia for a handful of concerts. I was excited. The album had gone platinum within a week, and ended up at number three on the charts. A year later it was nominated for an ARIA award for bestselling album. Having had no expectations for that record, it was particularly sweet. It was a good example of what can happen if you follow your heart and see something through with passion and dedication.

So on that score I was thrilled. However, I was also extremely nervous – terrified, to be honest. It would be the first time I performed in Australia with an orchestra, and I had no idea how people would react. And while the material was wonderful and I wanted to treat it with the respect it deserved, it was also challenging, and I was fearful of doing a bad job. Every nuance, every breath, every note would count. I couldn't muck this up.

Lucky for me, I had my wonderful band by my side – Paul, Kere, Nick and Chris, and two fabulous backing vocalists, Kelly and Talei Wolfgramm. As well, a young composer and arranger called Nicholas Buc would be the conductor. Nick turned out to be more than just a genius, and he was certainly one of those. He had such spontaneity and energy you couldn't help but enjoy yourself on stage with him. He was a wonderful addition to an already great team and I loved him to bits. Six years later, we are still working together.

I also had a fantastic new assistant who made all the difference. Tori Wood, it turned out, knew more about me than I did myself, having been a fan since she was a little kid. She was versed in all kinds of other things, too, her special subject being fashion (and don't get her started on lingerie!). Tori still helps out whenever I'm in Australia, and I'd be lost without her.

After a typical Arena Christmas, I gave two performances with the Melbourne Symphony Orchestra at Hamer Hall in Melbourne. Hamer Hall is my home crowd but I was still terrified that the show would be a disaster. I needn't have worried. Thanks to the band, the orchestra, Nick and a very supportive audience (some home crowds can be tough, but not *my* home crowd), everything went off without a hitch.

A few days later I was in Sydney, rehearsing with the Sydney Lyric Orchestra for three concerts at the Sydney Opera House. There is something special about performing in that beautiful building. With the success of the Melbourne concerts to bolster me, I could relax a little and enjoy it.

While we were in Sydney we made a video for 'Entends-Tu le Monde?'. It had been Vince's idea to shoot the clip in Australia and once again he had a cameo, playing a mysterious handsome man sitting up the back of a bus.

Soon after, we headed back to Europe to do promotion for *7 Vies,* which was coming out in February. But when we arrived it was clear that not much had been put in place. The upheaval at Sony was taking its toll. Vince, Bruce and I all felt that the marketing plan was weak and poorly thought out. Everyone at Sony seemed distracted and it was hard to get answers out of them. It was frustrating.

Nevertheless, the album did okay, reaching number 12 on the charts. But I was left feeling very unsure about my future with Columbia. I still had one more album owing to the label, according to my contract. It turned out they wanted it, very much, and I had several discussions with them about the next album.

But when Vince and I sat down and talked about it, we decided that under the circumstances there was no point continuing. I didn't want to go through that again, putting everything I had into a record only to see it fall through the cracks. At that point, my well was dry. With Valérie gone, I knew I wouldn't be able to summon up the strength and belief to record and promote a new album with conviction. So in the end I asked my lawyer to write a letter informing Columbia I wanted out.

The label's response was admirable and it's something I love about the French. They will never make an artist honour a contract if the artist's heart isn't in it. It's a sensible approach. Instead, Columbia decided they'd release a good old honest 'best of'. And that was that.

I visited the office and thanked all those who I'd worked with over the years. Most of them had already been retrenched or left. One who was still on deck was Virginie Couarc'h, who I'd worked with since the days of *In Deep*, and who had found our beautiful apartment in Batignolles. Virginie was very sad to see me go, and I was sad to say goodbye, but I was ready to move on.

There was perhaps another reason why I made that decision. Now we had Gab, Vince and I had been keen to give him a brother or sister, and that had been part of our plans for 2008. In fact I'd been pregnant briefly in 2007 but had miscarried at home in Clapham. Vince was away sailing with a couple of his fathers' friends to pick up a boat from Tunisia and bring it back to France when it happened. The next day I dropped Gab off at creche, caught a bus to the hospital, had myself checked out, picked Gab up and came home. (I got into trouble with Gab's godmother, Georgia Zaris, for doing that. Linda lived close by and was a good friend.) Anyway, I felt lost, and like a bit of a failure. But it wasn't meant to be.

And then, in 2008, I had another miscarriage. I guess I'd been crazy busy but I was particularly stressed that year over what was going on at Columbia and also more broadly in the industry. *Songs of Love and Loss* had sold well, but I was questioning my place in the world. Where did I fit in now?

Vince and I were sad and disappointed to lose two pregnancies, but I have always been philosophical about things like that. Nature is a powerful force and there's no point questioning it or fighting it. As the French say, *La nature est bien faite* – nature is well made. And it is. Miscarriage is common and women all over the world go through it every day. It was hardly something extraordinary. It was difficult, nevertheless, and it became more so once it actually sank in. But it is what it is. I guess I could have tried IVF, but I wasn't sure it was right for me.

I dealt with it all the way I deal with most things. I just kept going. EMI wanted a second album. Gab was more than enough to keep us busy and laughing every day. And who knew what else might be around the corner? Another one of those seven lives, perhaps. I still had a couple more to go, surely.

CHAPTER 30

Living a Lifetime Together

Life had slowed down a little, at least enough to enjoy some family time. I was back in London working on the follow-up to *Songs of Love and Loss*. It had been the number one Australian album over Christmas, so EMI were all geared up to do another one. So geared up, in fact, they wanted a bit more say regarding the choice of songs. But John O'Donnell never overstepped the mark. 'I trust you. Just do what feels right,' he'd say.

The songs ended up all being favourites of mine, anyway. First up was the Lulu track 'Oh Me Oh My'. I'd always loved Lulu – such a soulful and honest singer, she was never too fancy but always kept it real. Then there was 'Close to You', a Bacharach–David song made famous by the Carpenters (and didn't Karen Carpenter have the voice of an angel!). I'd always admired Deborah Harry – she was such a risk-taker, and 'Call Me' was nothing less than a smash hit. We pared back Alice Cooper's 'Only Women Bleed' to its essence to bring out the emotion. 'I Hope I Never', by Tim Finn, a truly great songwriter, is one of my favourite Split Enz tracks. Then there was Joni Mitchell's 'Both Sides, Now', Elton John's 'Your Song' and an original, a song I wrote with Paul Manners and his offsiders, called 'Living a Lifetime Together'.

Duck, Paul Guardiani and Simon would be on board again, and we were all excited about the recording, because this time I planned to sing live in the studio with the London Studio Orchestra. The concept was to capture the excitement and buzz of a live performance.

It sounded like a great idea, but the pressure was enormous. We recorded seven songs in one day at Air Studios. Simon Hale did the arrangements and conducted. He was superb, driving the session and keeping everyone on track. I got the feeling the musicians enjoyed having me in the room with them and they were very complimentary. There was a mood of spontaneity and exhilaration, just as we'd hoped. Having been put on the spot regularly during more than thirty years of performing, I kept it together, and we recorded everything in just one or two takes.

Performing those songs with an orchestra seemed like a natural step for me to take. I was harking back to my pop roots and all those songs I grew up listening to on the radio, as well as my Italian musical roots, which took in opera, and my roots in musical theatre. For me, both *Songs of Love and Loss* albums encapsulated my musical heritage and my musical identity.

It also seemed a natural step to perform with the great Italian tenor Andrea Bocelli while he was in Australia. Andrea's unbelievably beautiful voice is one of my favourites on the planet. Having heard *Songs of Love and Loss*, he requested I sing the duets he'd made famous: 'The Prayer', which he recorded with Celine Dion, 'Canto della Terra', which he recorded with Sarah Brightman, and the Elvis song 'Can't Help Falling in Love'.

Singing duets with Andrea was an absolute honour, but it was challenging. Even though Italian is my first language, I'd rarely sung in it. For me, it's not just about getting the pronunciation right – which wasn't a big ask for me in Italian, anyway – but communicating the emotion. Italian is an incredibly emotional language – I would have to be able to infuse those words with the passion they promised. It was a new test, but it was wonderful to return to my Italian roots and pay tribute to them in the best way I knew how.

Andrea and I first sang together at a big concert in Lithuania, just days after I'd finished recording *Love and Loss 2*. Then, in August, we sang together in concerts in Australia and New Zealand. Before each performance Andrea would warm up in the bathroom of his dressing-room. To keep his vocal cords moist, he'd have the shower going full bore and the entire place would be filled with steam. Andrea was very funny – his imitation of an Australian accent was the best I've ever heard.

Singing 'The Prayer' in Italian with Andrea gave me goosebumps every night. *Che bella lingua!*

Back in London we were putting the finishing touches to *Songs of Love and Loss 2*. Gab was nearly three and had begun attending the nursery school around the corner. He was starting to pick up a Clapham accent to add to his Australian and French turns of phrase. Gab was even more multicultural than I was as a kid, back when I'd be speaking Italian to my parents one minute and broad Australian to my mates the next. Gab just seemed to slot in wherever he was.

I made a quick trip to Australia for the release of *Songs of Love and Loss 2*. The album went gold virtually overnight and reached number 12. Then I was back in London for a break before an Australian concert tour the following March. I thought we could have a bit of quiet family time together. It was a good plan, but it didn't last. Not long after we returned, a man in a dark suit appeared on our doorstep in Clapham. He looked like something out of the secret service, but he was just there to deliver an envelope. It was addressed to me, so I sat down at the kitchen table and opened it. Inside was a letter from President Sarkozy of France, informing me that I had been awarded a Chevalier de l'Ordre National du Mérite for my services to France.

My first reaction was, *Someone's taking the micky here – I wonder who?* I called out to Vince to come and see. 'Check this out,' I said. 'Is it a gag?'

Vince read the letter. 'No, of course it's not a gag,' he said. Then he gave me a big hug. 'You're being knighted, French-style!'

I rang Bruce. He got on the phone to the French embassy in London. It turned out the honour was the second highest in the land, after the Legion of Honour. That blew me away. I'd be up there with Marcel Marceau, Jacques Chirac and Jacques Cousteau. I was speechless for at least ten seconds, which is still a record. I felt unworthy, honoured, grateful, moved. France had not only opened its arms to me but its heart too.

When Gab heard I was to be made a *chevalier* he thought I'd have to start wearing armour and riding around on a horse. When I explained I'd still be wearing jeans and a T-shirt for most of the time and getting around the usual way, he was extremely disappointed.

The French embassy in London suggested I receive my honour there. But after I gave it some thought, I decided I wanted to be decorated in France. It just made sense and it wouldn't feel right to do it any other way. The French government agreed to my request and said they'd inform me when and where the ceremony would take place. In the end, it wasn't until three years later that I was decorated at a wonderful ceremony at the Palais de la Culture by the Minister for Culture, Frédéric Mitterrand. We invited family and friends and afterwards Vince and I took everyone out to dinner across the road. It was an extraordinary evening.

*

Receiving such an honour from the French got me thinking. Who was I and where did I belong? I'd always considered myself Australian through and through. You wouldn't hear me with a trans-Atlantic accent any day soon. Then there was my Italian heritage, which was such a big part of who I was. And now I had strong and binding ties to France, a nation that had become my second home, even when I was living in London and dreaming about Australia. Strongest of those ties was the fact that my nearest and dearest were both French. Vince and Gab had parents, grandparents, uncles and aunties, cousins and friends in France. In a year or so Gab would be starting school. We had to think about where would be the best place for him.

In the end we decided it was time to move to Paris. Vince was missing his homeland and Gab needed one. So we began the search for a house, somewhere not too far from the centre but with a bit of space and peace and quiet. It took a while, but eventually we found a place we both loved. Built in the early 1930s, it had a beautiful garden and was full of charm, despite the fact it had poky rooms and was unbelievably run-down. (We only discovered *how* run-down once we moved in.) It would need more than a makeover, but Vince and I spotted its potential immediately. On our second visit I could see Vince was already knocking down walls in his mind to open up the rooms and bring the outdoors in (during summer, at least!).

When we told friends and associates that we were moving back to France, people thought we were mad – it can be such an administrative nightmare over there. Even my French accountant counselled against it. But we weren't moving for tax reasons or anything like that. We were moving for family. It was an easy decision.

Another thing happened around that time that got me thinking again about identity. Bruce was contacted by someone from the SBS television show *Who Do You Think You Are?*, enquiring whether I'd be interested in being the subject of an episode. *Who Do You Think You Are?* explores a person's family history. The show is a journey of discovery, often literally, as they take a person back to the place their ancestors lived or worked. The subjects of the show are regularly surprised, amazed or even shocked by what is revealed. An underlying theme of the show is that most of us are probably *not* who we think we are, and that when you scratch the surface most of us have multicultural heritage. For example, we may think we're bog Irish, only to find out we have Spanish blood. Or we think we're Arabic until we find out our great-grandmother was Jewish. It can make for some gripping television. Before they commit to have you on the show, however, they research your family to determine whether there's actually a story there to tell.

I said yes straight away. Then I wondered whether I'd done the right thing. There was no doubt I had a lot of questions about my heritage that remained unanswered. I knew very little about my grandparents, or any of my ancestors, in fact. Having grown up so far from my parents' homeland, we

Arena girls knew only snippets of family stories. Mum and Dad never talked much about the old days. Now I questioned why. Was it just because our immediate extended family was already enough to keep up with? And maybe, having left Sicily, Mum and Dad were simply more focused on making a new life in Australia. But I couldn't help wondering: could there be skeletons in the closet that might be better left alone? In any case, it was too late. I'd already given the show the go-ahead.

I didn't hear anything from the show for months. When I finally heard from them, I was informed the researchers had hit a dead end. In the meantime, we moved house. Silvana, who was still working for Sharon Osbourne and had moved to LA, began dating our darling friend Matt, the hair stylist who had tried so valiantly to cut Gab's hair. As well, through necessity, I had to release the demos of my fourth Sony album, the one they'd rejected. It wasn't something I'd ever planned to do. But a fan announced on my website that she'd bought the demos from a private seller in the UK for quite a large sum of money. She was offering to burn copies on request for other fans.

I was shocked. Bruce contacted her and asked her not to make any copies as the rights belonged to me. In the end, we decided I'd have to release the material myself through my website. Called *The Peel Me Sessions 2003*, it was a little piece of history that I knew the fans would enjoy.

Two more albums came out in 2009: my French best-of, called *The Best and le Meilleur* (The Best and the Best) and a live

CD and DVD from the Songs of Love and Loss 2 tour called *The Onstage Collection*.

We finally moved into the house in Paris around the end of the year. The wiring in the place was horrendous and the first time it rained we had to stock up on buckets to catch the leaks. But at least the boys were back where they belonged.

Not long after, I had a third miscarriage. By then I'd heard from *Who Do You Think You Are?* again. They'd found enough information to make a show and were ready when I was. Soon some of my questions about my family and my identity would be answered. So why was I so scared?

CHAPTER 31

The Man With the Child In His Eyes

The people from *Who Do You Think You Are?* told me they'd be flying me to Rome, but not much more. I may as well have been blindfolded – I had no idea what would happen or what I'd find out.

In Rome, I met the researcher Anthea Bulloch, who had done all the legwork in Italy for my episode, and Jane Manning, who was the show's director. We spent just a night in Rome. The next day we flew to Catania in Sicily.

I had expected to go to Sicily, but I was still nervous. I realised I didn't know much about my family at all and now I was about to bust open the vault. Who knew what was in there?

But I had to admit I was deeply curious, too. I'd been named Filippina after my grandmother Filippa, and yet I knew almost nothing about her. It wasn't until we began work on the show that Mum revealed that she thought Nonna was an orphan. Mum said she knew nothing more. When it came to Nonno, my grandfather, whose name was Francesco Catalfamo, all Mum had was a piece of paper a relative had sent her that said the Catalfamos had been traced back to Sicilian nobility of the fourteenth century.

When Mum showed me this document I couldn't believe it. I also couldn't understand why she'd never told us. Then she revealed that her grandfather had come from a place called Santa Lucia, which was also news to me. Mum hadn't told us, she said, because she genuinely didn't think we'd be interested. When I thought about it some more, I could see her point. Often it's not until you reach a certain age – when you have children of your own, perhaps – that you become interested in your ancestry. If she'd tried to talk to me about it when I was a teenager I probably would have swiftly nodded off. When you're a kid all you're interested in is the now.

Mum's document intrigued me, not so much because it suggested we were related to nobility, but because I thought it might help explain something about the Catalfamos. We always had the sense that the Catalfamos were aloof – a complex, darker breed. I have a dark side too, and I'd always wondered about it. Nonno, in particular, was a severe, brooding character. As I mentioned previously, when I met him as a little girl I thought he was very grumpy indeed. Now, at last, we might find out why.

When we arrived in Sicily we drove to Valguarnera, the little town in the middle of Sicily where both my parents grew up. We were standing in front of the church where my parents were married in 1957 when Anthea revealed that it was in fact my parents' fifty-third wedding anniversary that day. My parents' wedding had been unusual by most standards, because my father was not actually present. He was in Australia, having travelled to the other end of the world two years earlier. So Mum and Dad were wed by proxy. It was actually quite common among young Sicilians at the time, due to the number of people emigrating.

Dad had come out to Australia to cut cane in the far north, thanks to an agreement between the Australian and Italian governments. World War II had wreaked devastation and disruption on Italy, and poverty and overcrowding were rife. To ease the problem, the government of Italy actively encouraged its citizens to emigrate. Meanwhile, Australia was looking for new citizens, in the belief that the nation needed to 'populate or perish'. Australia didn't want just anyone, though. At first, the government intended that nine out of ten immigrants be British. It very quickly became clear, however, that this was unrealistic, so the policy was broadened to take in 'northern Europeans'. When still not enough immigrants applied, the policy had to be revised again, to finally allow southern Europeans to emigrate. The plan was that southern Europeans would preferably work in the tropics up north. Those were different times, but the only name for it is racism. The funny thing is, it never worked, anyway, and now the southern city of Melbourne is home to Australia's largest Italian and Greek communities.

There was a mass exodus of southern Italians from their homeland during that time. Originally, my dad travelled to Australia with the plan to make some money and then return to Italy. He worked hard in the cane fields but found that the pay was extremely poor. One thing led to another and soon he was working for General Motors in Melbourne. By then Dad realised he could make a good life in Australia, and that's when he suggested that Mum come out too.

Mum's move to Australia changed the course of history for the Catalfamo family, because she was later followed by six of her siblings, leaving just two behind in Sicily.

So who were the Catalfamos? In Palermo, the capital of Sicily, I learnt that the document tracing the family back to Sicilian aristocracy was fake. We were not related to nobility. Not that it bothered me. What did was the fact that we still didn't know any more about that side of the family.

In Palermo I also met Joe Manusia, a retired American detective who researched Sicilian genealogy. He'd found out a lot about the Arenas – so much, in fact, that in one day I gained 427 new relatives. That cracked me up.

He'd managed to trace Dad's family back more than 300 years. When we looked at the family tree, there was one constant: *contadino*, or farmer. Most of the Arenas were farmers. That hardly came as a shock. Dad and his brothers have the most wonderful gardens. The Arenas all live from their gardens, still, and have always been salt-of-the-earth kind of people. Clearly it was in the blood. Joe also found that at least some of them had been very successful and well-to-do.

But what about those complex Catalfamos? It turned out Joe Manusia had discovered something interesting about my great-great-grandmother, Carmela Catalfamo. I would have to travel to Santa Lucia, where the Catalfamos originally came from, to hear more. So off we went to the north-east corner of Sicily.

In Santa Lucia I visited the city archives, where the records showed that Carmela had adopted six foundlings, babies that had been abandoned in 'foundling wheels'. Poverty was so widespread in Italy at the time that nearly 40,000 babies were abandoned every year by parents too poor to look after them. By roadsides all over Italy the authorities set up foundling wheels, small wheel-shaped shelters where people could leave their babies to be cared for by others.

In fact, Carmela had not only taken in six foundlings to be reared alongside her own five children, but had given those foundlings her own family name, going against accepted custom. Usually foundlings were given a made-up name by authorities. By giving her own name to her 'foster' children, Carmela ensured they could not be discriminated against. According to the show's researchers, Carmela was the only person historians had ever come across to do this. It was just never done.

Hearing this information touched me. To know that your great-great-grandmother was the kind of person who not only took in orphans but made sure they were treated like her own children was gratifying and inspiring.

But what struck me even more powerfully was that history was again repeating itself. Because, just like Carmela, my own mother had been taking in strangers – the old people in the nursing home. I had to admit that sometimes I'd resented the fact that Mum was so committed to her elderly clients. Why she felt such a powerful commitment to them, I never really understood, and it was a question that had nagged me over the years. To be honest, sometimes I'd felt that Mum put her clients before us. Of course she never did. Mum was trying to look after everyone, juggling her responsibilities and commitments to the best of her ability. Out of compassion and a sense of duty she had dedicated herself to a community as well as her own family, putting others first above herself. In these times of individualism and fracturing communities, Mum could teach us a thing or two about what it meant to be part of a community and to give of yourself. She'd done an extraordinary job caring for the elderly, who are so often neglected in our society. It made me very proud.

Carmela had later moved her family to Valguarnera, where my grandfather, her grandson, was born. In Valguarnera I met my mother's cousin, Pippo, who remembered my grandfather well.

'I remember he was very strict,' I said to Pippo. 'I didn't like the way he spoke to my mum.'

Pippo agreed. 'He was strict. He was a hardworking man.' Then he dropped a bombshell. 'You see, Pina,' he said, 'your *nonno* worked in a sulphur mine from the age of six.'

Apparently, Nonno's father had died when he and his brother, Pippo's father, were very young. After their father's death, the two little boys were sent to work in the sulphur mines. It was likely that, in return, their mother had received a loan from a miner for whom the boys then worked. That was extremely common. The interest rate charged was often so high, the children were indentured to the miner for years. This is what had happened to my grandfather and his brother.

If you google 'sulphur mining in Sicily' you'll be directed to websites on child slavery. The fact was, until as late as the 1930s, the sulphur mines in Sicily were filled with child labourers who were effectively slaves. They worked eighteen-hour days and slept in the mines with the rats. (Pippo explained that the rats were actually the miners' friends, because rats knew well before humans when danger was imminent, so if the rats were making a run for it, you did too.)

But it got worse. The mines were horrifically hot, and so the miners and the children worked naked. Salvatore Di Vito, the mining historian who showed me around the ruins of the sulphur mine, explained that men and boys working naked in such close contact resulted in a 'somewhat uncertain' morality, as he put it. Salvatore said that, with the miners working for sometimes months away from women, there were undoubtedly cases of abuse and pederasty.

As a child, my grandfather had been handed a platter of pain, his childhood an unimaginable living hell.

It explained a lot about the man I'd never understood. He'd suffered horrifically and of course it had shaped his character.

Back in town, I was invited to visit the house that Nonno had lived in with my grandmother. I still remember when we stayed there – it had seemed dark and creepy, although I recalled there was a lovely terrace on the roof. This was where I'd had my fifth birthday, when Nonno had seemed so grumpy as I blew out the candles.

The house's new owner welcomed me in and showed me around. Then he led me to the roof. When he bought the house he was told that the previous owner – my *nonno* – had regularly taken his gramophone up onto the terrace and played opera records to the whole town. He'd stood up there soaking in the music. Nonno was a huge Rossini fan, my mother told me later. In fact, he adored music, especially opera.

I always knew I had a connection with Nonno. Even though I thought he was grouchy, I was drawn to him in a way I never understood as a child. And now I knew for sure that one of those connections was music. Nonno and I not only loved music, we *needed* music. Music healed us, both of us.

Another connection was work. Like Nonno, I'd worked from a very young age. Of course, unlike him, my work had been wonderful, exciting, fun. And yet, we shared that common bond. Neither of us had what might be called a normal childhood.

At last I felt that I understood Nonno. But my grandmother, my *nonna*, was still a mystery. I'd met her during that trip to Sicily when I was little, but had not seen her again before her death in March 1993. Ultimately, we discovered she'd been a foundling, an abandoned child. Nonna had initially been placed with an unmarried woman but sadly, when Nonna was around eight years old, that woman had died. My grandmother spent the next ten years of her life in the care of the nuns. Believe it or not, I always had a sense of abandonment around Nonna and that her origins were unknown.

Who Do You Think You Are? answered many questions about exactly that – who I was. I discovered things about my family I never knew. In fact, my whole family benefited from the knowledge that emerged from the making of that show, and we owe so much to all those involved. Thanks to their work, I better understood my grandfather and my own mother. I also understood why my parents left Sicily for Australia and why they never returned. I'd heard so many stories, many involving my own family, of struggle, poverty, even slavery. Australia had given our family freedom and a life we could have never had in my parents' homeland. We Arenas would be forever grateful for those opportunities. I realised that was why I would always be Australian first and foremost, whatever had happened or would happen, wherever I was and whatever I did. Because that's who I am.

I know now why I can sing.

It's where I come from,

This past within.

A land so rich, its beauty rare,

Where souls survived

But wept despair.

I pray we all can move along

But take with us

What made us strong,

To show the world it can be done.

This beautiful song,

Let it be sung.

CHAPTER 32

Higher Ground

It was summer in Paris and, while we hadn't yet managed to do anything to the house to 'bring the outside in' as per Vince's grand plan, the weather was beautiful. We probably should have been out enjoying the day, but it being Sunday I was still in my dressing-gown and Gab in his pyjamas, even though it was lunchtime.

My phone bleeped. It was a message from Salvatore Anzalone, a Belgian concert promoter and old friend of Vince's. Sal and I had been working together for quite a few years.

'Cadel's wearing the yellow jersey.'

'What's the yellow jersey?' I texted back.

'*Quoi?* Cadel Evans has won the Tour. He can't lose now unless he falls, which he won't. It'll be the first time an Aussie has won.'

I rang Sal.

He faked outrage (or did he?). 'What do you mean you don't know what the yellow jersey is?' he yelled down the line. 'It's the Tour de France and Cadel Evans has won! What're you gonna do about it?'

'What do you want me to do? It's Sunday and I'm at home in my PJs cooking lunch.'

'Call someone,' he said. 'You should be there. You should sing.'

He was right, of course. I should, and I would. I was by no means a cycling aficionado but I did know that winning the Tour de France was an incredible achievement. I was fairly sure there was no tougher sporting event on the planet. You had to be almost superhuman to finish it, let alone win it. Being Australian, I was also aware of just how much my nation hated sport – NOT! This Cadel Evans was clearly already a national hero and his victory deserved to be celebrated properly here in France.

'I'll call the Australian ambassador,' I told Sal.

I'd met the ambassador, David Ritchie, on various occasions. He was a lovely gentleman. 'Where are you, darling?' he said when I rang. 'You should come down. Cadel has won!'

'What are you doing about the national anthem?' I asked.

'Someone's gone back to the office to pick up a disk. We'll just play that.'

'We can do better than that,' I said. 'I could sing, if you like.'

'Really? You'd do that?' David was up for it, I could tell.

'Yep. I'd *love* to.'

At that moment Vince walked in the door. I quickly told him what was going on. As I talked I could see his brain ticking over. He was cooking something up.

'Let me call Barbara,' he said.

Barbara was a friend of Vince's sister Sophie. She also happened to work for the company that organised the Tour. In fact, she was one of the key contacts.

Vince called Barbara, who called someone else, who called France 2, the TV station broadcasting the event. France 2 knew me well – I'd appeared on their station countless times – and they knew how I worked and what I could do.

Barbara came back to say they loved the idea.

We had an hour to get there. I ran upstairs and rifled through my wardrobe for something appropriate to wear. I found an Australian flag top that the stylist Nicole Bonython-Hines had given me on a shoot years earlier. Vince got Gab out of his pyjamas. Then we jumped in the car and gunned it. For the first time in history we got every green light. We made it in twenty minutes.

At five o'clock on that balmy Sunday evening on the Champs-Élysées in Paris, Cadel Evans was declared the winner of the Tour de France. He was indeed the first Australian ever to win the race.

With tears in my eyes, I sang 'Advance Australia Fair' a cappella. It was a momentous occasion and I felt incredibly proud – proud of Cadel, proud to be Australian, and proud to be able to honour Australia and France in the best way I knew how. It had seemed the logical and natural thing to do.

Afterwards, I talked to Cadel. He was extremely emotional, which I could completely understand. When I came to know more about the man, I felt an affinity with him. He'd worked hard for years to win that race. He'd had ups and downs, but he'd never given in. And of course, he was Australian, like me. That really meant something.

The person who got the biggest shock was my manager, Bruce. He was in the UK and had no idea what had gone on. Suddenly every media outlet was on the line wanting to get the inside story.

The funny thing was, Michel Drucker, 'France's Michael Parkinson', who had always been such a great supporter of mine, had spotted Cadel years earlier. Michel was a cycling fanatic. 'Watch that Cadel Evans,' he said to me once. 'He'll win the Tour one day.'

'Who'll win the what?' I think I said. Well, now I know.

That year, 2011, I'd given concerts in France and Australia. Both countries were now dear to my heart. While I'd made France my home, there was no denying that Australia would always be 'home'. And now Cadel's win had brought the two countries together in a beautiful way. These days, I no longer felt conflict or doubt about who I was or where I belonged. The fact was, I'd been a citizen of the world for so many years,

I could feel at home in Paris, London, Melbourne, Sydney, Sicily, LA, Corsica – wherever I laid my hat. I was at a place in my life where I could look back on my past without regret. I no longer cared if people continued to call me Tiny Tina forever. In fact, I looked back on that little girl with great fondness. She'd just followed her heart and done what she loved most. There had been something very genuine and innocent about *Young Talent Time*. It had shaped my past, present and probably future. It helped make me who I am.

So when, not long after Cadel's victory in the Tour, I received a call from someone at Channel Ten, asking me whether I'd be involved in a new series of *Young Talent Time*, I said I'd give it serious consideration. After some thought I decided I could only participate if I was confident the show was done well, with thought, love and effort. I didn't want to get involved with anything that was knocked together, or not in the spirit of the original YTT.

Then I heard that John Young himself would be involved, and I was sure the show *would* stay true to the original. And if John was involved I couldn't possibly say no. I would be forever indebted to John Young for getting me started. When I was growing up on national television, he was always there for me, teaching, nurturing, mentoring. If it hadn't been for John, I wouldn't have had the career I'd had. In fact, I thought of him as my second dad. He had his own two daughters, Anna and Fleur, and then there was me, his surrogate daughter. So if John wanted me to do it, I couldn't refuse.

It was exactly how I'd felt a year earlier when I was asked to induct him into the ARIA Hall of Fame.

'Yes,' I'd said immediately. 'I'd be honoured.' And I was. I felt it was well overdue, to tell the truth, but these things take time, and most things happen at the right time for the right reasons. Now was definitely the right time and John certainly deserved it. He'd not only been a pop sensation in the early 1960s, but had gone on to pen some of Australia's best-known number-1 hits, songs like 'The Real Thing' for Russell Morris and 'Smiley' for Ronnie Burns. He had fifteen gold records on his wall and six Logies on his mantelpiece. John had been instrumental in the early days of Australian rock 'n' roll and yet he'd never properly been recognised for all he'd achieved. In fact, I think he lost credibility in the industry when he started YTT, and yet that show had launched many careers and promoted the pants off thousands of songs, most of them selling as singles in shops like 100 Puckle Street in Moonee Ponds, where I'd bought my first record.

So on 27 October 2010 I inducted John Young into the Hall of Fame. As part of the ceremony, I sang one of his own compositions, 'Here Comes the Star', a poignant song about the loneliness of fame. John was humbled and deeply touched by all the love in the room that night. I guess for him, it felt like things had come full circle.

And now, with a new series of *Young Talent Time* on the cards, it felt like things were coming full circle for me, too. Of course, I no longer qualified to be a member of the team.

I was a tad too old. Instead, I'd be a judge and mentor. There would be two of us – the other judge and mentor would be the Emmy award-winning American dancer and choreographer Charles 'Chucky' Klapow. Chucky's first high-profile performance was at the age of twelve. He began to choreograph by the time he was fifteen, and danced in *Austin Powers* and with Michael Jackson for the 'This Is It' tour, as well as choreographing three *High School Musical* movies. Chucky was also a gorgeous person, generous in spirit, articulate, interesting and interested.

Chucky was highly qualified to be a judge on a talent show, and I felt that I was too. Aside from my career experience, YTT would not be my first time as a judge and mentor. I'd been a guest judge on *Australian Idol*, working with Ian Dickson. We made a funny pair: he'd tell someone they were awful while I tried to give them positive and practical feedback. But Dicko always did it in such an endearing way you loved him nevertheless.

Dicko and I judged some Idol tryouts in London together with Darren Hayes from Savage Garden. One young woman fronted up and sang 'Chains'. Dicko told her it was 'rubbish'. I just said I was flattered, but she didn't need to sing one of my songs. Funnily enough, 'Chains' has become a favourite among talent show contestants all over the world, so I've been told. I guess it gives a singer the opportunity to strut their stuff.

Anyway, after much discussion I signed on the dotted line for a new series of *Young Talent Time*. The show would air from

January to May 2012. To do it, I would need to be in Australia for at least six months. It wasn't the best timing: we'd finally had our renovation plans approved for the house in Paris and building was due to begin. Regardless, Vince, Gab and I packed up our belongings and headed down under.

In Melbourne we stayed with Mum and Dad until we found a house to rent – in Moonee Ponds, of course. We got Gab into a school around the corner. Gab slotted in like a local within days. In fact, he absolutely loved school in Australia. I think the Australian approach to education suited him. In France even the littlies feel pressure to succeed and do well, and it's stressful for them. The Australian way seemed a bit more nurturing. They seemed to let little kids be little kids for a little bit longer.

Gab also got the chance to come to work with me, and he absolutely loved every minute. He'd sit in my judge's chair and give feedback to imaginary contestants, telling them what they'd done well and what needed work. The crew would fall about laughing – Gab kept everyone entertained.

So Gab was as happy as Larry. Vince found himself on a plane a lot, travelling between France, LA and Melbourne. In LA he was looking in on Silvana and Matt. Silvana had fallen pregnant in the second half of 2011, but the baby, little Louis, had come three months early, at just twenty-six weeks. It was tough for them all. (A year later, Louis was tearing around Dad's garden, getting into everything, just like Gab had a few years earlier.)

In the end, the new *Young Talent Time* was a beautiful experience. The host, Rob Mills, who'd been in the top five of the first season of *Australian Idol* in 2003, was terrific. The team of kids were gorgeous and incredibly talented. Everyone, from the smallest contestant to the executive producer, had a great time on that show. It was such a friendly set and you couldn't have had a more interesting, hardworking and loving bunch of people.

The focus was on family entertainment. The tricky thing was finding the right timeslot. They'd started the show in January, when people were still in holiday mode. The original timeslot was early on a Sunday evening, but I suspect families were still at the beach when the show aired. In the end they moved the show twice, the second time to Friday evenings, which again seemed an odd choice.

I was a bit miffed when it wasn't renewed for a second season, but that's television. It's a business. Still, I'd done it for John, and I think we did him proud. For me, it tied off a loose end. It was lovely to revisit *Young Talent Time*, this time from a different perspective, and to give something back to kids who had a dream just like I had.

What I hadn't expected was the love and appreciation I received. I hadn't realised just how many people saw me as some kind of role model or felt that I'd somehow contributed to their journey. It was humbling, and yet I felt ready to take on that role, to lead by example, to give back.

On the final night, the team did a wonderful job, singing and dancing their hearts out. The boys gave a fabulous rendition of a great song by the incredible Stevie Wonder. It's a song about moving ahead, about striving to survive and to flourish. I've always loved the track and always loved the sentiment. 'Higher Ground' could be the theme song to my life.

CHAPTER 33

Reset All

It had been a long time between drinks. Not literally, of course (Vince and I were always partial to a good bottle of red, or a glass of champagne, or an aperitif or two!), but metaphorically, because I hadn't released an album of new material in English for eleven years. In the interim, so many things had changed, starting with me. Since *Just Me*, I'd 'reset all', so to speak, with a second career in a new land, a new language, a new life, and new loves-of-my-life in Vince and Gab. Then there was the music business. It had changed too, beyond recognition, perhaps. Even the way people listened to music was different. Once, we bought albums and played them from beginning to end, over and over. Now people would download music a song at a time, adding each one to a playlist that in some ways was like wallpaper, a backdrop that added a bit of colour but didn't really impinge on the important business of living. For me, though, music *was* living, it was life, it was *my* life.

When I walked away from my French recording contract three or four years earlier, the well had been truly dry. I had nothing to give, and when that happens, you won't hear from me. Now, though, I was busting to write and record another original album in my own language and in my own way.

Vince, Gab and I were back in Paris, living in our friends Laurent and Brigitte's apartment around the corner while work proceeded on our house. From the other side of the world my new manager, Grant Gillies, began to hook me up with other songwriters, people in the UK and Scandinavia. Grant had come on board not long after the new *Young Talent Time* finished. He and I had met years ago, when he was label manager at Jive Records. My friend Morena worked with him and we'd met at an industry event. We'd reconnected at Channel Ten, where Grant was then working as marketing director. Not long after YTT folded, he left the network to set up an artists' management company.

Around the same time, I'd decided I needed an Australian manager again, especially because I was keen to make another original album, although I didn't have a recording contract. My Australian ties were as strong as ever – stronger even – and I'd been heading down under every year to give concerts and reconnect with fans and family. Whenever I did, I'd stay with Gab's godmother Georgia Zaris and her dog Rufus (Australia's most flatulent dog).

The global financial crisis had rocked Europe, and it drove home to me just how lucky Australians are, and what a country of opportunity my homeland was. Then there was the sunshine and the beach … I began to imagine a life where we lived six months in Australia and six months in France. Gab might be French by birth but he loved Australia – not only school, but the mood, the air – something. Vince was another matter. He's French through and through, and for the French their culture is like oxygen – it keeps them alive. He couldn't imagine living so far away from home for too long.

On the Arena family front things were changing too. After a lifetime of hard work and commitment to others, my parents finally retired. They hung on to the house in Moonee Ponds, which I will always think of as our family home, but sold the business. It was great to think that they were at last going to have some time to smell the roses, relax (although that was impossible to picture) and do some of the things they'd wanted to do but never had the time. Nancy had always kept an eye on them, and continued to do so, in between work and ferrying Sofia to her various engagements. Sofia was growing up into quite a little lady, and some people said that with her long dark hair and perky smile she reminded them of me in my YTT days. She certainly had *brio*.

Silvana and Matt were back in London, now with Louis, who had never looked back and was bigger and bouncier than ever. So, as always, the Arena clan were scattered around the world. But it's true that home is where the heart is, and for all of us that would forever be Australia.

Paris, or to be specific, our run-down house in Paris, was keeping Vince and me busy. The building works seemed to be progressing at a snail's pace, and we wondered if we'd ever move back in. The once beautiful garden was now a builder's lot, and nothing appeared close to finished. As the winter of 2012 descended, things ground almost to a halt. It felt as if we were being held hostage, caught up in a situation over which we had no control, our destiny entirely in others' hands. Meanwhile, the little apartment we had so generously been given grew chillier and chillier. Wrapped up in jumpers and scarves, I'd huddle over the heater, imaging I was sitting on Bondi Beach under an umbrella, taking in the surfers, the sparkling waves, the cloudless blue sky. A European winter is tough if you don't have proper heating. A trip to Stockholm to write saw me in head-to-toe thermals. If you think Paris is cold in December, try Sweden!

Unlike the house, which was looking more and more like a bombsite, the album was coming together. In fact, by early 2013 I had enough material for two albums. A visit to Australia to do more concerts gave me a chance to catch up with friends, family and old acquaintances. One such acquaintance was John O'Donnell, the man who had given me carte blanche when we were recording *Songs of Love and Loss*. I'd always admired John. Personable and artistic, he had a passion for the arts and that's what seemed to drive him.

We caught up for breakfast at a cafe overlooking Sydney's Circular Quay one morning in late summer. Having left EMI a few years earlier, John had since returned to the fold, and he was interested in hearing the new material. I promised to send it to him.

At home in France we finally moved into the house. Sure, we had no kitchen and I spent my days with a sponge in my hand as tradies drilled and hammered, traipsing dirt through the place all day every day for weeks. But it was great to be home. Grant was on the case with the album, and eventually had some good news: John O'Donnell wanted to do a deal. In fact, he wanted to do a deal for four albums.

I was over the moon. My well was no longer dry – in fact, it was full to the brim and overflowing. Watching Gab grow up, sharing a life with Vince, creating a home together, performing and keeping in touch with fans had recharged my musical batteries. Now they were at 100 per cent and I was raring to go.

I'd always known I'd make another album, eventually, somehow. Now was the right time. I was forty-five and ready to get started again. It made me think of when we were kids and, when a record finished, we'd grab the arm and put the needle back at the beginning to hear the song over. I'm sure that's how Nancy trained me – she'd play those records again and again and I'd memorise every word. Well, now I was ready to go round again.

But for me, going back to the start would also be a chance to rethink. I wanted to get back to basics, to focus on what's important and leave out the rest. In fact, one of the songs I'd co-written for the album was called 'Reset All'. I liked the idea that when things get too complicated or aren't working anymore, you need to go back to the beginning, to simplify, return to what you know in your heart works. Having lived through the GFC in Europe, I couldn't help thinking we all needed to 'reset all', on every level. It had struck me lately that while our lives were full of ways and means to communicate, we seemed less able to connect. There was so much white noise we could no longer hear each other.

I don't know about you, but I believe music has a role in all that. Through music we can reconnect. And with this album I wanted to tune out the white noise and focus on what I think is important in good music – melody and a story that make you *feel*. So, following my friend Laurent's suggestion, I decided to call the album *Reset*, after the song.

No doubt, this time around it would be different again. And who knew how things would pan out? As I said, the music industry is a whole new ball game. What hadn't changed for me was music itself. In my mind, a great song is a jewel – small but exquisite, lovingly cut to reveal its inner beauty, holding within it an entire world. And to hear great songs will always soothe my soul, move me, inspire me, allow me to *connect*. To sing great songs is a privilege, for sure.

But singing my *own* songs is what I love. It's a necessity for me, like three meals a day and a few rays of sunshine. I don't know what I would do if I couldn't write and sing. It makes me who I am, regardless of where I happen to be or what language I'm speaking. It has done since I wrote my first song and sang it to myself in the shower. It's as natural for me as breathing. Filippina Arena sings to live and lives to sing. That's just the way it is.

I think Nonno would understand. And Nonno would be proud. But guess what, Nonno? Not only that. Now I can dance.

TINA ARENA

Album Discography

ENGLISH LANGUAGE STUDIO ALBUMS

Tiny Tina and Little John
With John Bowles
Vinyl LP, Pisces, 1977, Australia; CD, Standard Records, 1998, Australia

Rock & Roll Love Letter/Ring Ring/Do Ron Ron/High Hopes/Ma (He's
Making Eyes at Me)/Let Your Love Flow/Somewhere Over the Rainbow/
Jeans On/Heartbeat (It's a Love Beat)/Calendar Girl/That's Rock 'N'
Roll/Anything You Can Do/I'm Your Little Boy/When I Kissed the
Teacher/Ben/Everybody Needs a Rainbow/Everything Is Beautiful

Strong as Steel
CD, Avenue Records/EMI, 1990, Australia; Standard Records, 1996

Woman's Work/I Need Your Body/Close to My Heart [1990 only]/
For the Sake of Talking [1990 only]/Rumour Has It [1990 only]/
Images of Love [1990 only]/Strong as Steel/The Machine's Breaking
Down/I'll Be There/Stagefright/I Believe (When I Fall In Love It Will
Be Forever)/I Need Your Body (Original 12" Mix) [1990 only]/The
Machine's Breaking Down (Club Mix Hot Dr. Mix) [1990 only]/Wouldn't
Change a Thing [1996 only]/Best for You [1996 only]/On the Line [1996
only]/ You Make Me Feel Good [1996 only]/Be a Man [1996 only]

315

Don't Ask
CD, Columbia, 1994, Australia; Columbia, 1994, Europe; Columbia, 1995, UK;
Columbia, 1996, Europe; Epic, 1996, US

Chains/Heaven Help My Heart/Sorrento Moon (I Remember)/Wasn't
It Good/Message/Show Me Heaven [Japan, Europe and US only]/
Love Is the Answer/Greatest Gift/That's the Way a Woman Feels/Be a
Man/Standing Up/Chains (S&M Radio Mix) [Europe 1996 only]

In Deep
CD, Columbia, 1997, Australia; Columbia, 1998, France; Columbia, 1998, UK;
Epic, 1998, Japan; Epic, 1998, US; Columbia, 1999, France

Burn /If I Didn't Love You/Sixteen Years/In Command/Not for Sale/Unsung
Hero/I Want to Live With You/Welcome to My World/I Want to Know
What Love Is/Flashback/Now I Can Dance/Stay/Burn (Acoustic Version –
Hidden Track)/I Want to Spend My Lifetime Loving You [France, Japan
and UK only]/No Shame [France, Japan, UK, US, only]/Whistle Down the
Wind [Japan, UK, US only] Aller plus haut [France only]/Les Trois Cloche
[France only]/Segnali di Fumo [France only]/Chains [France 1999 only]

Just Me
CD, Columbia, 2001, Australia; Columbia, 2001, France & Belgium

Dare You to Be Happy/Soul Mate #9/But I Lied/God Only Knows/Symphony
of Life/You Made Me Find Myself/If You Ever/Tangled/I'm Gone/Something's
Gotta Change/Coeur de Pierre [France and Belgium only]/Tu es Toujours Là
[France and Belgium only]/Si Je Ne T'Aimais Pas[France and Belgium only]

Songs of Love and Loss
CD, EMI, 2007, Australia

The Look of Love/I Just Don't Know What to Do With Myself/So Far Away/
To Sir With Love/The Man With the Child In His Eyes/Do You Know
Where You're Going To/Love Hangover/I Only Want to Be With You/
The Windmills of Your Mind/Everybody Hurts/Woman/Until/Wasn't It
Good (live) [deluxe edition only]/You Made Me Find Myself (live) [deluxe
edition only]/Les trois cloches (live) [deluxe edition only]/Now I Can Dance
(live) [deluxe edition only]/Sorrento Moon (live) [deluxe edition only]

Songs of Love and Loss 2
CD, EMI, 2008, Australia

Oh Me Oh My/Only Women Bleed/Every Breath You Take/
Close To You/Call Me/Baby It's You/Nights In White Satin/I Hope
I Never/Both Sides Now/Wouldn't It Be Good/Your Song/
Living a Lifetime Together/Downtown [digital only]

The Peel Me Sessions 2003
CD, Positive Dream, 2009

Talk to Me/Your Love Has Never Failed Me Yet/Peel Me (Like an
Orange)/Transparency/Drunk with Love/Doesn't It Feel Good/
No Apology/Take Me Apart/(Sweetest) Love Hangover

Reset
CD, EMI, 2013, Australia

Love You Less/Still Running/You Set Fire to My Life/Let Me In/
Out of the Blue/Don't Hide/Patchwork Heart/It's Just What It Is/
Don't Look Back/Bring Me Love/Only Lonely/Destination Unknown/
Reset All/I Can Breathe [deluxe edition only]/Lose Myself [deluxe
edition only]/You Set Fire to My Life (acoustic) [deluxe edition only]

FRENCH LANGUAGE STUDIO ALBUMS

Un Autre Univers
Columbia, 2005, France

Aimer Jusqu'à l'Impossible/Tu Aurais dû Me Dire (Oser Parler d'Amour)/
Je M'appelle Bagdad/Si Tu Veux Mon Coeur/J'ai Envie de Savoir/S'il
Faut Prier/Il y a des Jours/Un Autre Univers/Et Puis Après (with Henri
Salvador)/Changer/Si J'avais le Temps/Jamais Non Jamais/Simple Désir

7 Vies
CD, Columbia, 2008, France

Entends-Tu le Monde?/Tu Pourras Dire/7 Vies/Danser la Vie/Ombres
Chinoises/L'un Pour L'autre/Ta Vie/S'il M'est Donné/Hollywood
Boulevard/Je Vois ta Lumière/Ailleurs/Dis-moi/N'oublie Pas

COMPILATION ALBUMS

Souvenirs
CD, Columbia, 2000, Australia

I Want to Spend My Lifetime Loving You/Love's Funny That Way/
Show Me Heaven/If I Was A River/Whistle Down The Wind/No More
Tears (Enough Is Enough) (live with Donna Summer)/Burn (live at the
Olympia)/Sorrento Moon (I Remember) (live at the Olympia)/Chains
(Live at the Olympia)/Live (For the One I Love)/Les Trois Cloches/
Segnali Di Fumo (with Luca Barbarossa)/Aller Plus Haut/Aller Plus
Haut (video)/Les Trois Cloches (video)/If I Was a River (video)

Greatest Hits, 1994–2004
CD, Columbia, 2004, Australia

Italian Love Song/Chains/Burn/Wasn't it Good/Sorrento Moon (I
Remember)/Now I Can Dance (single edit)/Soul Mate #9 (single version)/
Heaven Help My Heart (radio version)/Symphony of Life/That's the
Way a Woman Feels (The New Horns Mix))/If I Didn't Love You/I
Want to Know What Love Is/Dare You to Be Happy (remix)/Show
Me Heaven/If I Was a River/Never (Past Tense) (radio edit)/I Want to
Spend My Lifetime Loving You (with Marc Anthony)/Take Me Apart

Bonus CD (limited edition only)

Aller Plus Haut/Les Trois Cloches/Tu es Toujours Là/Cœur de Pierre/Si Je
Ne T'aimais Pas/Je Te Retrouve un Peu (with Jay)/Symphonie De L'âme (single
version)/Ti Voglio Qui (radio version)/Segnali di Fumo (with Luca Barbarossa)

The Best et Le Meilleur
CD, Columbia, 2009, France

Aller plus Haut/I Want to Spend My Lifetime Loving You (with Marc
Anthony)/Aimer jusqu'à l'impossible/I Want to Know What Love Is/
Les Trois Cloches/Je M'appelle Bagdad/Night Fever/Tu es Toujours Là/
Entends-Tu le Monde?/Live (For the One I Love)/Symphony of Life/
Chains/L'un Pour L'autre/7 vies/Tu Pourras Dire/Tu Aurais Dû Me
Dire (Oser Parler D'amour)/Et Puis Après (with Henri Salvador)/
This Universe/Out Here on My Own (duet with Patrick Fiori)

Album Discography

LIVE ALBUMS

Vous Etes Toujours Là
CD, Columbia, 2003, France

Je Te Retrouve Un Peu (with Jay – studio version)/Si Je Ne T'aimais Pas/
Sorrento Moon/Aller Plus Haut/Les Trois Cloches/Burn/Tu Es Toujours
Là/Symphonie De L'âme/I Want To Spend My Lifetime Loving You
(with Roch Voisine)/I Want To Know What Love Is/Chains/Woman/
You Made Me Find Myself/Coeur De Pierre/Never (Past Tense)
(bonus track, The Roc Project feat. Tina Arena – studio version)

Greatest Hits Live
CD & DVD, Sony BMG Columbia, 2005, Australia

Soul Mate #9/Take Me Apart/If I Didn't Love You/That's the Way a Woman
Feels/I Want To Know What Love Is/Wasn't It Good/Les Trois Cloches/
Burn/You Made Me Find Myself/Italian Love Song/Symphony of Life/
Sorrento Moon/Heaven Help My Heart/Chains/Dare You to Be Happy

The Onstage Collection
CD & DVD, Liberation, 2010, Australia

The Look of Love/I Only Want to Be With You/Wouldn't It Be Good/
Only Women Bleed/Je M'appelle Bagdad/I Want To Know What
Love Is/I Want To Spend My Lifetime Loving You/Wasn't It Good/
Burn/Maybe This Time/I Just Don't Know What to Do With Myself/
Nights in White Satin/Chains/Call Me/Symphony of Life

Symphony of Life
2 CDs & DVD, Ambition Entertainment/EMI, 2012, Australia)

CD 1: Arenature Overture/Living a Lifetime Together/Oh Me Oh My/The
Man with the Child in His Eyes/I Just Don't Know What to Do with Myself/My
Husband Makes Movies/Don't Cry for Me Argentina/The Prayer (with Anthony
Callea)/I Want to Spend My Lifetime Loving You (with Anthony Callea)
CD 2: Wasn't It Good/Burn/Sorrento Moon (I Remember)/You Made Me
Find Myself/Je M'appelle Bagdad/Only Women Bleed/GoldenEye/Maybe This
Time/Symphony of Life/Cry Me a River/Chains/Both Sides Now/Call Me

319

ACKNOWLEDGEMENTS

This book would not have been possible without the assistance of many people who generously gave of their time, their memory banks, their photo albums and files.

First, I would like to thank my family. Without their support and advice I couldn't have had any kind of career – or written this book. To my darling parents, Franca and Joe – thank you, thank you, thank you. Without your love and support I couldn't have achieved anything. A special thanks to Mum for keeping every clipping and costume and allowing me to use the family photos.

To my sister Nancy – thank you for everything. You got me started in music and always listened and gave advice when I needed it. Thanks for sharing your memories, which were much clearer than mine; and for trawling through all the family photos and getting them ready for publication – a huge job, I know! Thank you also to Walter, for helping Nancy out. And a big thanks to my sister Silvana, and Matt for sharing the ride, your memories and your family snaps.

To John Young, my mentor and lifelong friend who gave me my first gig when I was just eight years old – thanks for everything!

Acknowledgements

To my manager Grant Gillies – I couldn't have done it without you! You make it all so easy and fun. Thanks also to Mike Brady, who recalled far better than I ever could how we had those hits with 'I Need Your Body' and *Strong as Steel*. The lovely Geoffrey Schuhkraft helped me piece together the stories around my trips to LA, Japan and around Australia, and generously lent me his photos. To Ann-Marie Meadows, who travelled with me all around the world, despite her fear of flying – thanks for sharing your memories and your photos.

Thanks also to my former manager, Bruce Pawsey; my assistant in Australia, Tori Wood; Janine Kerr; Emmanuel Candi at Sony Music Entertainment Australia; Peter Karpin; John O'Donnell at EMI Music Australia; Wade Goring at Foxtel; Jane Manning and Anthea Bulloch for sparking my interest in tracing the family history and telling my story; Robin Eastwood and Julie Raffaele at Artemis International for supplying images; and Rafa Sanchez, who generously mailed from Spain an amazing collection of clippings and video that he has gathered over the past twenty years; Nicole Groch, for sharing her photos; and Andrew Mulcahy, for supplying even more pictures. Thanks also must go to the extraordinary photographer Pierre Baroni, for agreeing to photograph me for the cover of my book.

I am indebted to a circle of friends in Australia, France, London, Los Angeles, New York and Sweden. The diversity of these spirits means my life is rarely dull. Thank you for welcoming me, or us, with open arms every time we pass

through: Jacques, Val, Natalie and Laurent Robert; Stephane
DuMontier; Ludovic and all the gang at the Val; Brigitte and
Laurent; Margaux; Charles; the Kadoches; Georgia Zaris;
Lauren Liistro; Mattias Lindbloom; Anders Wolbeck; Linda
Gregoriou; Stefan Tyra; Nic Buc; Michael Angel; Gil Buresi;
Fabienne; Sophie Hare; Steve and Karen Birbeck; Paul; Lia;
Olivia and Ava Toscano; Heather Cairns; Marianne Harris;
Tim Page; Kelvin and Lynn Rann; all the gang at Les Enfoirés;
and Salvatore Anzalone. If I've left someone out please don't
hate me for it!

I am also indebted to Fiona Henderson, who loved the idea
for this book and pursued it with a passion; as well as Catherine
Milne and Katie Stackhouse at HarperCollins, for making the
process *almost* painless!

Thanks to Jude McGee, who so graciously enabled me
to put this story into words. I trusted my instinct when we
embarked on this storytelling journey together. I'm glad I
waited for the perfect wordsmith to come along. It was worth
the wait – thank you!

And last but by no means least, a huge thank you to my
partner, confidante, and collaborator Vincent Mancini – an
unbelievably patient man who has taught me many things; and
to Gabriel, my son, who singlehandedly keeps it all very real.

INDEX

'Strong as Steel' 55, 60–1, 66, 68, 147
'Symphony of Life' 209–10, 211, 222, 223
'Take Me Apart' 230
'Talk to Me' 230
'Tangled' 203
'That's the Way a Woman Feels' 112
'To Sir With Love' 263
'Tu Aurais Dû Me Dire' (You Should Have Told Me) 244
'Tu Es Tourjours Là' (You Are Always There) 212, 213, 220, 223, 228, 244
'Turn Up the Beat' 43, 45, 72
'Unsung Hero' 118
'Until' 263
'Wasn't It Good' 82, 104, 125
'Whistle Down the Wind' 137, 165
'Woman' 205, 243, 263
'Woman's Work' 68
'Wouldn't Change a Thing' 119
'You Made Me Find Myself' 204
'You Make Me Feel Good' 119
'Your Song' 279
Songs of Love and Loss 262–4, 268, 270, 273, 277, 278–81, 286, 310, 316–17
songwriting 41, 69, 71, 75, 80–1, 88–91, 117–19, 120–1, 200–7, 209, 228, 241–2, 279, 308, 312–13
Sony 2, 75, 79–80, 83, 85, 89, 93, 96–7, 99–101, 111, 120, 124, 131, 140, 141, 142, 146–8, 152–3, 157–8, 169, 176, 179, 182, 201, 214–15, 228, 230–2, 236, 272–3, 275, 285
Sorrento 45, 90, 98
Southern Sons 134
Souvenirs 201, 318
Split Enz 279
Springfield, Dusty 34, 56, 230, 259, 262
Springfield, Rick 15
Springsteen, Bruce 77, 134

Stardust, Alvin 6
Starmania 175
Starr, Ringo 41
Steinman, Jim 139, 140
Stenlake, Ian 221
Stewart, Rod 50, 91, 122, 181
Sting 202
Stone, Judy 29
Straw 245
Streisand, Barbra 34, 35, 56, 91, 111, 123, 142, 148, 157, 159, 162
Strong as Steel 60–1, 68, 75, 79, 84, 120, 315
Summer, Donna 34, 36, 56, 91, 157–9, 160, 162, 201
Sweet 6
Sweet Charity 33
Sydney Olympic Games 2000 191–4, 198–9, 202
Sydney Opera House 29
Symphony of Life 319
Szeps, Henry 221
Taliefero, Crystal 134
Tapis Rouge (Red Carpet) 175–9
Tarrant, Chris 99
Taylor, James 91, 92
Te Kanawa, Dame Kiri 137
Television House 21, 25, 85, 120–1
Thomas, Chrissy 170, 234
Tiësto 228
Tiny Tina x, 4, 22–3, 27, 33, 40–1, 43, 46, 49–50, 56, 60, 67, 80, 180, 301
Titanic 139, 178
The Tonight Show with Jay Leno 113
Top of the Pops 99, 139
Toppano, Peta 53
Tour de France 297–300
Tunisia 256–7
Turner, Tina 55, 183
Twain, Shania 141
Tyler, Bonnie 41, 137, 138, 139, 202
Tyson, Dave 89–91, 117–18, 121
Un Autre Univers (Another Universe) 243, 253, 258, 317
Valguarnera, Mitch 289, 292
Vannoni, Mitch 100
Vega, Carlos 91
Veneruso, Jacques 213, 244
Vergnes, Thierry 249, 257

Versace, Donatella 189
Vettese, Peter-John 207, 208–12, 271
Vidal de Fonseca, Emmanuelle 213
Vous Êtes Toujours Là (You Are Always There) 228, 319
Wa Wa Nee 170
Ward, Christopher 89
Warren, Diane 55, 147
Webb, Jimmy 34
Webster, Nikki 192–3
Wembley Stadium 2, 142–3
Wendt, Jana 34
Werfel, Steve '42, 72, 88, 119, 217
West End x, 138, 178, 182, 187–90, 200, 265–8
Wheatley, Glenn 57, 128
Whistle Down the Wind 137–9, 141
Who Do You Think You Are? 284–5, 286, 287–96
Wilde, Kim 43
Williams, Robbie 123
Williamson, John 191, 193
Winehouse, Amy 123, 213
'Wizards of Oz' showcase 78–9, 81
Wolfgramm, Kelly 274
Wolfgramm, Taleri 274
Wonder, Stevie 56, 127–30, 135, 306
Wood, Tori 274
World Music Awards 1, 113, 176, 187, 189
World's Best Selling Australian Artist 113
Wyman, Bill 122
Yeston, Maury 53
'You Asked for It' tour 107
'You Asked for More' tour 107
Young, Anna 301
Young, Fleur 301
Young, John x, 16–17, 19, 21, 27, 28, 34–5, 36, 85, 120–1, 142, 301–3
Young, Penelope 230–1
Young Talent Time (YTT) ix–x, 1, 16–22, 24–8, 30–40, 41, 49, 56, 85, 120, 122, 192, 256, 301–3, 305–6, 308
Zammit, Steven 26
Zaris, Georgia 276, 308